THE COMPLETE IDIOT'S GUIDE® TO

Tantric Sex

by Dr. Judy Kuriansky

ALPHA

To all those who are working toward more love ... and peace ... thank you.

Copyright © 2002 by Dr. Judy Kuriansky

THE COMPLETE IDIOT'S GUIDE TO & Design is a registered trademark of Penguin Group (USA) Inc.

International Standard Book Number: 0-02-864175-2
Library of Congress Catalog Card Number: 2001097252

05   04   03   8   7   6   5   4

Interpretation of the printing code: the rightmost number of the first series of numbers is the year of the book's printing; the rightmost number of the second series of numbers is the number of the book's printing. For example, a printing code of 02-1 shows that the first printing occurred in 2002.

Printed in the United States of America

Publisher
Marie Butler-Knight

Product Manager
Phil Kitchel

Managing Editor
Jennifer Chisholm

Acquisitions Editor
Mike Sanders

Development Editor
Lynn Northrup

Production Editor
Billy Fields

Copy Editor
Rachel Lopez

Illustrator
Hrana Janto
Jody Schaeffer

Cover Designers
Mike Freeland
Kevin Spear

Book Designers
Scott Cook and Amy Adams of DesignLab

Indexer
Brad Herriman

Layout/Proofreading
Svetlana Dominguez
Mary Hunt
Michelle Mitchell

Contents at a Glance

**Part 1: An Introduction to Tantric Sex:
The Spiritual Path to Sacred Love**   **1**

1 What Is Tantric Sex?   3
*Tantra and tantric sex as a pathway to love, sacred sex,
transformation, healing, and bliss. How the West is reviving and embracing ancient Eastern techniques. The benefits of tantric sex. A test of readiness for tantric sex.*

2 The Basics: Yes, Yin Yang, Yoni, and Yab Yum   19
*Sex as energy not activity. Now, how do you activate and
use it? Achieving balance and union of opposites. Do opposites attract? The love position of yab yum. New terms
for sex that honor your love.*

3 Spinning Your Wheels and Breathing to Ecstasy   29
*New ways to breathe your way to bliss. How energy cen-
ters in your body bring you to transformation. Creating
the inner flute and using your third eye. Symbols and
sounds that help your practice.*

4 Awaken and Worship the God and Goddess in You   43
*You are a divine being! Getting to know the ancient deities
and finding the god and goddess in you and your partner.*

Part 2: Getting Started in Sacred Sex   **59**

5 Prep Your Body Temple of Love   61
*Your body as your temple of love, learning to love it, get-
ting to know it and use it for higher loving. The mirror exercise and love muscle workouts. A test of your spine.*

6 Amp Up or Damp Down Your Sexual Energy   73
*Controlling your energy to relax or activate. Techniques to
help you do that: the sacrum tap, the chakra thump.
Dancing up an energy storm and getting your pelvis
moving.*

7 Setting the Stage for Your Tantric Nights of Pleasure   81
*Making time for lovemaking and preparing the sacred
space for your tantric nights of pleasure. Cleansing the
tantric way. Rituals to sanctify your love temple. Dedica-
ting your lovemaking and dressing the god/goddess way.
Setting your intentions to get ready for the best nights ever
to come.*

8   Practices for Beloveds to Reach Bliss   95
    What is bliss? Spark your love connection with simple
    techniques like the eye lock and heart tap. Stimulating
    your senses and using them to turn you and your part-
    ner on.

9   Breaking Through Blocks to Bliss   107
    Solutions to common problems that get in the way.
    Making time for love through 10-minute connects and the
    morning blessing. Solving anger, battles over control and
    fears of separation. Letting go of past abuse through emo-
    tional release. Seven ways to balance male and female en-
    ergies. Take the Sex Relations Review.

Part 3: Making Major Progress on the Path to Ecstasy   119

10 Giving Her the Best Nights Ever   121
    The value of taking turns. How to make her night different
    from all other nights. The Date Checklist. Boudoir basics
    to please her. Six promises to make to your Goddess.
    Getting her to relax and moving her energy. When love
    and love liquid flows. What women want most.

11 Giving Him the Best Nights Ever   133
    A checklist to prepare for his best nights ever. The four R's
    to please him: relax, relieve, reassure, reward. What to do
    and say on the first night and beyond. Helping him sur-
    render to love and pleasure. Secrets to arouse his passion
    with exciting ways to stimulate his lingam and God spots.

12 Make Lovemaking Last ... and Last ... and Last   145
    How long is a man supposed to last? Test his and her re-
    actions to lovemaking length. Myths about lasting longer.
    The keys to ejaculation control. How the partner helps.

13 A New View of Love, Sex, and Orgasm: The Big TTO   159
    The new focus on conscious love. Approaching sex, the
    sexual response cycle, and orgasm in a new way. Different
    kinds of orgasm. The power of the TTO, the tantric trans-
    formative orgasm. How to connect sex energy to love en-
    ergy. The ooo-ahh path to passion and the total body
    orgasm, cosmorgasm, and mega-orgasm. Spots to feel the
    big O. Orgasmic waves that keep on coming.

14 Getting Fit Together for Tantric Sex   171
    Exciting new routines for physical activities to do together.
    Yoga poses to help your love practice. The new trend—and
    value—of belly dancing for men and women. How love-
    making is a workout. The benefits of a new technique of
    Yogaboxing.

Part 4: Going Deeper: More Love and Better Sex Than You Ever Imagined   185

15 Make It Juicy with Magic and Play   187
Games lovers can share. Fun ways to enjoy connecting. Dancing for and with each other. Toys and gifts in sacred loving. How to achieve sex magic in lovemaking.

16 Advanced Tantric Lovemaking Techniques   201
What makes a technique advanced? An exercise for time- less love. The maithuna ritual and kundalini snake dance. Advanced yoga poses, lovemaking positions and new erogenous zones. Oral pleasure, bringing in divine en- ergy, and tuning in to vibes that create more intimacy.

17 Sexual Healing to Set You Free   215
The special techniques of sexual healing to heal your hurts to rebuild trust and release your love and joy. Instructions for the healer and the receiver. What happens in a healing. How you, too, can be healed.

18 Sex, Song, and Videotape   229
The value of stimulating eyes and ears in sacred sex. CDs and videos that complement your tantric mood. Recom- mendations to help you on your path.

Part 5: Dating and Mating Tantra Style   241

19 Singles, Sex, and Tantra   243
You don't need a partner to follow the tantric path to bliss. You are the beloved. How to take yourself on a tantric date. The search for Mr./Ms. Right tantra style. Who is the perfect tantric partner? Unusual couplings that really work. Where to go to find a tantric match and how to bringing in your soul mate.

20 Tying the Knot Tantra Style   257
The unique rituals in marriage ceremonies, tantric style. What tantric brides and grooms wear. Who comes, what they say in their vows, and priests and priestesses who preside. Dedications to each other. Special participation of the guests. Ideas that you can use.

21 When He Resists or She Strays   271
What to do when you are enthused about this tantric path but your partner doesn't share your interest. Deciding what's best for you and your relationship. Understanding and dealing with affairs the tantric way. The energy booster and other ways to survive affairs and differences, and get back on a loving track.

Part 6: Tantra for Everybody in the New Millennium   281

22 A Lifetime of Tantra: Learning to Love at All Ages   283
How tantra leads to longer life. The value of tantra for all ages. How tantra is helpful in mid life and menopause. How college kids and teens are taking to tantra. The techniques of tantra to raise healthier kids and how tantric principles can be integrated into a school system.

23 Lifestyles and Situations: Tantra for All Relationships   293
The pros and cons of cybertantra. How a tantric lifestyle works regardless of your situation or relationship status. The new tantric sex workshops for gay men. The value of tantric sex in case of disability. Healing relationships with parents and families.

24 Which Path Is Right for You?   303
Who's teaching what? Making sense of the various tantra traditions. The noted contemporary teachers and the importance of having a guide or teacher. Questions to ask about a workshop and ways to keep your tantric practice going. Retreats, gatherings and the new trend of exotic escapes.

25 A Healing Force for Now and the Future   319
The healing force of tantric sex in racial tensions, generational tensions, teen sex, abuse, and drug use. How you are not alone: creating tantric community and family. New hope to help heal the world.

Appendixes

A Glossary   327

B Workshops, Web Sites, Teachers, and Tantra
Communities   333

C Tantric Tools   343

Index   353

Contents

**Part 1: An Introduction to Tantric Sex:
The Spiritual Path to Sacred Love   1**

1 What Is Tantric Sex?   3

What Is Tantra? 4
Sacred Sex the Tantric Way 4
How Tantric Sex Frees Your Mind, Body, and Soul 5
Tantric Sex as the Path to Healing 6
Tantric Sex as Magic 6
A Powerful Chemical Cocktail to Bliss 6
Find and Follow the Pathways of Energy 7
How the West Revived Eastern Tantric Sex Practices 7
Sacred Sex 10
Myths About Tantra and Tantric Sex 11
Why Tantric Sex Now? 12
Twelve Benefits of Tantric Sex Practices 13
Are You Ready for Tantra? 15
The Ten Pledges of the Tantric Sex Path 16

2 The Basics: Yes, Yin Yang, Yoni, and Yab Yum   19

Yin and Yang: What Is Male and What Is Female? 20
The Circle of Coupled Consciousness 20
Shiva and Shakti 21
Getting in Touch with Opposites 22
Achieving Balance and Union of Opposites 22
Position Yourselves for Love in Yab Yum 23
Sex as Energy—Not Activity 24
My Partner, My Beloved 24
*What Do You Call Your Sex Organs? The New Terms
  for Yoni and Lingam* 25
A New View of Desire 26
Empowered to Say "Yes" or "No" 26
Taking Care of Your Body Temple 27

3 Spinning Your Wheels and Breathing to Ecstasy 29

The Importance of Your Breath 29
Why We Don't Breathe Correctly 30
The Chakra Wheels 31
Breathe Through the Chakras 33
The Third Eye as Window to the Soul 37
Making All the Connections from Coccyx to Crown 37
Your Inner Smile 38
Be Both Participant and Observer 39
   Mantras 39
   Yantras 39
   Mandalas 40

4 Awaken and Worship the God and Goddess in You 43

What Is "God/Goddess"? 44
Integrate All Your Roles 44
Seeing Beyond the Superficial 45
The Importance of Worshipping Each Other 46
Clearing Up Confusion About Gods and Goddesses 46
Getting to Know the Ancient Goddesses 46
   Major and Well-Known Goddesses 46
   Other Goddesses Around the World 49
Gods from Different Cultures 51
Modern-Day God/Goddess Icons 53
Gods and Their Goddess Counterparts 53
The Essence of the God/Goddesses Within You 54
Using Deities in Your Sex Practice 55
Festivals and Other God/Goddess Gatherings 55
   Fertility Festivals in Japan 55
   Burning Man Festival in Nevada 56
   Goddess Gatherings 56
Temples 57

Part 2: Getting Started in Sacred Sex 59

5 Prep Your Body Temple of Love 61

Your Body as the Bridge to Bliss 61
   Building Body Love: Through the Looking Glass 62
   Describe Your Sexual Parts Inside and Out 63

If Your Penis or Yoni Could Talk 64
Go on a Genital Exploration 64
The Two Colors of Tantra: Merging the Sexual and
  the Physical 65
The Yoga Connection 66
Some Simple Yoga Movements 66
Hold It: These Are Called Bandhas 66
Love Muscle Exercises for Men and Women 68
Follow a Conscious Workout 68
The Spinal Tap 69
Food for Thought: You Are What You Eat 70

6 Amp Up or Damp Down Your Sexual Energy   73

Ways to Calm Down 74
Air Yoga as a Stress Reducer 74
Amping Up for Good Loving 75
Control Your Breathing 75
Practice the Sacrum Tap 75
Do the Chakra Thump 76
Practice Streaming 76
Dance Up an Energy Storm 76
Get that Pelvis Moving! 77
Fantasize 78
Let Yourself Go! 78
Do the "Shakti Shake" 78
Take Lama Breaths 79
Ask Your Partner for Help 80

**7 Setting the Stage for Your Tantric Nights
of Pleasure   81**

Making Time Enough for Love 82
The Conscious Cleanup 82
The Tantric Bathing Ritual 84
God and Goddess Dress Up 86
Your Ideal Romantic Setting 87
Prepare Your Sacred Lovemaking Space 88
Change Your Setting 89
Music to Make Love By 89
Building an Altar 90

Honoring Rituals to Sanctify Your Space 90
Quiet the Mind 92
Set Your Intention Together 92
Going Out on Your Tantra Date 93

8 Practices for Beloveds to Reach Bliss   95

What Is Bliss? 95
Synchronizing Your Energy 96
Look into My Eyes: Eye Gazing 97
The Heart Hold 98
The Partner Passion Pod 99
Stimulating the Senses 99
Call It Sacred: Finding Your Tantric Love Triggers 102
Sex in the Flow Lane 102
Advanced Body Exploration 103
Her "Yoni Show" for Him 103
His "Love Arrow Show" for Her 103
Making Sacred Water Magic 104
Staying in Bliss: The Afterplay 104

9 Breaking Through Blocks to Bliss   107

When Big Emotions Burst Forth 108
Making Time for Each Other 109
Couple's Morning Blessing 109
The Ten-Minute Connect 109
Diffusing Your Anger 110
Overcoming Feelings of Separation 111
Balancing Your Male and Female Energies 111
The Sexual Relations Review 111
Seven Ways to Balance Sexual Energy 113
Frustration Over Who's on Top 115
Getting Past Desperation and Attachment 115
Purging Panic and Obsessions 116
More Ways to Clear Blocks 117

Part 3: Making Major Progress on the Path to Ecstacy   119

10 Giving Her the Best Nights Ever   121

The Value of Taking Turns at Pleasure 122
What Do Women Really Want? 122
Step 1: Set Your Intention *122*
Step 2: Remind Yourself That This Is Her Night *123*
Step 3: Be Prepared to Serve Your Goddess *123*
Step 4: Face Your Fears *123*
Step 5: Decide How You Will Call On Her *123*
Boudoir Basics 124
Night of Pleasure 1: Promises to the Goddess
in the Pleasure Palace 125
Relaxing Her 125
Night of Pleasure 2: Getting Closer 127
The Resolution Phase 129
Night of Pleasure 3: When Love and Love Liquid Flow   129
The One Thing Women Need Most *131*
The One Thing Women Want Most *131*

11 Giving Him the Best Nights Ever   133

Night 1: Taking Your Man into Tantric Bliss 134
Preparing Him for Pleasure 134
Leading Him to the Tantric Love Temple 135
Preparing Him for His Night of Love 135
Step l: Put Him at Ease *135*
Step 2: Bathe Him *136*
Step 3: Enter the Love Temple *136*
Step 4: Promise Him Pleasure *136*
The Tantric Shiva Massage, a Time to Surrender 137
Languishing Over His Lingam 138
The Second Pleasure Night 139
A Variation on Massage *140*
Include More Lingam Strokes When Pleasuring *140*
Pleasing His God Spots *141*
Building His Sexual Charge *141*
The Secret to Moving His Energy *142*

The Third Night of Pleasure 143
Entering His Sacred Space *143*
Exploring and Exciting His God Spot *143*

12 Make Lovemaking Last ... and Last ... and Last 145

How Long Is He Supposed to Last? 146
When It's All Over Too Fast 146
Her Reaction to Three-Minute Sex *146*
His Reaction to Three-Minute Sex 147
Why Men Come So Fast 149
No Expectations, Please! *149*
Ejaculation and Orgasm Are Different *150*
The Stages of the Male Sexual Response Cycle 151
Traditional Control Tactics 151
"Sealing the Penis," or Sexual Kung Fu 152
Tantric Sex Versus Other Methods of Prolonging
  Lovemaking 153
The Transmutation Breath 154
Tips on How She Can Help 155
If He Ejaculates Before She Is Ready 156

13 A New View of Love, Sex, and Orgasm: The Big TTO   159

What's Love Got to Do with It? 160
A New View of Orgasm and the Sexual
  Response Cycle 160
The Cosmorgasm *162*
The Mega-Orgasm *162*
The Clearing Orgasm *162*
Reaching Multiple and Simultaneous Orgasms *163*
The Tantric Wave *163*
The Stock Market Orgasm *164*
How to Have the Big TTO 164
Taking Sex Drive to a New Level 165
The Shiva Shakti Mudra *165*
Variations on the Shiva Shakti Mudra *165*
Connecting the Sexual Energy to Other Energy
  Centers 166
Using Movements to Send Sexual Energy *166*
Using Sound to Transmute Music Energy *166*

Where Do You Feel the Big O? Alphabet Orgasms 169
The G Spot 169
The X Spot 169
The AFE Zone 169
The PFE Zone 169
The Anywhere-in-Your-Body Orgasm 170

14 Getting Fit Together for Tantric Sex   171

The Importance of Physical Activity Together 171
The Love Muscle Exercises for the Man and
    the Woman 172
Partner Pelvic Thrusts 172
I Could Have Danced All Night 173
An Eight-Step White Tantra Twosome Routine 173
Couple Connect 174
Circling Couple Celebration 175
Squat-to-Stand Support 175
Partner Pelvis Press 176
Dangling Duos 176
The Couple Cobras 178
Lovers Table 178
Couple Cuddle 179
Bedroom Bodybuilding 179
Yogaboxing 181

**Part 4: Going Deeper: More Love and Better
          Sex Than You Ever Imagined   185**

15 Make It Juicy with Magic and Play   187

The Spirit of Play 188
How Much Juice Is There? 188
The Importance of Play in Sex 188
Affirmations About Joyful Sexual Union 188
Laugh Your Way to Better Health 189
Dancing for Each Other 189
Mirror, Mirror 190
The Hand Dance 191
Using Your Body Parts 191
Belly Dancing 192

Ecstatic Dance 192
The Temple Dance 193
Feasting on Your Love 193
Games Lovers Play 194
Creating Sex Magic Through Tantric Sex 196
Toys for Tantric Play 197
Gifts from the Heart 199
Where to Find Tantric Love Toys and Gifts 200

16 Advanced Tantric Lovemaking Techniques   201

What Makes a Practice "Advanced"? 201
A Slow Ride into Timeless Love 202
The Magical Maithuna Love Ritual 203
The Snake Dance 203
Advanced White Tantra Twosome 204
Advanced Passion Positions and Acts 206
Enflaming of the Dragon Goddess 207
The Kabazzah 208
The Full Stop 208
The Two New Erogenous Zones 208
Tongue Fu 209
Mudras 209
Advanced Visualization in Tantric Sex 209
Advanced Tuning In: You, Too, Can Be Psychic! ...210
Eight Steps in Deity Yoga 210
Base Chakra Pleasuring 211
Advanced Aids in Tantric Play 212
Entering the Time and Space Machine 213
Past Lives Connected to God/Goddess 213
Astral Projection 213

17 Sexual Healing to Set You Free   215

What Is a Sexual Healing? 216
Who Can Be a Healer? 216
What Happens in a Healing 217
Healing the Goddess 217
When the Goddess Love Liquid Flows 219
Healing the God 219
Overcoming the Two Major Hurdles in His Healing 219
Instructions for His Healer 220

Healing the Pain of Abuse 221
Handling Emotions in a Healing 222
Rules for the Healer 222
Rules for the Receiver 224
At the End of a Session 224
Are Healings Effective? 226

18 Sex, Song, and Videotape   229

Tantric Music 229
What Makes Tantric Music Special? 231
Let the Music Flow Through You 232
Sounding Chakras 232
Chants That Charge Your Connection 233
Tantric Videos That Tantalize as Well as Teach 234
The Kama Sutra Series: Videos with a Tantric Twist 235
Honoring the Goddess on Video 236
Other Videos 236
Tantra-Related Workouts to Watch 237
Related Videos on Sex 237
Tantra on Radio, TV, the Silver Screen, and
   the Internet 238

Part 5: Dating and Mating Tantra Style   241

19 Singles, Sex, and Tantra   243

You Are the Beloved 244
Meeting Your Match 245
Conscious Flirting 245
Who Is Mr. or Ms. Right? 246
*The Beloved Shows Up in Surprise Form, If Only
   for Now* 247
Quiz: Are You Ready for Your True Tantric Sex Partner? 248
Sensing, Not Scoring 249
Finding Your Soul Mate on the Tantric Path 249
Getting Ready for the Beloved 251
Bringing in the Beloved 251
Where to Go 252
Two Love Lessons You Wish You'd Learned When
   You Were Young 253
Safe Sex When Practicing Tantra 254

20 Tying the Knot Tantra Style   **257**

The Unique Aspects of a Tantric Marriage Ceremony 258
Feast for the Tantric Wedding 259
Music for the Tantra Marriage 259
Guest Participation 260
Special Ceremonies for Tantric Lovers 260
Christina and William's Tantric Marriage Ceremony 260
Rundy and Lisa's Four-Day Wedding Ritual 265
Mark and Patricia's Hindu Fire Ceremony 267
Keeping the Fires Burning 268

21 When He Resists or She Strays   **271**

When One of You Is Convinced But the
Other Isn't Sure 272
Hell No, I Won't Go! 273
Know What's Best for You 274
Honor Your Agreements 274
Don't Sneak Off to a Tantra Talk 274
Share Your Growth 275
When the Going Gets Tough 275
When a Relationship Has to End 275
Tantric Tolerance 276
What to Do About Tantric Sex Affairs 276
An Affair as Energy Booster 277
Considerations About Tantric Affairs 278
The Energy Booster Checklist 279

**Part 6: Tantra for Everybody in the New
Millennium**   **281**

**22 A Lifetime of Tantra: Learning to Love
at All Ages**   **283**

Want to Feel and Look Young Again? 283
The Real Fountain of Youth in Amrita Flow 284
Tantra in Older Years 284
Facing the Changes 285
Easing Her Time Through Menopause 285
When He Has a Mid-Life Crisis 286
*Seven Keys to Happier Life Transitions Through
Tantric Love* 287

Filling the Empty Nest 288
When a Partner Dies 288
Tantra for College Students 288
Tantra for Teens 289
Healthier Kids When You're a Tantra Parent 290
How the School System Can Be Tantric 291
The Payoff of Sensory Training at All Ages 292

23 Lifestyles and Situations: Tantra for All Relationships   **293**

Cybertantra 293
  The Pros of Cybertantra 294
  The Cons of Cybertantra 295
Seeing Beyond the Physical 295
  Lasting Love for Seemingly Odd Couples 295
  Facing Society's Opinions 296
The New World of Sexuality 296
  Tantric Sex for Men Who Love Men 297
  Tantric Sex for Goddesses 298
Tantric Love for Those with Disabilities 299
Healing Relationships with Your Parents 300
Tantra with Your Pets 300
Tantra with Your Plants 301

24 Which Path Is Right for You?   **303**

The Importance of Guidance 304
Finding the Right Guide 305
The Different Traditions of Sacred Sexuality 308
Osho: The Spiritually Incorrect Mystic 310
Different Trainings 310
Types of Healers and Other Practitioners 311
Starting and Keeping Up Your Practice 312
  Continuing Your Tantra Education 312
  A Few Things to Be Aware Of 313
Costs 315
Do Tantra Weekends Work? 315
New Trends in Tantric Experiences 316
Integrating Tantric Sex with Other Techniques 317

25 A Healing Force for Now and the Future   **319**

You Are Not Alone 320
Sending Energy, Especially in the Face of Tragedy 320
Healing the Cycles of Abuse 322
A Healthy Way to Get High 323
Tantra as a Healing Force in the Face of Illness 324
How Tantra Promotes Tolerance and Diversity 324
How Tantric Sex Can Help Heal the World 325

Appendixes

A Glossary   **327**

B Workshops, Web Sites, Teachers, and Tantra Communities   **333**

C Tantric Tools   **343**

Index   **353**

Forewords

It's exciting for me to see the tantric perspective coming more and more into mainstream thought. People may be drawn to tantric practices hoping to enhance their sexual satisfaction. It does an amazing job of improving what you already know and enjoy, but it also takes sexuality to another dimension entirely, an experience way beyond "normal."

Tantra is much more than a sexual teaching. Tantric practice can transform every aspect of your life, helping you to expand your physical health and vitality, emotional healing and expression, psychic sensitivity, satisfying relationships, creativity, productivity, and abundance. It is not unusual for someone to tell me after a few months of tantric involvement that he or she feels like a different person, much less stressed, much more comfortable, more joyful.

Dr. Judy is uniquely qualified to be a major tantric communicator, to be the means through which this message goes forward to a broad population. Through her studies and research, her writings, her years on radio and in the media, she knows her subject and knows how to capture people's interest. She speaks directly of sexual matters, but also appreciates the deeper potential of tantra.

In this book Dr. Judy has presented a broad overview as well as specific things you can do to begin your personal exploration. Tantra is really a spiritual path, leading to self-discovery, to realizing you are much more magnificent than you ever guessed. If you have the courage to try something new, this book will guide you through your first steps, get you started on a great adventure.

Bodhi Avinasha

Founder of Tantrika International and author of *Jewel in the Lotus*

Tantra is a way of life that is needed now even more than ever before in our times. In the face of intense intolerance, fear, and pain, what is essential is tolerance, love, and healing. Dr. Judy delivers this message in an intelligent and sensitive way—an impressive combination evident in her all of her work. She is the perfect professional to communicate these principles to help millions of people—and the world.

Besides overcoming fear, this is a time to finally get past sexual repression. The "sexual revolution" which began in the early sixties is now an accepted part of sociological history. While many feel that this revolution is dead, having tried all there is to try sexually and growing bored with it, I believe that the sexual revolution was the initial phase of a "sexual evolution." The 60s' seeds of a woman's right to pleasure and power in the world flowered in the 80s. As we move forward into the twenty-first century, we are beginning to understand that feminine energy is awakening our consciousness and healing the planet. Tantric wisdom states that as a woman awakens her sexual center (second chakra) she naturally awakens her feminine and spiritual powers. It is time to embrace this wisdom.

At the foundation of our sexual structure is the typical early conditioning which filled us with guilt, fear, insecurity, and shame. This conditioning still drastically affects our ability to receive and transmit love and energy sexually, both to our partner and to ourselves. Even if we have a beautiful sex life much of the time, the foundation is still shaky and results in periodic relationship problems, sexual insecurities, and a lessened ability to enjoy sexual sharing. It is time to reverse this conditioning, to allow us to journey into the ecstatic spiritual potential of sexual love.

Tantra is one of the missing links for these puzzles. It is truly time for men and women to join together in their quest for sexual harmony. It is time for the dark age of sexuality to end; for each of us to take the light and consciousness we've all awakened and put it into our sexuality, thus transforming its very nature.

Dr. Judy is a gifted therapist and writer, doing valuable work in the world. In this important book, Dr. Judy provides us with clear, easy to understand concepts and techniques of tantra, both ancient and modern. Learn to practice them well and you will become a master in the art of love. You will watch your sexual love life become infused with more consciousness, energy, intimacy, pleasure, and the connection where the two become one.

Charles Muir

Director, Source School of Tantra, Maui, Hawaii; www.sourcetantra.com

Introduction

Tantra is a way of life whose time has come. The word itself has been showing up in popular culture on TV shows, radio, and even in movies. It's no surprise, given a few factors. Our world has accelerated and new ideas are fast in coming in all arenas. Digital advances in our technological age are replacing person-to-person contact, leaving people isolated. And war in our new century has threatened our sense of safety and security. In the face of this, tantric practice offers hope.

Tantra is actually an idea that originated thousands of years ago, but it is still applicable to our life and needs today. It's a way of life that brings back true, deep, and intense connection. It's a spiritual way of being, consistent with today's increasing interest in spirituality. Most of all, it's a practice that emphasizes love—something we all want and need.

What exactly is tantric sex? That's what *The Complete Idiot's Guide to Tantric Sex* is all about: explaining the way of life the ancients knew and that we are rediscovering. In these pages I will guide you through the basic things you need to know to practice this exciting and profound way of loving—and some advanced techniques, too! I'll tell you about specific tools that you can put into practice right away that will work for you, no matter what other path you are on in your life. You'll see—these practices will immediately infuse you with new peace, insight, and joy.

One of the most important things you'll discover in these pages is that tantric sex is about far more than sex. It is about using sexual energy to create more love, and sacred sex as a means to *sacred love*. I had this special message printed for me by a street artist during one of my recent trips to China. It is a custom-made wording and depiction and I am delighted to share it with you here. The beauty of the lettering shows how the art of truly loving also promises to make our lives more beautiful.

A message of "sacred love" printed in Chinese lettering.

Many of the exercises described in this book can be done either alone or with a partner. That partner can be anyone of your choice, from a different background, or from the same sexual orientation. Since tantric sex stimulates and encourages creativity, I encourage you to be creative in adapting the exercises for your own spiritual practice, and then to integrate them into your practices with your partner.

In addition, be aware that there are many disciplines even within the field of tantra and tantric sex. These might differ only in slight ways such as instructing you in different ways to breathe (imagining a different pathway up and down your spine or through your body); or they may vary in more significant ways such as having a different emphasis (either on the more physical realm or on the more spiritual realm). I'll describe different approaches for you and give you some guidelines on how to make your choice.

The journey through this book promises to be an enlightening one, expanding your knowledge and your ability to love in new and exciting ways. You need not change anything drastic about your life; you can maintain your religion, beliefs, or any aspect of your lifestyle and just blend simple practices into the fabric of your life; or you can become immersed in a more major way. All is your choice, as you are the master of your destiny. Just by reading these pages, you will embrace more bliss in your life.

How to Use This Book

The chapters in this book are divided into six parts that take you through the practices of tantric sex and how you can integrate them into your life.

Part 1, "An Introduction to Tantric Sex: The Spiritual Path to Sacred Love," gives you the basics you need to know about tantric sex and how these ancient practices from the East can really work now, in the West. These four chapters teach you how to breathe, where your energy centers are, how to truly honor yourself and your partner, and how to prepare for a union of male and female divinity.

Part 2, "Getting Started in Sacred Sex," tells you exactly what to do to turn your home, your inner self, and your body into a place of worship and a clear channel for experiencing bliss. These five chapters give you specific things to do to set the stage for your tantra dates, and practices for beloveds to reach bliss.

Part 3, "Making Major Progress on the Path to Ecstasy," takes you deeper into your practices for spiritual growth and healing. These five chapters reveal a new view of sex and orgasm, how to truly make lovemaking last, what to do to get fit together, and all the steps to having the most exciting and fulfilling nights together.

Part 4, "Going Deeper: More Love and Better Sex Than You Ever Imagined," frees you to have the most playful and magical lovemaking and loving. These four chapters give you specific fun things to do together games to play, how to make magic, and more routines to tune up your love muscles and your whole body, to move to higher states of consciousness.

Part 5, "Dating and Mating Tantra Style," confronts the issues in relationships that you'll face on the tantric path. These three chapters help you find the mate you're looking for if you're single; and if you're in relationship, you'll learn how to handle differences in your desires, and how to make the happiest celebrations together you can ever imagine.

Part 6, "Tantra for Everybody in the New Millennium," addresses ways to integrate tantra into your life. In these four chapters, you'll learn how tantra can enrich your life no matter what your age, lifestyle, or relationships status; how to harness this new loving energy; and how to create a strong healing force for you, your beloveds, and the planet.

In addition, you'll find three helpful appendixes: a glossary of tantric terms, resources, and tantric tools.

It's always good to ground yourself in some clear points when you're learning something new that could change your life, so I've included boxes that offer you information and advice to help you make this blissful transformation really stick:

Tantra Tales

It's always interesting to learn about others people's stories. These boxes tell you about the experiences of other men and women who have decided to try out this new way of tantric relating, and how they—and you—can be successful.

Tantra Tutorial

With a new approach to life, love, and sex come new terms and concepts. These boxes clarify new words and ideas that you need to know, and answer some questions you might have about the practices as you embark on your new journey in consciousness.

Ecstasy Essentials

Ecstasy might sound simple, but it's not always so! These boxes tell you what you need to know to make it easier for you to embrace these higher states of consciousness and bliss that tantric sex makes possible.

Dr. Judy's TantrAdvice

Every page of this book is filled with advice, but in these boxes, I add a few extra pointers. These include things you can do to enrich your life and loving, as if I were answering one of your questions and giving you some helpful suggestions in person.

Blocks to Bliss

Because the practice of tantra is transformative, there could be some conflicts and controversial issues that arise along the way. These boxes prepare you for those dilemmas so you can avoid them and clear your path.

A Personal Note About My Own Journey

I am deeply grateful to everyone who has been part of my evolution at all stages of my life that has led to my latest reawakening into the more spiritual world. I'm amazed to reflect on some events that happened decades ago and are manifesting lately, consistent with the path of tantra. Like my dear childhood friend Rhea Ross insisting that I go with her to study yoga with Swami Satchidananda and Swami Muktananda over 30 years ago, when doing so was avant garde among people I knew. I've since visited the samadhis (graves) of these masters. Years ago too, spiritualist Judy Hevenly insisted I come with her to receive shaktipat from Gurumayi. And it was ages ago that I went to classes with Mantak Chia, Chinese master of the Taoism of sex (now living and teaching in Thailand), which proved to be my introduction into this tantric path that I have so intensely studied in more recent years. Also many years ago, my friend Laurie Sue Brockway (a true goddess and now a minister who also works with the Red Cross, as I do, during emergency disasters) kept telling me how "we just have to go to California to take one of Charles Muir's workshops in this terrific new thing called 'tantric sex.'" I've since been to many of Charles' seminars and his teacher trainings, and become a good friend of this gifted teacher.

For years in between those early tastes of tantra and now, I followed a most traditional professional path as a senior research scientist at the New York State Psychiatric Institute at Columbia Medical School. I did work on schizophrenia, depression and cross-cultural psychotic disorders with a brilliant British psychiatrist, Dr. Barry Gurland. In the late 1960s and early 1970s I became the protégé of the first professionals working in what was then the "new" field of sex therapy, who were collaborating with the "grandfather" and "grandmother" of sex therapy, Masters and

Johnson. This led to becoming one of the founders of the first medical-centered based organization of sex therapists; working on the sub-committee about sex for the American Psychiatric Association's Diagnostic and Statistical Manual, led by the eminent Robert Spitzer; running women's groups to teach women to have orgasm in 10 sessions with another pioneer in sexology, Dagmar O'Connor; and with my co-therapist and dear friend Dr. Larry Sharpe, writing some of the first professional papers about diagnosis, evaluation, and outcome of sex therapy. Along the way, I got my Ph.D. in clinical psychology at N.Y.U. and was fortunate to study "The Psychology of Love" with my supervisor and his wife, Irv and Sue Sarnoff.

The next phase of my work in the field of sex became more public as the host of radio call-in advice shows. This started over 20 years ago, on WABC Radio, but some of you are most familiar with my national radio show "LovePhones." Everyone has their favorites of the LovePhones radio calls, and so many of them come alive in the stories in my book *Generation Sex*. I am forever grateful to everyone who shared their touching stories—crying and laughing together—with my "radio family," co-host Chris Jagger, Badger, Jimmy, Sam, and Steve Kingston who started it all.

We talked about tantra on the radio years ago! How glad I am to have been able to do that—to have everyone using terms like "goddess" and "honoring," and to have broken radio ground by having the first sacred spot massage and female ejaculation to happen on radio airwaves (by tantra experts and friends Carla Tarantola and Sasha Lessin).

Acknowledgments

Tantra is about gratitude. I am ever so deeply grateful to my lifelong beloveds who have supported me from the core and taught me true unconditional love, including my mother Sylvia; my brother Robert and sister Barbara; Edward; and my "daughter" Alissa Pollack, whose beautiful energy infuses this book and everything I do, and who enriches my life every day with the best example of loving and support that I am blessed to have. Her light and devotion is a shining example of the love that is possible in this world.

Tantra is also about seeing the god and goddess in the people around you. I cherish all my friends, true gods and goddesses, who are such divine beings and who have taught and shared much love and growth with me in sisterhood and brotherhood. They include Jaiia Earthschild, Marci Javril, Voltage, Matt Feinberg, Laurie Handlers and Joshua Smith, Margot Anand, Carla Tarantola, Sasha and Janet Lessin, Brian Courtney, and many more, including those tantra teachers who so enthusiastically contributed their work to this book, like Carla and John, Laurie and Josh, Robert Frey, and Steve and Lokita Carter. I am especially grateful to the dear ones there for me at the beginning of this book, like dear friends Carla and John and my dear "sister" Nancy Froio, who offered brilliant inspiration the very first day this book was started during our third-level teacher training with Bodhi Avinasha; and to the dear ones who were there at the end, especially those tantrikas and dakas who read this manuscript and offered their love, support, suggestions, and gracious encouragement and enthusiasm for its contributions that went deep into my heart: Antoinette Asimus, Laurie Handlers, and Brian Courtney.

I offer the most profound of blessings and gratitude, too, to master tantra teachers and dear friends Charles Muir and Bodhi Avinasha, who have profoundly influenced my transformation. I have also been greatly affected on my path by "communicating" with Osho (who "left his body"); my training in Tibetan Tamang shamanism with Larry Peters and his shaman Amma; and my many trips to India, Japan, China, and Nepal, lands infused with astounding temples and god/goddess energy. Those trips led to quite an awakening about Hinduism and Buddhism, my friendship with Guru Rinpoche, and my "taking refuge" with a Buddhist lama Thrangu Rinpoche, who gave me the Buddhist name that translates into "Lake of Love."

This book is a labor of love, and I have felt the hand of spirits, divine beings, and angels guiding me in such a spiritually enlivening zone while doing this writing, that days passed with no need for sleep as the life force cursed through me. My sincerest gratitude to all of them, including wise ones who offered support, like Norah Beraja and Spiritual Counselor Carole Maracle (my most profound love goes out to her now on the other side).

My gratitude extends to all my Chinese friends who greatly enrich my life these days, and offer me an amazing view of how love can transcend all language and culture. These include all my friends at Liaoning Education Press who published my other books, *The Complete Idiot's Guide to Dating* and *The Complete Idiot's Guide to a Healthy Relationship* in Chinese; my colleagues at the Shanghai Center for Reproductive Health Instruction; and my other Chinese colleagues who are dear friends, such as Zhang Zhigang and Dr. Peicheng Hu.

The physical world also matters in getting a book together, hence my gratitude to the talented artists who contributed their brilliant work to this manuscript. I had been waiting for years to work with Hrana Janto, having first seen her goddess drawings so many years ago. This book has made that a reality, and now you can share her artistry. How amazing that not only is she connected to goddess, but also knew so much about tantra (and was as much a night owl as me!). And to Meadow and Al, who also contributed inspired art with a generous spirit to this volume. I shall always cherish Meadow's three couples on their journeys to tantric love!

Deepest gratitude to all at Alpha Books involved in this project: from my acquisitions editor Mike Sanders, who was kind, supportive, and helpful at every moment; to production editor Billy Fields; to my "old" friends (because I've written several in this series): publisher Marie Butler-Knight, publicists Gardi Wilks and Vicki Skelton, and development editor Lynn Northrup, who contributed great ideas, loving support, and hard work at all hours (a combination I love!).

My deepest gratitude, too, to all the men and women who have participated in the workshops and classes I have led, who have shown their trust, shared their innermost feelings, and shown such courage in their transformation; and to everyone on this journey bringing love and light into their own and others' lives. A note of appreciation and praise, too, to my students at Columbia University Teachers College, Cathy Sullivan, Kristyn Simon, and Jessica Costosa, who worked on the report about the first research on this work; and to Kiyoko Sasaki, who gave so generously of her kind and capable soul and helped me up to the last minute. I'm proud of them as shining examples of the new generation of healers!

This book was finished in momentous times, when terrorism struck New York and shook the world, and when war consequently broke out. Thousands sacrificed their lives in the terrorist attacks so the world could pay attention to the need for love and peace. The energy of that message infuses these pages. It made this effort timely, as people reach out now for safety and security, and the message of tantra—of trust and love—offers hope to heal our individual lives, our relationships, and our planet.

Illustrators

Hrana Janto is an illustrator and painter who specializes in sacred art, on subjects about mythic, folk, and fairy tales, and in styles from fantasy to ancient history. A goddess herself, Hrana created paintings of goddesses for the deck of cards in *The Goddess Oracle: A Way to Wholeness Through the Goddess and Ritual* (Element Books/ Harper Collins, 1997) and also teaches dance. The creator of the cover art, the Dr. Judy icon, and the majority of beautiful drawings throughout the book, her work has also appeared on calendars, logos, and in children's books and magazines.

Other artists who contributed the anatomical and some other drawings: Meadow is an illustrator, painter, and sculptor whose work is in the collection of the Smithsonian Institute in Washington, D.C. She has been shown in dozens of solo and group exhibitions in museums and galleries nationwide, from the New York Academy of Art to the American Crafts Museum. Her erotic artwork and poetry appeared in a book about women. A practicing reverend, Meadow is fulfilling her life's dream: establishing the first women's sculpture park, also a healing center and wildlife sanctuary called "Woodrock Sanctuary," the first park of its kind in this country. Meadow collaborated with Al Hughes, a New York fashion illustrator who branched out to write and illustrate children's stories and to draw humorous space beings and celebrity caricatures that have been featured on ABC news.

Testimonials

Here's what people are saying about Dr. Judy's speeches, workshops, seminars, and keynote speeches, as well as *The Complete Idiot's Guide to Tantric Sex*:

> "*The Complete Idiot's Guide to Tantric Sex* is an empowering, satisfying, beautifully written book on sexuality today. I invite all of you who really want authentic pleasure in your life to read this empowering worldview on sexually."—
> B.Courtney, contractor, California

"Dr. Judy's new book on tantric sex is a wonderful act of service for the world and presents an impressive unified view of tantra as it is practiced and taught today, offering a wealth of techniques and opportunities to individuals and couples to integrate sex and consciousness."—Antoinette Asimus, executive director, Tantrika International

"This is the definitive book on tantra. Dr. Judy is so complete in her writing that one no longer has to sort through bits and pieces from competing schools of thought. She has included it all. What a great work and what a pleasure to read it."—Laurie Handlers, co-founder, Butterfly Workshops

"I learned more from Dr. Judy's lectures than any other experience. I am forever transformed. She taught with brilliance, sensitivity—and made it so much fun. We cried and laughed!"—Student in New York tantra seminar

"The audience was riveted to Dr. Judy's keynote address at our event. It was full of fascinating information and really good humor and got us all out of our chair! Everyone wants her back!"—Texas executive, program chair

"Dr. Judy gave us rich information and we loved how she teaches, very unique. It changed my way of work and my way in my marriage."—Medical doctor in training class in China

"Dr. Judy changed my life in such a short time. She gets right to the core of the problem and really cares."—"Janine," radio listener

Trademarks

All terms mentioned in this book that are known to be or are suspected of being trademarks or service marks have been appropriately capitalized. Alpha Books and Penguin Group (USA) Inc. cannot attest to the accuracy of this information. Use of a term in this book should not be regarded as affecting the validity of any trademark or service mark.

Part 1

An Introduction to Tantric Sex: The Spiritual Path to Sacred Love

You're about to embark on a wonderful journey! Would you like to feel more intense excitement than ever before? Experience more love for yourself and others than you ever imagined possible? Have the best sex ever—truly, because it's not just sex; it's much more?

If you answered yes, get ready to be transformed, to feel freer, and more enthusiastic about yourself and your life. I can make these promises to you because I know it's possible and because I have seen inspiring transformations happen to men and women of all ages, young and old, when embarking on the exciting journey you can make in this book.

In this part, I'll introduce you to the ancient arts of lovemaking that started in the Eastern parts of the world thousands of years ago but that were lost over the centuries until now—when we in America are reviving them. You'll learn powerful breathing techniques, ways to generate powerful surges of sexual energy through your body, how to honor yourself and your partner, and all the basics to get started on the tantric path into deeper intimacy and higher states of ecstatic consciousness!

Chapter 1

What Is Tantric Sex?

In This Chapter

➤ What is tantra and tantric sex?

➤ How tantra affects your senses, spirit, mind, body, and soul

➤ How tantra is compatible with the modern Western way of life

➤ Fact or fiction: correcting myths about tantric sex

➤ The benefits of tantric sex

➤ Quiz: Are you ready for tantric sex?

Are you ready to experience bliss like you've never felt before? Imagine a sexual experience in which light flashes explode in your brain and every cell in your body feels alive. Imagine exploding with pleasure at even the slightest touch anywhere on your body. Imagine being in a sexual embrace of such utter joy and peacefulness that you "melt" into one another and then expand to feel "at one" with the entire universe.

If you would like to have those experiences, you're reading the perfect book! I'll take you through the world of tantric sex in which such experiences are possible and attainable. You will learn the basics teachings that bring you to these high states of pleasure and consciousness, and actual step-by-step practices you can perform immediately to reach these states of bliss and enlightenment.

The ancient practice of tantric sex is enjoying new popularity in America, making this the perfect time for you to harness what you already know about love and sexuality and take it to the next level. The world we live in is more ready than ever for tantric sex because of our new appreciation for deeper spiritual practices. In addition, as life is increasingly driven by technology so that person-to-person contact is diminishing, there is more desire for the intimate, meaningful contact that tantric sex offers. Read on through these chapters to achieve just that!

What Is Tantra?

To understand *tantric sex*, first you must understand what *tantra* is. The word "tantra" comes from ancient Sanskrit language meaning "expansion through awareness." Tantra is a spiritual path that involves very specific practices that use breath, sounds, movements, and symbols to quiet the mind and activate sexual energy, directing it throughout the body to achieve states of consciousness and bliss. Tantra traditions come from ancient practices in India, Nepal, and China. Whereas once they were reserved for royalty, now they are for all of us.

The practices also help heal past hurts, often stored in sexual centers of the body, so that you can be more fully present in the moment and open to love. When practiced together, the techniques bring about a powerful flow of energy between you and your partner, which energizes your being and expands your love for each other and the universe.

Tantra Tutorial

Tantra is a Sanskrit word meaning the teachings and practices that use energy to lead to a high state of bliss and enlightenment. **Tantric sex** applies the teachings of tantra to the sexual union in order to reach these high states.

Sacred Sex the Tantric Way

Feel your sex center now and sense any energy flowing there. Press yourself against the chair if you are sitting, or squeeze the muscles of your buttocks if you are standing. Therein lies a powerful energy generator, according to the tantric sex tradition—but the path does not end at just physical pleasure. Imagine feeling volts of electricity surging in your sexual area, which you could direct to your heart to feel more love—or to your mind for mind-blowing orgasms that last endlessly and put you in a state of complete joy and bliss.

Tantric sex involves the practice of various meditations and exercises (including yoga) to arouse and channel tremendous energy within the body, cycle that energy with a partner, and send it out into the world. It is intended for personal fulfillment, interpersonal intimacy, and connection to the entire world of beings. The energy generated by tantric sex can be used for either pleasure intended for blissful enlightenment or for healing. In Parts 1 and 2 I'll discuss tantric sex for pleasure. In Part 3 I'll tell you how to harness that pleasure for healing.

Achieving bliss is a major goal in tantric sex.

So what is tantric sex? It can be any and all of the following:

➤ Achieving a balance between male and female energies within the self and with a partner.

➤ Sexuality that directs energy toward free expression and breaks barriers internally and interpersonally. This is attained by elevating sex acts into a divine practice and uniting as beloveds for whom every touch and movement is considered a divine gift.

➤ Aligning with another being and with the world through divine sexual experience.

➤ Celebrating sexual union as an honoring of all beings and creation.

➤ Practices that liberate the soul to experience the highest levels of bliss.

Blocks to Bliss

The term "tantric sex" is often misinterpreted and potentially dangerous for the uninformed because it is used to refer to a mixture of different paths, as a buzzword for wanton sexuality, and as an excuse for sexual affairs, sex addictions, and sex for sale.

How Tantric Sex Frees Your Mind, Body, and Soul

As in any meditative practice, a crucial key to achieving the wonderful benefits of tantric sex is to quiet the mind; you will learn many methods of doing this in this book. Tantric sex is *mindful* in that you pay attention to what you're doing in the exchange between you and your partner. Being mindful induces a sense of respect and reverence for the experience, which lends itself to honoring each other as god and goddess, as you will learn in Chapter 4, "Awaken and Worship the God and Goddess in You." Consistent with mindfulness—but not at all contradictory—is the goal of tantric sex to get out of your mind and release your body. Through this kind of release you can freely express yourself and feel deep states of love outside of sexual pleasure that touch your soul.

Tantric Sex as the Path to Healing

An advanced use of tantric sex is for healing the body, mind, and spirit. Men as well as women suffer various hurts, rejections, and abuses—either real or perceived—from previous relationships. Through exercises and rituals explained in this book, tantric sex can be used to heal these hurts and free the body, mind, and spirit to feel peaceful, empowered, and open to love without fear, guilt, embarrassment, shame, or anger.

As you will see, specifically in Chapters 9, "Breaking Through Blocks to Bliss," and 17, "Sexual Healing to Set You Free," sexual healing involves three steps:

1. Identifying past hurts (either real or imagined) through sexual stimulation and meditation.
2. Releasing powerful emotions attached to these hurts.
3. Replacing the hurt with positive experience and emotions.

Dr. Judy's TantrAdvice

You might enjoy renting the popular movie *Bliss*, which is about the healing and personal growth that is possible through tantric practice. However, be aware that the true spiritual aspects are barely touched upon and the story is obviously skewed to conform to the needs of a marketable Hollywood drama.

Tantric Sex as Magic

Throughout this book and specifically in Chapter 15, "Make It Juicy with Magic and Play," I'll guide you through rituals and creative new techniques that will heal your hurts, make you feel young, and expand your ability to love and experience joy.

A Powerful Chemical Cocktail to Bliss

Tantric sex practices affect you in many dimensions—your senses, spirit, mind, body, and soul. Real changes occur in the body that are consistent with ecstatic states, including the flow of chemicals that lead to euphoria. These include *endorphins* (called "the pleasure chemical"), *oxytocin* (called the "cuddle chemical"), *phenylethlyamanime* (another pleasure chemical), and *adrenaline* (an activating chemical). Different practices stimulate the nervous system to create either excitation or relaxation.

Although tantric sex practices have not been studied in the laboratory, other related research has shown how certain activities that alter the brain and body are routes to bliss. Meditation, key to certain tantric practices, has been extensively researched and shown to have positive effects on brain wave activity, specifically causing relaxation responses. In preliminary research, a California sexologist measured women's brain wave activity during relaxation, imagery, and tantric-related masturbatory activity and showed that women who practice tantric activities can induce brain waves during self-pleasuring that are associated with pleasurable altered states of consciousness.

Find and Follow the Pathways of Energy

In tantric sex you discover energy pathways in the body and concentrate on controlling the movement of that energy within those pathways. You interweave those energies with your partner to dissolve feelings of separation and to become united. As you will discover in Chapter 2, "The Basics: Yes, Yin Yang, Yoni, and Yab Yum," tantric sex brings together key glands in the brain (the pineal and pituitary glands) that correspond to energy centers, or chakras. When this happens, you will see how grand it is!

How the West Revived Eastern Tantric Sex Practices

Ancient Eastern cultures have been practicing some of these sacred sex traditions for centuries. Unfortunately, through political upheavals, religious objections, and cultural changes in those societies, the practices were suppressed or forgotten. It's amazing that these practices are being revived now in America and being returned to their origins by key figures in the field—as well as by me in my current extensive work in the Orient. I call this the "Enlightenment Road" for new thinkers, bringing precious new ways of life from one country to another, much like traders brought their wares along the famous "Silk Road" through China centuries ago.

Blocks to Bliss

Don't get so carried away in the pursuit of bliss that you forget that the goal behind the practice of tantric sex is the attainment of wisdom, enlightenment, and the benefit of all mankind, not just individual pleasure.

Me with Chinese colleagues answering calls on a Shanghai hotline.

Signing books at a national Chinese book fair.

Although meditation from Eastern gurus such as Swamis Muktananda and Sachidananda became popular about 25 years ago, and tantric sex practices were similarly introduced by Easterners such as Mantak Chia, the practices became mainstream only about a decade ago. Tantric sex practices were revived mainly by students of related arts of yoga and meditation in the West, who came upon teachings of tantra and integrated them into their own practices.

Although tantric practices were developed in the Eastern part of the world, they are particularly applicable and appealing to the Western world today. Here are 10 ways tantric sex has modern-day appeal to the West:

1. Tantric sex promises simple steps and instant results, which are appealing to Westerners who are conditioned to "instant" lifestyles (instant coffee, fast food, instant gratification) and quick fixes.

2. The practices are based on channeling and using desire, rather than denying desire. Most Westerners don't like the idea of abandoning desire, but adapting it to reach higher states is acceptable and even appealing.

3. The practices don't require the traditional retreat from society. Mainstream Westerners are not willing to find ecstasy and enlightenment by joining an ashram for years of quiet meditation, shaving their heads, wearing orange robes, or giving up worldly goods.

4. Tantric sex is based on the principle of transformation of energy; Westerners are familiar with this concept in physics, electronics, and modern technology.

5. Westerners like to control (things, themselves, others); tantra harnesses control by practices that channel energy into different body parts and for specific purposes.

Tantra Tales

Perhaps one of the most notable bridges between Eastern and Western thought in our time is the Indian mystic Osho, who knew he had to adapt the most austere Eastern meditation practices to make them more appealing to Westerners. He set up a retreat center in America in the 1970s. His lectures were peppered with jokes and included freeform dancing to live bands and celebration, and courses taught subjects like psychic massage, aromatherapy, and astrology.

6. Tantric sex practices encourage experience and self-determination, practical day-to-day rituals, and a step-by-step approach to achieving higher states of peacefulness, bliss, and consciousness rather than blind faith, which is not as appealing to Westerners accustomed to questioning belief systems.

7. Tantric sex starts with individual practice, which generates into practice with a partner that can then benefit the whole society. This is consistent with the individualism that is the basis of Western society.

8. Tantric sex hails self-discovery, a practice consistent with the Western obsession with self-improvement and self-mastery.

9. Tantric sex honors the human body, consistent with Western appreciation and focus on the body. Far from being a hindrance to enlightenment, the body is considered the vehicle for bliss.

10. Tantric sex practices encourage heightening the senses through beautiful clothing, attractive surroundings, and stimulation of all the senses, which is consistent with Western obsessions with worldly pleasures.

Sacred Sex

Sacred sex refers to the connection between two *higher selves* for the intention of a divine union—not for physical thrill, lust, or intent to use another person for personal sexual or emotional satisfaction. The coming together of two beings is considered an act of godliness, to be taken seriously and done with great reverence, serving as a bridge between the physical world and the spiritual world and reached via the vehicle of the body and breath.

Several different types of tantra are practiced and taught in modern times. Some of these preserve the ancient traditions; others have adapted some practices to suit more Western or modern ways. However, most of the ideas are based on similar principles, such as:

➤ Sexuality is sacred.

➤ All beings are connected and equal.

➤ Sexual energy can be directed and channeled for the benefit of the individual, couple, and all beings.

➤ Sexual union is the road to higher consciousness and ecstasy.

➤ The breath is the key to releasing this powerful energy.

Even if you know nothing of tantra yet, you might know about, have heard a friend talk about, or had a taste yourself of an experience in which you were making love and "melted into" your partner, or "felt at one with the universe." Tantric lovemaking leads to this merging of the self with the beloved and the universe. This can be a challenge, because it requires suspending the rational mind—the thinking, worrying, critical part that defines who we think we are and our daily interests, needs, and problems. Oh, the mind struggles against giving up its worrying—after all, as tantric teacher Bodhi Avinasha says, "If it gave up worry, might the mind then be out of a job?" The mind constantly tells you, "I need this"; "I should do that"; "I don't like this." Tantric sex gives you a chance to stop the ego and the mind from this longing and worrying.

Ecstasy Essentials

Critics claim that Westerners have diluted or tainted the practices of tantric sex from the pure form that originated centuries ago. Westerners actually should be credited for reviving (even if somewhat revising) practices that were neglected for centuries.

Tantra Tutorial

To release the ego, you can call upon your **higher self,** or the wise part of you that is above judgments, worldly fears, and fear of the unknown. In quiet moments, some people find it easier to visualize this self as actually above the head, looking down on the problem or situation and witnessing it.

Myths About Tantra and Tantric Sex

Because tantra celebrates sexuality, it has become ripe for criticism and misunderstanding. Here are some myths and truths about tantric sex:

Myth: Tantric sex is all about sex.

Truth: Tantric sex practices sometimes do not even include genital contact—they are really about energetic and spiritual contact between partners. Intercourse or the connection of genitals only serves to heighten the energetic connection when a couple is ready for that intimate stage.

Myth: Practicing tantra means you give up pleasure.

Truth: This myth is the opposite of the mistaken belief I just addressed that tantra is all about sex; neither extreme is true. Tantra does not require a renunciation of pleasure, even though some yogic practices do; rather tantra is an enhancement of joy and pleasure. The tantric sex path does not see desire as something to be denied, as if you have to mimic the image of the Buddha sitting silently meditating cross-legged, alone, not thinking of anything—and giving up sex. Instead, tantra recognizes the powerful force that sex plays in our lives and harnesses it to achieve states of bliss beyond just physical pleasure.

Myth: Tantric sex encourages indulgences of the appetites, which leads to affairs or orgies.

Truth: Tantric sex does not advocate indulging uncontrolled sexual or other appetites, or multiplying your desires and wallowing in pleasure. In fact, it trains us to control desire to channel it to higher purposes. What's more, connection between two people is meant to be considered very seriously and commitment highly regarded. Although some people use tantric sex as a way to rationalize having sex with many different people or many people at once, this is not the spirit of true tantra. Sexuality is not meant to be flittered away mindlessly or thoughtlessly, but honored and intended for the purpose of higher states of consciousness, rather than simply physical stimulation or satisfaction. You could even say that you can resist sexual contact with others because you are trained to be able to connect with others emotionally and spiritually, without having to engage bodies in sex. In a true tantric practitioner, a newly liberated libido does not act out promiscuous desires.

Dr. Judy's TantrAdvice

To understand the difference between allowing pleasure rather than grasping for it, imagine a person you desire in front of you. First, picture stepping forward and grabbing for that person, who stays out of your reach. Feel your frustration and heart pounding. In contrast, picture staying in place and seeing that physical being dissolved into a ray of light that either comes to you or not. Experience a more peaceful and expansive feeling within yourself.

Dr. Judy's TantrAdvice

If a married woman feels attracted to another man, instead of having an affair, in tantric practice she would watch her feelings, meditate on them, and follow the force of that fantasy to bring new energy into her sex life with her husband.

Blocks to Bliss

Beware of anyone, tantra teacher or otherwise, who demands that you follow them rigidly; give up your life, friends, or family; or sign over your finances.

Myth: Tantric sex turns you into a sex maniac.

Truth: Tantric sex does release your sexual energy and give you full permission to express yourself—so the tendency to act out sexually is possible, but only if you misuse the practices. If you learn the practices responsibly, you will overcome any tendencies to have random, meaningless sex.

Myth: Tantric sex is for Easterners and is not consistent with how we see sex in the West.

Truth: As I mentioned earlier in this chapter, tantric sex practices are actually quite consistent with our Western way of thinking. The focus on the individual, the acceptance of pleasure, and clearly defined steps are a perfect fit with the way Westerners currently live their lives. Tantric sex retools these approaches to be more aligned with the road to true ecstasy.

Myth: Tantra is a religion and a cult that will trap or brainwash you.

Truth: Tantra is neither a religion or a cult. The genuine ethical tantra teachers do not want to control you; they merely guide you in a series of practices that you choose for yourself and adapt into your life.

Myth: It takes a long time to learn how to do tantric sex.

Truth: One of the beautiful aspects of the tantric path is that the practices can be put into effect immediately and results noticed. In just one weekend workshop you can learn enough basic ideas and practical exercises to immediately improve your sex life and general feelings about yourself, which will generate to every part of your life.

Why Tantric Sex Now?

Several factors have led to the popularity of tantric sex in our modern times:

➤ In the last two decades of the twentieth century, couples and singles suffered great distress and frustration over relationships and searched for solutions in all directions. Self-help books and courses have become increasingly popular as people seek solutions to finding and keeping the love they want. People could choose from a growing number of approaches once considered "alternative" or "pop psychology," but that are now much more mainstream. The options are innumerable, as is evidenced by the growing number of self-enrichment and alternative health and healing centers.

➤ Co-dependency and addictions of all kinds, which stem from lack of love and true intimate connection, have escalated. Sufferers and health experts are seeking, and willing to try, many new kinds of solutions to these problems.

➤ We are moving away from the view of relationships as "dysfunctional"—which emphasizes only negative patterns of behavior—toward a more positive view, which focuses on the potential for healthy interactions.

➤ People have increasingly turned to medications to relieve depression and anxiety (disorders that have reached epidemic proportions), yet found these solutions disappointing.

➤ Pressures of corporate downsizing, increased consumerism, and technological advances have put increasing strain on relationships, causing loneliness and isolation and turning people toward Eastern philosophies, which shun materialism.

➤ The growing interest in improving relationships and attaining a deeper connection between lovers has led gradually to the resurgence of the Age of Aquarius, with its interest in what's come to be called *spirituality*. This spirituality focuses attention on the deeper parts of one's soul, instead of just rational reasons for coupling or particular ways that couples can stay together.

➤ World tensions, terrorism, and war have increased people's distrust and distress, and therefore a desire for peace both internally and in their daily life. Tantra stands for that trust and peace, in the internal and external worlds.

Tantra Tutorial

Once "alternative" but now more mainstream methods for personal growth and health range from bodywork or massage techniques to past-life regression (imagining eras in which you might have lived previously that helps explain your relationships, problems, or goals in the present).

Twelve Benefits of Tantric Sex Practices

Devoting yourself to any practice has to have payoffs. There are many dividends from investing time and energy into tantric sex. Tantric sex practices can help you achieve the following:

1. **Expand your possibilities for love.** Tantric sex shows you how to deepen the physical and spiritual connection with your partner, and nurture and love yourself.

2. **Rejuvenate your health.** Practicing tantric sex has physiological and psychological effects that maintain—and regain—health. For example, breathing techniques bring more air into the body, nourishing the tissues and muscles. Research has shown a link between the effects of relaxation, meditation, and spirituality and better physical and emotional health. People who are spiritual have lower blood pressure, lower levels of anxiety and depression, more stable hormone levels, and better functioning immune systems.

3. **Tap into the fountain of youth.** For all the health benefits mentioned previously, practicing tantra can make you feel and look young again.

4. **Empower women.** Many women suffer from low self-esteem. They might have a poor body image or they might give in to sex when they would really like to say no or not tell their partner what they really want. In tantric sex, women are treated with the respect and honor they desire and deserve.

5. **Empower men.** So many men worry about their penis size, and how long they last in sex. Many also don't know how to commit or really please a woman. When men feel more empowered in sex, they become more confident and open to being more caring in their relationship.

6. **Help you achieve true satisfaction from sex.** When the sex act is over, are you ever left with the feeling that you're not really finished? This is often because the sexual act does not go beyond the genitals—it does not touch the heart. In tantric sex, you can reach the state in which every cell in your body feels nurtured from the soul connection you feel with your partner. When sex happens with this kind of heart connection, both body and mind are fed.

7. **Alleviate anxieties and depression.** Statistics show millions of men and women suffer from anxiety and depression, including symptoms like fatigue, listlessness, and sleeping and eating disturbances. Tantric sex provides an enormous source of energy to the body and peacefulness to the mind that overcomes these problems.

8. **Elevate sex.** When you elevate sex to a level of sacredness, it takes on a richer dimension than a mere physical act.

9. **Prolong pleasure.** Tantric sex techniques make lovemaking—including the afterglow—last a long time. This occurs not only through ejaculatory control but by learning to direct sexual energy anywhere in the body or into spiritual manifestations.

10. **Heal past emotional wounds.** Tantric sex can help you heal past hurts from all kinds of painful or traumatic experiences in which you felt betrayed or abused.

Instead, it helps you create experiences of being honored and respected in sex and in life in general.

11. **Deepen your connection to others.** Tantric sex gives more meaning to life and enriches your relationships.

12. **Affect the world positively.** Your personal gains cause you to generate more positive and loving energy outwardly, extending to everyone you come into contact with, even altering the energy of the planet (since all things on a meta-physical or spiritual level are interrelated).

Tantra Tales

Michelle noticed that her husband was less enthusiastic about their sex life after only two years of being together. She admitted that she had grown more inhibited, spending less time touching him and only allowing intercourse without giving him the oral pleasure he once enjoyed so much. Learning tantric sex practices turned all this around. Michelle committed herself to becoming a better lover, offering to massage her husband all over, experimenting with new ways of pleasing him, following her instinct and sensing what he would enjoy.

Are You Ready for Tantra?

How do you know whether you're ready for tantric sex practices? Take this quiz to see whether these practices will be consistent with where you are now in your spiritual journey. Share this quiz with your partner to see if he or she is also ready to begin these practices.

The "Are You Ready for Tantra?" Quiz

Check Yes or No for each of the following questions:

1. Are you willing to change the way you have sex now to have a deeper, more meaningful experience? ❏ Yes ❏ No

2. Do you believe that how you breathe affects your sexual experience? ❏ Yes ❏ No

3. Do you think that women can have multiple orgasms but men cannot? ❏ Yes ❏ No

4. Do you think a man should be a "man" and a woman should be a "woman," with no crossover in those roles? ❑ Yes ❑ No

5. Do you think that a man has to ejaculate to achieve pleasure? ❑ Yes ❑ No

6. Do you want lovemaking to last longer? ❑ Yes ❑ No

7. Do you think you must have an orgasm to be satisfied in sex? ❑ Yes ❑ No

8. Do you need a certain type of lover to be happy? ❑ Yes ❑ No

9. Do you want to have sex with your partner on a high spiritual level? ❑ Yes ❑ No

10. Do you think that your loving can influence more peace on earth? ❑ Yes ❑ No

Scoring: Count the total number of Yes and No answers you have to the preceding questions, according to the following:

Number of Yes answers to questions 1, 2, 6, 9, 10: _____

Number of No answers to questions 3, 4, 5, 7, 8: _____

My total score = _____

My partner's total score = _____

If your total score is more than 5, you are really ready for tantric practice. You believe in channeling pleasure for higher purpose and want to use lovemaking to achieve an energetic exchange with a partner. You are willing to enthusiastically participate in tantric training and are ready to learn the skills that will enable you to use your sexuality in a sacred way.

If your total is between 3 and 5, you have the potential to start tantric practice and would benefit greatly from taking a tantric course. Read on to learn more about tantric sex, and spark your interest and commitment to harnessing the potential you already have.

If your total is less than 3, you have skepticism about how to harness sexuality, but still should read on and consider how to integrate these new, exciting practices into your life.

The Ten Pledges of the Tantric Sex Path

Once you have committed to the path of tantric sex, see how the following pledges feel to you. Hopefully, a peaceful feeling washes over you (your breath more even, mind restful) as you read these sentences:

1. I pledge to explore the divinity within myself.

2. I pledge to honor the god and goddesses divinities in others.

3. I pledge to explore my sensuality and sexuality as a way to rejuvenate my organs of blocked emotions.

4. I pledge to balance my inner being, my relationships, and my environment.

5. I pledge to apply my balance and bliss for the good of the rest of the world.

6. I pledge to discover my sensuality for harmonious relationships.

7. I pledge to remove emotional obstacles from my past or present, to free me to express my inner being and joy.

8. I pledge to connect with my inner child for joy.

9. I pledge to be both a healer and a lover for my partner and myself.

10. I pledge to use my sexual energy wisely and judiciously for increased self-confidence, gentleness, power, pleasure, harmony, and freedom for myself, my beloveds, and others in this world.

The Least You Need to Know

➤ The practices of tantric sex can lead you to more satisfying, blissful sex; but even more important, to higher states of consciousness and better relationships.

➤ Although tantric sex practices originated in ancient Eastern cultures, they can be easily integrated into the Western way of life.

➤ Tantric sexual practices have many physical, emotional, interpersonal, and spiritual benefits.

➤ Anyone can follow tantric sex practices as long as they are willing to make changes in their attitudes and behaviors and make a commitment to an honorable and respectful way of life.

Chapter 2

The Basics: Yes, Yin Yang, Yoni, and Yab Yum

In This Chapter

➤ Achieving balance and uniting male and female, yin and yang, Shiva and Shakti

➤ A test of opposites

➤ The lovemaking position of yab yum

➤ Sex as energy, not just an act

➤ New terms for lovers and sex organs

➤ Setting boundaries of "yes" and "no"

Now that you are embarking on the study of tantric sex, you'll find yourself changing how you view certain aspects of yourself, your relationships, and the world—a paradigm shift from what likely is familiar or comfortable for you. Through your new exploration, you will learn to look beyond the physical being to see the divinity in every man and woman. You'll view sex as sacred and spiritual rather than simply a physical act. What's more, you'll learn a new language of love as you progress to higher states of consciousness and bliss.

As you embark on this journey, suspend any limiting beliefs of how you think you have to be, what you think you need from a lover, and what has to happen in sex for you to be fulfilled. As you read this chapter, allow yourself to embrace new ideas about who you are, what a really happy partnership entails, and how to have truly great sex.

In this chapter I'll introduce you to those basic concepts and practices of tantric sex that are important to your understanding of this exciting new way of life and loving. Get ready to stretch—I promise it will be worth it!

Yin and Yang: What Is Male and What Is Female?

I'm sure you're familiar with traditional stereotypes of men as assertive and powerful, and women as soft and nurturing. We also know too well the criticisms that men don't express feelings (thinking that's a "female" thing to do), and that women don't speak up or take credit for what they do (characteristics considered more "male"). Fortunately, an increasing number of men and women are allowing themselves a broader range of behaviors.

Tantric sex might seem to affirm these opposite characteristics, since a fundamental principle of tantra is that male and female are considered polar opposites. According to Eastern theory, yin represents feminine characteristics and yang represents masculine traits. However, that's not to say that a woman can't be "yang" and a male "yin." Rather than taking this principle literally, try to imagine male and female as energies. The path to bliss in tantra is the union of these two powerful forces.

Ecstasy Essentials

Tantra asserts that all problems, fears, and unhappiness in relationships derive from the feeling that we are not whole and are searching to complete the unfulfilled parts of ourselves. Yet each of us has the capacity to embrace our male and female energies, to become whole, and to come together in a healthy union.

The Circle of Coupled Consciousness

You've undoubtedly seen the circular yin yang symbol before, with one white and one black side. It's the classic Chinese symbol of the male and female energies uniting into a whole. According to Eastern theory, the circle represents the union of yin as the feminine or female energy and yang as the masculine or male energy. Yang is the force of father, heaven, sky, and all that is logical and penetrating. Yin is the feminine force of the earth and mother, representing aspects of being that are nurturing and receptive.

Yang is quick to fire whereas yin is slow to heat. Think of how similar this is to the typical sexual response cycle of men and women—he's always so ready for sex while she needs more romance to get in the mood. (In fact, men need only three minutes to get excited, whereas it takes women fifteen minutes to reach equivalent arousal.)

Yang corresponds to the upper part of the body, including the throat, brain, and power center, while yin is linked to the heart and lower body (the womb and sexual organs). (I'll discuss more about these energy centers in the next chapter.) Again, these ideas are consistent with stereotypes that men are more "in their heads" and into power, while women are more in touch with their body and emotions. Tantric sex practices give you specific tools, disciplined practices, and fun games that bring these two parts and characteristics into balance—to assist your journey to cosmic bliss.

The Chinese symbol of the union of yin and yang.

Shiva and Shakti

Another common image in tantric tradition is the Hindu couple in the form of Lord Shiva and his female consort, the Goddess Shakti. He is considered the mighty creator, and she the essence of energy. Their symbolic union inspires us to expect to be treated like a god or goddess, and to surrender to the god or goddess in our partner. (I'll discuss more about how honoring in this way leads to sacred love and magical sex in Chapter 4, "Awaken and Worship the God and Goddess in You," and in Part 3, "Making Major Progress on the Path to Ecstasy." There you'll learn exactly how to treat each other to have awesome and enlivening loving experiences.)

Lord Shiva and Goddess Shakti.

Shiva's male energy also represents bliss, and Shakti's female energy represents wisdom—another magical combination of two essential elements necessary to reach enlightenment. The perfect pair is often depicted in statues and paintings in many entwined positions—embracing, sitting, standing, balancing on one leg, or dancing, with Shakti wrapped around Shiva's body or hiked on his hips. (Dancing, as I'll tell you later in this book, is a sacred ritual to free the spirit and facilitate enlightenment.) The pair also might be sitting inside a *lotus* (a plant in the water lily family, considered in Hinduism to be the source of life).

Getting in Touch with Opposites

To reach the ideal balance of opposite energies, first you must recognize any divisions you have made. Look at the following list of stereotypic characteristics. Circle the ones that you identify with or that best describe you. Read the opposite quality and see if you can imagine being like that as well. Add some other qualities you can think of.

Strong	Weak
Happy	Sad
Active	Passive
Angry	Peaceful
Hateful	Loving
Cold	Hot
Light	Dark
Logical	Emotional
Sun	Moon
Other: _____	
Other: _____	

> **Tantra Tutorial**
>
> The left side of the body is considered the receiving side (yin); therefore many tantric sex practices I tell you about in this book are meant to be done while gazing mainly into your partner's left eye, or by visualizing energy entering through your left hand and flowing out toward your partner with your right hand.

Imagine going from one extreme to the other, and then what it would be like to embrace both characteristics.

Achieving Balance and Union of Opposites

An ultimate goal of tantric sex is to balance polarities, which you explored in the previous exercise. Different cultures might use different terms, but all similarly search for balance of opposites and use rituals to achieve sacred union of male and female energies. Some of these practices seem esoteric to us; others are familiar. For example, prayers invoke both energies, as in "God's will be done on earth as it is in heaven." In tantric practice, energy from heaven (also considered male—yang or "father" energy) has to unite with energy from earth (also considered female—yin and "mother" energy) in a cosmic circle, in order to reach the desired higher states of bliss.

People often ask me whether opposites really attract. Think of your past relationships. Have you and your partner been opposites in any way? Perhaps one of you was the pursuer and the other the pursued. Perhaps one was more emotional and the other more rational; one more extravagant and the other more prudent. These couplings are common and represent the self seeking balance. These relationships can certainly work, and being different can create excitement, but it's unhealthy to seek an opposite to fulfill a part of you that is lacking (as in the case of a woman choosing a man who is extremely logical because she feels too emotional).

Tantra Tutorial

In ancient times among certain groups, **androgyny** (being both male and female) was honored, and **hermaphrodites** (people born with genitalia of both sexes) represented perfection.

Position Yourselves for Love in Yab Yum

The Hindu term *yab yum* refers to the position you might have seen in tantric art: The man sits with legs crossed and the female straddles in his lap, their legs are wrapped around each other and if possible, meet behind the back (the same position is called *Cranes with Necks Intertwined* in Chinese). Yab yum represents the union of opposites, like the male and female forces of yin and yang. This position accomplishes several goals, as it …

➤ Enables lovers to look directly in each other's eyes.

➤ Aligns their energy centers (something I'll discuss in the next chapter).

➤ Gives easy access to each other's bodies.

Dr. Judy's TantrAdvice

When assuming the yab yum position, choose a place to sit that is comfortable for you. Experiment (try sitting in a chair). Use a pillow to be more comfortable and aligned, especially if one partner is much shorter than the other.

Couple sitting in yab yum position.

Sex as Energy—Not Activity

Sex in the Western world has all too often been a matter of performance (how much the woman moans, how long the man lasts) or behaviors (such as oral sex or intercourse). Tantric sex redefines what sex is—not as an action, but as movement of energy within you individually, and between you and your partner. The practices guide you to generate sexual energy, transform it into love energy, and transmit it to your partner and even to the universe. (I'll discuss this further and give you specific techniques on how to do this in Part 3.)

My Partner, My Beloved

Tantra is about sacred love; so, the partner is considered a *beloved* to be honored, cherished, and loved unconditionally. Use the term "beloved" when you speak to your partner and see how just the word alone arouses loving feelings. Say, "John, my beloved, I would like to ...." Also, when speaking about your

Dr. Judy's TantrAdvice

A man's energy "enters" the woman (and vice versa) through penetration or the exchange of body fluids; an important reason to be selective about with whom you have a sexual embrace or physical encounter.

24

partner to someone else, refer to him or her as "My beloved ...." It might seem strange at first, but you will also be sending out that loving energy to the person with whom you are speaking, who will share in that love.

What Do You Call Your Sex Organs? The New Terms for Yoni and Lingam

Tantric sex also gives you a new vocabulary for the genitals, to honor the sacredness of those parts of the body and their role in sex. I'll tell you about these shortly, but first it's important to identify how you already feel by the labels you use. Look over this list of names for the female and male genitalia and add any others you can think of. Circle the ones that you feel sound positive, and make you feel good about yourself and your body, or your partner's body. Put an X through the ones that you feel are negative and pejorative.

Ecstasy Essentials

Tantric sex is commonly associated with the *Kama Sutra*, the ancient Hindu texts of love that contain advice on love and many positions for lovemaking. Some of these will be presented in Part 3, where I'll tell you about many specific practices for pleasing your partner.

Vagina	Clitoris	Pussy
Momma lips	Down there	Jewel gate (Japanese)
Pleasure pot	Mystic rose	Doorway of life (Chinese)
Chalice	Sacred cave	Kohe (Hawaiian)
Cunt	Other: _____	Other: _____

Now do the same for words that refer to the male genitalia:

Penis	Phallus (Greek)	Prick
Pecker	Whonker	Thing
Johnson	Whacker	Peter
Family jewels	Arrow of love	Jade flute (Chinese)
Wand of light	Other: _____	Other: _____

Consider using these words for genitalia (as I will be doing throughout this book) from the tantric sex traditions:

➤ **Yoni** is a Sanskrit word meaning "womb" and "source." It refers to the vagina, a woman's sacred temple.

Dr. Judy's TantrAdvice

Using tantric terms might feel stilted to you or your partner at first, but with practice it will become more comfortable and infuse you with positive energy. Honoring words convey more respect. Practice saying, "I adore your lingam" or "What a beautiful yoni."

Ecstasy Essentials

Asking permission of your partner for any sexual act (or anything else) you would like honors the other person and is a rule of tantric sex. I'll discuss this in more detail in Chapters 10, "Giving Her the Best Nights Ever," and 11, "Giving Him the Best Nights Ever," which cover pleasing your partner.

➤ **Sacred space** refers to the divine insides of the female, meant to be treated with great reverence, as it is the source of Shakti, female power and feminine divine energy.

➤ **Pearl** is a word for the clitoris.

➤ **Lingam**, **vajra**, or **thunderbolt** refer respectfully to the male phallus, and evoke the male energy of the Hindu Lord Shiva.

A New View of Desire

You feel desire every time you feel the urge to have something you think will make you feel better. "That chick is hot," you might say about how a woman looks, or "I want that guy," you might exclaim about a man you think will make your dreams come true. These desires can come from feeling incomplete, expressing the feeling that "If only I had (him or her, this or that), I would be happy," reflecting a neediness and driving you to possess someone or something. Ironically, once you have what you desire, you often become disillusioned; for example, you might search for someone prettier, richer, or more interesting. Through tantric sex practices you are no longer desperate, or attached to superficial needs, allowing you to create healthier relationships.

Empowered to Say "Yes" or "No"

When people are empowered to set their boundaries, both in sex and in general, they gain valued self-esteem. In tantric sex, you are in charge of your body and soul. A lover should always ask your permission to enter your sacred space, and you have the right to say yes or no. Are you ready to say no to being disrespected, pressured into sex, touched in a way that makes you uncomfortable? When you speak your truth in this way, your partner is empowered as well, by knowing your limits and how to please you. Are you also ready to say yes to longer lovemaking, ecstasy in multiple orgasms, deeper satisfaction and intimacy, spiritual love connected to blissful sex? If so, you've come to the right book!

Taking Care of Your Body Temple

According to tantra, your body is your temple. To reach enlightenment through tantric sex, you have to take care of that temple. Any fitness routine you prefer is helpful, although many tantric practitioners mix their sexual practices with some form of yoga (a gentle choice). Yogic poses have roots in tantric lovemaking positions from ancient texts (although they also became the route to asceticism and abstinence). Read more about useful, interesting, and fun routines you can use individually or with a partner in Chapters 6, "Amp Up or Damp Down Your Sexual Energy," and in 14, "Getting Fit Together for Tantric Sex. "

Tantric sex practices also balance the opposites of meditation and *activation*. This is done through breathing practices, which send breath through your body, as I'll tell you about in the next chapter.

The Least You Need to Know

➤ Tantric sex involves the union and balance of opposites, female and male energies referred to as yin and yang that symbolize dark and light, moon and sun, receiving and giving, heaven and earth.

➤ Yab yum, the position for lovemaking described in ancient Hindu texts in which the woman sits in the man's lap, helps align energies necessary for a powerful tantric love connection.

➤ Tantric sex is not simply an act but the buildup, movement, and transmission of energy through your own body and between you and a partner.

➤ Setting boundaries by saying yes or no to what you want builds self-esteem and empowerment that is essential for a healthy interaction with a partner in tantric sex.

➤ Honoring and respecting your partner is essential in tantric sex. It is accomplished by asking permission for any sexual act and in using terms like "beloved" to refer to your partner and "sacred space," "yoni," and "lingam" to refer to sexual organs.

Chapter 3

Spinning Your Wheels and Breathing to Ecstasy

> ### In This Chapter
>
> ➤ Powerful breathing techniques for better sex
>
> ➤ The chakra wheels keep spinning: seven energy centers in the body
>
> ➤ Seeing love more clearly through the third eye
>
> ➤ Sounds that evoke bliss
>
> ➤ Symbols that evoke ecstasy
>
> ➤ The inner smile necessary for joy

You will explore many sacred practices in this book; I promise all will be fascinating and fun. They will include using sights, sounds, and symbols in your journey to bliss. I'll tell you about these in this chapter.

However, all require one practice also presented in this chapter. It's something that you are doing at this very minute: breathing. Breathing properly and directing the breath is essential to reach the deepest possible intimacy and highest possible states of ecstasy.

The Importance of Your Breath

Proper breathing supplies necessary oxygen to your cells and frees emotions and sensuality. It can lead to euphoria and even orgasm. The breath is key to lasting longer in sex, having more intense orgasms, and feeling more intimate love. Sounds simple, doesn't it? Hold on! There's the problem: We hold our breath too much! How are you breathing now? No doubt it's shallow and barely expanding your chest. Shallow breathing is not healthy!

Here are three simple practices I teach people that you can do now for bigger breath:

➤ **The Source of Life**   Notice the place in your body from which your breath is coming. Is it from your throat, chest, or stomach area? Make a deliberate effort to make it come from deeper within your body. With each breath, trace the breath and bring your hand to where it stops before you exhale. Lower your hand and make the breath come from as low down as your genitals. That is key to firing up your sex energy.

➤ **Egg to Eagle**   This one is great to do if you're sitting. Exhale as you crunch down into a ball, bringing your elbows in close to your body and resting your hands gently on the back of your head. Feel the stretch across and down your back along your spine. Inhale, lifting up slowly, and stretch to bring your elbows as far back behind you as you can. Feel the stretch in your chest, throw your chest out, and arch your back. Feel all the air rushing into your lungs. Repeat.

➤ **The Bellows**   The goal of this exercise is to take in as much air as possible by imagining that your lungs are a bellows. Keep your arms comfortably by your side. Blow all your air out forcefully, making a loud "whoosh" and then suck in as much air as possible with as much noise. Continue, taking longer breaths and making louder noises. Feel better already? (These are sounds you will eventually emit during sexual experiences—freer sounds allow more intense sexual responses.)

Why We Don't Breathe Correctly

The more air you get, the better your body, brain, and organs are fueled; the more relaxed you are; and the clearer your thinking is. The fact is that many factors inhibit our breath. Are your clothes too tight? Don't be vain—my whole life changed for the better once I started wearing looser clothes, elastic waistbands, and easier-fitting clothes! Is your posture terrible? Do you slump, like I do, over the computer?

Some causes of poor breathing are more difficult to identify or change. Do you have a physical disorder? Side effects from medications? Undiagnosed food allergies? (My life and breathing also changed for the better once I realized how creamy foods created phlegm in my throat and inhibited my breathing—not good for my work on the radio!)

Dr. Judy's TantrAdvice

Don't worry (like I used to) if you yawn; that's a good sign your body is taking in more air!

Another fault lies in fear. Shallow air protects us with shallow feelings. Emotions can come flooding out with intense breathing. For this result, many tantric workshops include emotional release exercises.

Tantra Tales

One patient of mine, Kim, protested that her boyfriend did not love her enough. But when I asked her to take deep breaths and focus on her body sensations, she resisted. Whenever she complied, floods of tears would fall, revealing her pain as a little girl desperately wanting love but deep down being afraid that if she received it, she would lose it. So she kept the breath—and the love—at a distance. With encouragement and understanding, she was able to take deep breaths, allow the emotions, and feel more loved.

The Chakra Wheels

Energetics is the "in" word of the new millennium. It means focusing on energy. Physicists agree that everything in our world is energy. Think of how we talk about being drawn to someone "like a magnet," or feel "electricity" in their presence—all signs of energy.

According to tantric philosophy, energy centers known as *chakras* go along an imaginary axis down the core of our physical body from the bottom of our pelvis to top of our head. These are not physical entities but subtle energy fields associated with different qualities. If you could see them, they would look like energy forces spinning in a wheel out of seven different centers in your body. Being familiar with these chakras is crucial to all the practices you will learn in this book.

The second chakra, located in your genital area, is the seat of the powerful force that I will keep referring to throughout this book because it is key to all the practices that you will learn to control and direct—through breath and other movements—to bring you to deeper levels of intimacy and higher levels of enlightenment and bliss.

Tantra Tutorial

Chakra is a Sanskrit word for wheel, disc, or hub. Rather than being physical entities or points, they are best considered as centers or energy forces.

Energy centers, or chakras, and their aspects.

The following chakra chart shows the colors, sounds, and issues associated with each energy center. The questions in the chart reveal whether you have strength or blocks in that area. The idea is to focus on a particular chakra (area of your body) and recite the sound associated with it, or think about the particular color, to connect with the energy in that center.

Another approach in using this chart is to read the issues and questions and see which ones are relevant to you (either that you feel good or bad about them). Then focus on the chakra, color, and sound, in order to strengthen yourself regarding that issue. For example, if you're feeling stifled in expressing yourself (the fifth chakra), put your hand on your throat, visualize the color blue, and repeat the sound "ham" to give yourself more courage to speak up.

Chakra Chart Evaluation

Chakra	Color	Mantra	Issue	Question(s)
(1) Base	Red	Lam	Security	Do you feel insecure, needy, helpless? Or safe, secure, grounded?
(2) Sex	Orange	Vam	Energy	Do you feel undesirable and inhibited? Or sexy and alive?

Chakra	Color	Mantra	Issue	Question(s)
(3) Solar plexus	Yellow	Ram	Power	Do you feel weak, threatened, powerless? Or confident and worthy?
(4) Heart	Green	Yam	Love	Do you feel unloved and abandoned? Or loving and compassionate?
(5) Throat	Blue	Ham	Expression	Do you feel unheard, misunderstood, passive? Or expressive and truthful?
(6) Third eye	Purple	Ooo	Vision	Do you feel unclear, unauthentic, confused? Or inspired and intuitive?
(7) Crown	Violet	Omm	Enlightenment	Do you feel spiritually void and disconnected? Or enlightened, ecstatic, and cosmically connected?

In another exercise, you can chant the sounds one by one (they are ancient Sanskrit words) as a way to connect with each chakra, and therefore have an experience of moving your energy through your body.

Breathe Through the Chakras

Your breathing practices help you create a clear channel in your body through which air can travel past these chakras; cleansing, feeding, and fueling you. Air going through a clear channel in your body is called an *inner flute* because of its sweet flute-like sound. You then can send your breath to your partner, who will cycle it through his or her chakras and return it, fueling and empowering you both.

As you breathe, picture the breath going through the chakras. Try the following two exercises:

➤ The *complete breath* relaxes you. Inhale deeply into your lower belly and chest (until it pouches out like a contented Buddha). You can do this on your own or with a partner; either face to face or back to back. Sadly, many people resist doing this breath, feeling unattractive with their belly popping out, but it is a good breath to do in the middle of sex. Say, "Let's do the Buddha breath" and press your bellies and chests against each other.

➤ In contrast, as its name suggests, the *fire breath* fires you up. Take continual rapid breaths in and out of the nose (like snorting) causing your stomach to pulsate quickly. You can accelerate the energy even more by raising and lowering your arms (a familiar motion if you exercise on a stationary bike).

Once you get your individual breathing going better, you are ready to breath with a partner for more powerful love connections. One word of caution, however: Too much energy in the brain before you are prepared to handle it can cause you to literally "blow your fuse," like too many electrical appliances in an outlet. This results in headaches, confusion, passing out, or even a panic attack. For this reason, it's a good idea to take a workshop about tantric sex if you are going to practice the techniques intensely.

➤ **Synchronizing breath** In this exercise you breathe in and out at the same time as your partner to get on the same wavelength. Sit comfortably cross-legged facing each other on a pillow if necessary, as long as your spine is straight. Give each other a wink or touch to signal your pacing. After a while, close your eyes to sense each other's energy pattern.

➤ **Reciprocal breath** In this breath imagine that you are exchanging air, inhaling your partner's breath (or imagine breathing for each other). Sit in the yab yum position and inhale while your partner exhales; then exhale while your partner inhales.

Reciprocal breath: exchanging energy between beloveds.

➤ **Circulating breath** For this breath, inhale, imagining energy rising up from your sex center (second chakra) through your body (passing through all the chakras, as listed in the previous table), traveling to the top of your head, then back down to your genitals and the base of your spine on the exhale. Picture tracing a loop inside yourself and then out to a partner. Practices can be called by different names by different disciplines. Thus, the Hindu circulating breath is known to Chinese Taoists as the Microcosmic Orbit or the Golden Circle.

Tantra Tales

I've counseled many patients who start crying when they really look deeply in a loving partner's eyes and breathe. Don't be alarmed by this. The experience can trigger deep feelings about finally experiencing love you always wanted but never had.

Circulating breath: cycling energy through beloveds' bodies.

➤ **Bliss breath** Inhale deeply through your mouth and exhale naturally and continuously, allowing any natural sounds. Smile.

➤ **Ecstatic breathing** To do this breath, lie on your back with your knees up and inhale long, slow breaths through the mouth; counting to five, expanding the abdomen, and creating an archway under the small of the back. Exhale to the count of five, bringing your back to the floor and tilting your pelvis slightly upward. Allow the air to rush into the chest, opening your throat. Repeat rhythmically to create a wave-like motion throughout the body. Release any tightness in the throat, neck, chest, shoulders, abdomen, buttocks, or pelvis by purposefully tightening and then releasing the muscles in those areas. Allow sounds and feelings (sadness, anger, joy) to emerge freely on the exhale. This technique has been developed by Lori Star in her California "Celebrations of Love" courses (see Appendix B, "Workshops, Web Sites, Teachers, and Tantra Communities").

Tantra Tutorial

The cobra breath involves a particular pattern of breathing with moves and imagery that are powerful tools for mind expansion (invoking the shape of a snake). To ensure that tantra students are prepared for its powerful effects, some traditions, like Tantrika International, insist that this breath be taught orally and only by those given permission to do so by experienced tantra teachers.

➤ **Partner pelvic passion breath** I named this breath that way because it really perks up your passion by intensifying the energy created by the circulating breath with the pelvic holds that I will explain in Chapter 5, "Prep Your Body Temple of Love." An additional benefit results from pressing your heart chakras together. Lie side by side or sit face to face with the woman in the man's lap (yab yum position). Keep eye contact while you inhale and exhale together to a count of five, and draw the breath up from the base of your spine to the top of the head, and back down again. Create a cycle of breath with one of you inhaling while the other exhales. Imagine sending love out to your partner and receiving love from your partner with each breath. Gently press your heart areas together. You can amp up or damp down your arousal by pumping your pelvic muscles (see Chapter 5, for a full description of these) to force more breath—and therefore more energy—into your body.

Ecstatic breathing.

The Third Eye as Window to the Soul

No doubt you have heard the phrase "The eyes are the window to the soul." In tantra, the most effective door to your soul is not your real eyes, but that symbolic eye called the *third eye* (actually, it's behind your eyes, in the middle of your brain). Opening your third eye helps you delve deeper into your own being and connect on a higher level with your loved one. (Fortunately, more men these days seem to want the intimacy that women have always craved; that kind of connection is possible only when both people really want it to happen.) I often find myself putting my middle finger on that spot on my forehead to connect with the third eye deeper within, imagining breathing into it when I want to tap into deep relaxation and inner knowing.

Dr. Judy's TantrAdvice

To help you with different breathing patterns, play a CD to pace yourself. Excellent choices are any of Gabrielle Roth's CDs, the CD called "Tantric Sexuality," and Osho's "Dynamic Meditation" CD (see Appendix C, "Tantric Tools," for more information).

Making All the Connections from Coccyx to Crown

Your energy needs to flow in a clear channel, with the major checkpoints being the chakra energy centers. At one end is the base of the spine, at the *coccyx bone*. Just above it is a triangular area called the *sacrum* (you will later learn to tap it for energy). Also in this area is the *kunda* gland, the source of the powerful *kundalini* energy (or life force). You can see where these are in the body on the following illustration, and also in the anatomical drawings in other chapters.

The breath carries energy up the spine and into the brain. In various breathing patterns the breath goes past the primitive brain (*medulla oblongata*) and then you direct it to connect the vital *pineal* and *pituitary glands*. Through this connection, god and goddess (Shiva and Shakti) energy can meet in the magical place in between, called "the jewel in the lotus."

Tantra Tutorial

One of the best books about harnessing sacred sex energy for the purpose of enlightenment is *Jewel in the Lotus* by Sunyata Saraswati and Bodhi Avinasha (Sunstar Publishers, 1996).

The most effective breathing practice using the chakras is to imagine energy going through them in order, from top to bottom or vice versa; drawing breath up from the base (or earth) and to the top of your head (the sky)—or the opposite way, down from the top of your head to the base.

The breath needs to fol-low a clear channel up the spine and into the brain.

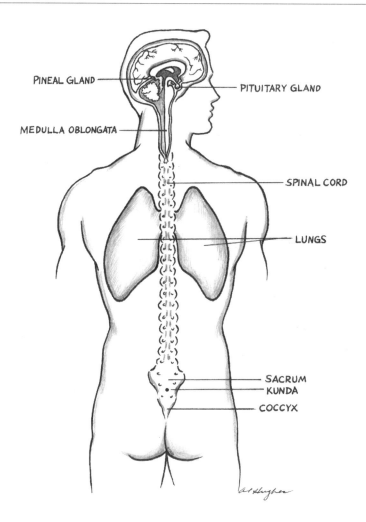

Your Inner Smile

Smiling is a powerful tool for happiness and bliss. It boosts your confidence and makes you and everyone around you happier. Research has even proven that smiling triggers the *limbic system* in the brain, which is the center for pleasure.

You know about the smile that is visible on your face, but there's another smile tantric practice teaches about. It's called the *inner smile*. You imagine it happening in the back of your brain, at the nape of your neck, in the primitive brain. Picturing it creates not only a positive attitude, but helps you reach the desired state of bliss that tantra is all about. Put your best smile on your face and imagine an equally broad inner smile when you look at your partner and at yourself in the mirror. This will boost your self-esteem and create good energy in your inner and outer world.

Try this exercise. Allow yourself to have any facial expression, even a scowl. Now purposefully put on an outer and inner smile and notice how your energy shifts. Make this inner smile during any of the exercises described throughout this book.

Be Both Participant and Observer

Key to stilling the mind for tantric sex (as well as many other meditative practices) is being in a mental state in which you are simultaneously participant and observer. This means that you are "doing" at the same time as observing yourself while you are acting. When you watch yourself act, it is called being the *witness*. This is a technique that helps you get over a common problem that interferes with good sex. So many men and women complain about distracting thoughts that cause sexual performance anxiety; for example, "How long can I last?" "Will I please her?" "Does he think I'm attractive?" To solve this problem, in tantra, you notice (witness) yourself having these thoughts (instead of fighting them as many people do, which only makes them more persistent!), and then simply refocus your attention on your breath and the sensations in your body.

Mantras

Mantras are spoken or silent sounds, or a series of sounds that trigger specific reactions in the body and mind because their vibrations correspond to specific chakras.

Repeat any sound and notice its hypnotic effect. Try drawing out the sound "om" and feel the vibration move from your body up into your head. The sound helps you focus your mind and move energy where you want it in your body. You probably already know how sound can affect you (and send you into other realms) when you listen to your favorite music and feel sensations in your body, or feel like you are carried into another world. Using sound in mantras allows you to control what you feel and where your mind goes.

Mantra sounds are usually short and repetitive (to help quiet the mind) and range from a single word ("om"), a line ("Om Mane Padme Hum") or a verse (such as the Lord's Prayer). You can recite a known mantra or make up your own. Any word or phrase that you enjoy saying will work fine.

Tantra Tutorial

The commonly used Sanskrit chant, "Om Mane Padme Hum," is the oldest and most famous Buddhist mantra, written on prayer flags and chanted thousands of times by Tibetan and Nepali people as well as tantra practitioners. It expresses the idea of enlightenment through union of male and female. Chant it for five minutes alone or with your partner to create a peaceful and delighted space.

Yantras

A *yantra* is a geometric figure that you concentrate on to still your mind and be stimulated by the particular state that the symbols are meant to evoke in you. The idea is to focus on the figure and then close your eyes, letting it be projected on your inner mental screen. There are symbols related to each of the seven different chakras. These yantras are used like mantras, to focus your energy on a particular issue related to that energy center.

The six-point Star of David is another popular yantra, which I will talk more about in Chapter 9, "Breaking Through Blocks to Bliss."

Mandalas

Mandalas, a kind of yantra, are patterns with concentric rings that come out from the center and contain symbols, figures, or forces of nature (like deities, waterfalls, or dolphins) that reveal mysteries of the universe. Psychoanalyst Carl Jung is credited with introducing mandalas into the West, using them as a therapy technique and map of the psyche to "uncover the mystery of the unconscious and the soul."

California artist Paul Heussenstamm, a master of painting mandalas (see the following illustration), often depicts patterns that evoke tantric sex imagery in the union of god and goddess surrounded in exquisite nature. Heussenstamm makes custom mandalas and teaches classes on how to make this art, in California and on journeys to countries like India and Nepal. "You don't have to think of yourself as an artist," he says. "Just close your eyes and notice the lights and colors that appear in the visual field. People draw what their mind has conjured up, and it gives you clues as to what's really in your soul." (See Appendix B for contact information.)

An original mandala by artist Paul Heussenstamm.

The Least You Need to Know

➤ Breathing practices are key to directing sexual energy to other parts of the body to connect with the beloved, maintain health, achieve ecstatic states, and melt into unity.

➤ There are seven energy centers called chakras throughout the body, each associated with colors, sounds, and issues. Tantric practices help you connect and use the energy in these centers to achieve desired feelings and connections in yourself and in a relationship.

➤ Practicing breathing exercises with a partner can greatly intensify your love connection and achievement of mutual sexual satisfaction.

➤ Quieting the mind and directing energy is key to reaching high states of consciousness in tantric sex and can be accomplished through meditation on sounds and designs.

Now THAT was worship!!

Chapter 4

Awaken and Worship the God and Goddess in You

In This Chapter

➤ The role of god and goddess energies in tantric sex

➤ Significant deities from varying traditions, cultures, and eras

➤ How to connect with divine forces within you

➤ How to use deity meditations

➤ Uniting your god and goddess as beloveds

➤ Festivals and temples that honor god and goddess energies

Tantra is a path to God—the feeling of divine blessing and presence in every aspect of your life, including sex. This connection with the divine is achieved by ecstatic union with a beloved as you both experience your own—and each other's—divinity. In tantra, every man and woman is a god or goddess. That means you are a divine being just as you are, with wisdom and abilities that need only to be recognized and released. Honoring yourself—and being honored—in this way gives us the self-esteem we all need but often feel lacking. Once you see the divinity within yourself, you can see the divinity in others.

This chapter helps you connect with the essence of the god and goddess in yourself and your partner because it is so important to your practice of sacred sex and to your goal of enlightenment. I will introduce you to different gods and goddesses related to tantric practice, and techniques of using their divine energies on your journey.

What Is "God/Goddess"?

In tantra the terms *god* and *goddess* refer to treating yourself and others with the respect and honor you would extend such revered beings. Through this honoring in tantric sex practices, your divine consciousness will embody the power of the universe.

Deities in tantric practice are essentially archetypes of spirits, guides, angels, and light beings that are symbols of various energies, qualities, or relationships. Other terms for male and female deities are deva and devi, daka and dakini, priest and priestess. Although deities are portrayed as external beings, they can be considered projections of qualities within our own nature.

The word "goddess" is widely used in the tantra community but has become more mainstream lately, used to refer to a woman who is proud of and in touch with her power as a feminine force. The goddess embodies a range of qualities of a woman, from being soft and nurturing to being strong and fierce. The term "god" is not used as popularly, possibly partly due to the reverence in Judeo-Christian tradition for "God" as a superior being.

Some traditions promise that you can be gods or goddesses in another life, or only by changing in some way to become more divine. Tantric sex poses that being god or goddess is your birthright. You are divine now, without change.

Being a god or goddess refers to your energy, creative force, and cosmic power. Every woman is a goddess. That means she is the embodiment of all that is feminine to be honored and worshipped. She is a lover, seductress, healer, and nurturing mother, as well as a hunter and wild woman. She must reveal and embrace all these parts of herself and be similarly honored. Similarly, every man is a god, the embodiment of many roles, including being a provider, protector, and a symbol of power; as well as being nurturing, healing, and surrendering. He must embrace and be honored for all these parts. These qualities are present in all people, regardless of age, race, culture, status, or any characteristic. We either display these qualities or they are available as potentials.

Blocks to Bliss

Even if you are skeptical, deities and spirits might be helping, supporting, and guiding you. Suspend disbelief for the moment to notice how these energies might help heighten your experience of love and blissful sex.

Integrate All Your Roles

As a start on your path to embracing god/goddess within you, think of all the roles you play in your life and how you feel about yourself. Are you a parent? An entrepreneur? Are you feeling nurturing? Sexy? Powerful? Introspective? Review your qualities in your mind or write them down. I often have participants in my workshops make a collage of their roles (as shown in the following illustration, for example), with themselves in the middle surrounded by symbols or photos or written words for their feelings.

After you read about the gods and goddesses in this chapter, go back over your list and write in the names of deities you most relate to. For example, if you wrote "sexy," write in Ishtar; if you feel "powerful," write in Shiva.

Integrating the goddess self.

Seeing Beyond the Superficial

You know the experience of judging others or being judged, by looks, job, or stock portfolio. Likely you know the pain of statements such as "She's too fat" or "I need a guy who has more money." Your body or bank account becomes your eligibility quotient in the wide world of dating and mating. But in the tantra world, there are no such criteria; you are encouraged to see beyond superficial characteristics into the divinity of each being.

Three essential steps in worshipping the divine according to the tantra tradition are ...

1. Embrace the divinity within yourself.

2. Acknowledge divinity in your partner. Tantric sex emphasizes the equality of both male and female deities to achieve necessary balance of energies.

3. Unite god and goddess in the union of you and your beloved. This achieves the perfect balance of male and female energy necessary to achieve bliss and higher consciousness.

The Importance of Worshipping Each Other

Through my years of work as a therapist, I know how happy people become when they are acknowledged. Do you know what it feels like to be truly appreciated? To be really noticed? To be deeply known as when someone "gets" who you are? Tantric sex takes acknowledgment one step further: to being *worshipped!* Worship doesn't mean blind obsession; it means loving unconditionally and limitlessly. Nor does it mean having power over someone who is your slave; it means serving each other equally from the highest state of personal power and mutual respect.

Think of all the compliments you would like to hear about yourself, and wonderful things you could say about your beloved. That's what it means in tantra to be worshipped like a god or goddess.

Clearing Up Confusion About Gods and Goddesses

All deities are involved with life and death. However, understanding their roles can be confusing because some have hundreds of incarnations or *manifestations,* which represent different aspects and therefore have different names. I remember being very confused by the most dramatic example of these—the Hindu Lord Shiva, who is also called Brahma and Vishnu, and who has more than a thousand different manifestations ranging from his Protector form to his more evil form called Bairab. Similarly, the power of the goddess Kali can be seen in her "light" form as powerful but also in her "shadow" aspect as manipulative and controlling. The goal is to accept and merge these aspects within yourself.

These qualities can be those you like or dislike, want to emulate or discard. As you read about them in this chapter, see which resonate with you. Do the exercises later in this chapter to understand their role in yourself and your relationships.

Getting to Know the Ancient Goddesses

Male and female divine figures can come from ancient cultures such as the Sumerian, Teutonic, Egyptian, Greek, and Roman. They can also come from modern times. Let's take a closer look at some of the gods and goddesses from around the world, starting with the goddesses.

Major and Well-Known Goddesses

Most goddesses represent fertility. Goddesses are loving and nurturing in their light manifestations; however, they also are portrayed as seductresses engaging in ritual prostitution. As you read through this list of goddesses from various cultures, circle names you find yourself drawn to:

➤ **Lilith**   A Near Eastern goddess portrayed in many legends as an independent woman refusing to be dominated by men (and therefore named for a music festival a few years ago that celebrated female artists). In one myth she is the first woman in paradise, but she did not submit to Adam as did Eve. In ancient Sumerian lore, she gained a reputation as a seductress and harlot, using her secrets of sexual techniques to lure men to the temples of Inanna, Ishtar, and Astarte to worship her, hail infidelity, and participate in tantric sexual rites.

➤ **Ishtar**   The "Exalted Light of Heaven," with her sweet lips and beautiful body, is known for her eroticism and sexuality but also depicted as the goddess of battle, carrying a bow and sword and riding on a lioness. Deriving from ancient Sumeria as Inanna, and later appearing in the Babylonian era as well as in Egypt, she is symbolized by the evening star and revered for her prophecy, leadership, and healing of the sick. In annual rites, this high Priestess unites with the king in sacred marriage.

Ishtar, the great goddess of eroticism.

➤ **Aphrodite**   The most popular goddess from Greek tradition is associated with love, desire, ultimate sexuality, and ecstasy, and is often symbolized by a dove, dolphin, rose, apple, or even an opium poppy. She is also popularly known as Venus, famous Roman goddess of love, known for purity, and supposedly invented by the Romans to turn the citizens toward chastity.

➤ **Artemis**   In Greek mythology, she is the virgin goddess of the hunt and the moon. She is the female counterpart to Ares, the god of war.

➤ **Guan-Yin**   This is the great Chinese goddess of compassion, whose statue is sold everywhere in China. I've been moved after seeing one of her tallest statues on Puduo Mountain, the site of three of her most revered temples; another statue of her is planned to be placed in the water at China's most expansive Buddhist gardens on the island of Hainan, meant to evoke the impressive welcome of our own Statue of Liberty.

Guan-Yin, Chinese god-dess of compassion.

➤ **The Virgin Mary**   She is the ultimate Christian symbol of purity and motherhood.

➤ **Hindu goddesses**   Various goddesses are of great importance in India and Nepal. I have witnessed ceremonies and seen temples to many of them, and also have many small statues that I keep in my home and even carry in my pocketbook. They include …

  ➤ Durga, the mother of goddesses.

  ➤ Tara, a goddess representing kindness and wisdom.

  ➤ Lakshmi, the goddess of abundance, wealth, happiness, and prosperity.

➤ Saraswati, goddess of the arts.

➤ Kali, the goddess of power and strength. I have witnessed many sacrifices at her shrine outside Kathmandu, Nepal, where goats and chickens are slaughtered and their blood offered to her statues, as a request for her protection.

Kali, Hindu goddess of power.

Other Goddesses Around the World

Almost every culture has goddesses that might be equivalent to deities from other cultures and eras. Even if your own background differs, you might identify with these entities (especially if you believe in past lives when you may have lived in those times and places). Here are several countries and some of the goddesses associated with them:

➤ **Japan**   The goddess Benzai Tennyo is associated with sexuality and fertility, but also with granting good fortune and with the art of music (similar to the Hindu goddess Saraswati).

➤ **Mexico**   Tlazolteotl is the Aztec goddess of love and sexuality whose worship included prostitution. In her dark side, she is associated with death and human sacrifice.

Tantra Tales

Some women today rename themselves with Sanskrit names of goddesses, such as Lakshmi, Kamala, and Usha. Or they may refer to a goddess to describe their own behavior. For example, one tantra friend of mine talks about her expressions of anger or confrontations with other people by saying, "My Kali came out!"

Tantra Tutorial

Greek goddess prototypes, such as Demeter as mother and Artemis as the warrior, are described in Agapi Stassinopolous's book, *Conversations with the Goddess: Revealing the Divine Power Within You* (Stewart, Tabori & Chang, 1999).

➤ **Ireland**   Maeve is considered a magical goddess of Ireland. On one hand she is associated with wanton sexuality, but on the other she is a warrior who uses her sexuality to win battles.

➤ **Scotland**   Riannon, a Welsh goddess often depicted mounted on a white horse or who transforms into a white mare for a marriage ceremony. In mythology, she was chased by a Prince who could not catch her until he asked her permission—a story evoking the importance of a man's surrender to the goddess (a key tantric sex principle).

➤ **Africa**   Mboze is the goddess of the Woyo people; she represents fertility through rainfall. Odude is a Northwest African goddess, whose name means "the black one" and who is often imaged as a serpent, evoking the tantric kundalini energy rising.

➤ **Israel**   The Hebrew goddess Shekinah, whose name means "creative force," is equivalent to the Hindu "Shakti," and is meant to establish balance. Ruth is a real woman revered to have saved her people in ancient times, and thus can be considered a goddess.

➤ **Egypt**   Qadesh is the goddess of love and sex from the Akkadian and Babylonian empires often depicted as a ruler of fertility in the animal world; her worshippers also practiced prostitution.

➤ **United States**   Mother Maui is the goddess of the New Age movement; Gaia is the goddess of the Earth; and Pele is the goddess of fire, often depicted as arising from a volcano. (Having spent much time on the island of Maui in Hawaii, I know firsthand the powerful goddess energy there, and recommend you go there to experience it, too.)

➤ **Thailand**   Tap-tun is celebrated in Thailand (and as Chao Mae Tuptim in China) with offerings of hundreds of symbols of lingams (male sexual organs).

➤ **Haiti**   The Voodoo goddess Erzuli, also called Empusae, is known as a sexual vampire, sucking out men's strength by seducing them while they sleep and inducing erotic dreams or ejaculation. She is worshipped in modern times with champagne and perfume.

➤ **Middle East**   The Islamic goddess Al'Lat (also called Hecate) is the feminine form of Allah and similar to the Hindu Lord Shiva in that calling her is like saying "the Lord" or simply "God." She symbolizes three aspects of the moon: the virgin, the mother, and the aging wise woman. Her reign ended when her shrine was taken over by the prophet Mohammed, signaling the change from matriarchy to patriarchy.

➤ **Near East** Cybele is reputed to perform both fertility and castration rites. Archeological finds dating back to 6000 B.C. prove her early worship, usually in the form of a black stone.

Remember to circle the goddesses whose energies you connect with. For example, I connect with Guan Yin because I spend so much time in China; all the goddesses in Nepal; the Greek goddess of the hunt, Artemis, which was the name of the women's rock band I played in; and the Welsh goddess Riannon, the subject of a Fleetwood Mac song I sang while in the band.

Gods from Different Cultures

Like goddesses, gods come from every culture, tradition, and era. Despite their association to a particular religion, many gods similarly represent a higher power, such as Jesus in Christianity, Allah in Islam, Buddha in Buddhism, or the Hindu Lord Shiva. See which ones you relate to:

➤ **Hindu gods** These include the most important, Lord Shiva; also known as Vishnu, god of all gods, with more than a thousand manifestations, including his dark side as Bairab. He is worshipped in the form of the Shiva lingam (a phallus) in temples throughout India and Nepal. As I mentioned in Chapter 2, "The Basics: Yes, Yin Yang, Yoni, and Yab Yum," Shiva's consort is Shakti (the female force); together they are a union of energy and enlightenment.

Another popular Hindu god is the oft-beloved Ganesh, known for his kindness and removal of obstacles, and well recognized as a boyish-looking figure with a human body and an elephant head.

➤ **Jesus** This is the Son of God and savior of the Christian people, who performed the ultimate self-sacrifice to deliver others from their sins.

➤ **Greek gods** As in the case of goddesses, there are many Greek gods, all of whom have equivalents in Roman culture. The highest god among all other

Blocks to Bliss

Some beings are considered to have given tantric sex a bad reputation. Aghora is a rebellious manifestation of the Hindu god Shiva, famous for orgies and cruelties, such that his devotees have sex in cemeteries. Bhogi supposedly volunteered as a human sacrifice to achieve sacred status; his dying wish was to have sex with many women.

Greek deities, Zeus is symbolic of power and domination. He is the archetype for the macho, alpha male. Other Greek gods include …

➤ **Eros** Called the god of love in Greek and Cupid in Roman, Eros evokes a familiar image as a cherub who mischievously aims arrows at people's hearts to make them fall in love. He also has been depicted as androgynous (not clearly male or female).

➤ **Dionysus** Called the god of lust in Greek times and Bacchus in Roman days, Dionysus symbolizes overindulgence of wine, women, and song, and is known for wanton feasts and drunken orgies.

➤ **Priapus** A Greek phallic god and son of Aphrodite and Dionysus, Priapus is known for his unusually huge erection; therefore symbolizing men's sexual potency (the word now refers to an erection that lasts too long!). In cases of impotence, venereal diseases, or other sexual problems, paintings or figures of private parts were offered to this god with prayers for healing. Virgins would also deflower themselves on his erect lingam. Many gods from other cultures are similar to him, such as the Roman Tutinus, the Egyptian Min, the Teutonic Frey, and the Japanese Sarutahiko.

➤ **Satyr** Related to Pan and Eros, Satyr is well recognized as the half-man, half-goat mythical creature who symbolizes unrestrained male passion and the pursuit of erotic adventures.

The unrestrained male passion in Satyr.

➤ **Hercules** Endowed with great strength and cunning, this Greek hero of classical myth is most often portrayed as a slayer of monsters and beasts.

➤ **Apollo** One of the greatest and best known Greek deities, Apollo is called Mars by the Romans, and is pictured as a handsome young man. He is god of the sun, music, poetry, medicine, and fine arts. We know his name well as the series of manned spacecraft, one of which landed on the Moon, marking one of the greatest achievements of our time.

➤ **Ares** The Greek god of war, he is equivalent to the energy of the female warrior, Artemis.

➤ **Egyptian gods** Ra is the god of the Sun, and another god, Osiris, is infamous in stories of dismemberment, incest, and adultery.

➤ **Japanese gods** These include Musuri-Kami, a Shinto deity honored at annual fertility festivals where hundreds of people march through the streets toting huge phalluses made of stone or wood.

Modern-Day God/Goddess Icons

Modern-day figures (alive or dead) also serve as cultural icons of gods or goddesses, usually because of their media exposure. Some believers think that the spirits of ancient figures are channeled through these people. Modern goddesses might include Marilyn Monroe and Madonna (the rock star) as sex goddesses, Mother Teresa as the Chinese goddess of compassion Guan-Yin, or even Barbara Bush as the strong mother energy of the Hindu goddess Durga. Modern-day sex gods might include Sean Connery or John F. Kennedy Jr.

In the following exercise, write down a few modern-day figures you think embody energies you either like or want:

Your Modern-Day Diety Exercise

Name of Person: **Qualities This Person Evokes in You:**

_____   _____

_____   _____

_____   _____

Gods and Their Goddess Counterparts

Tantra is a partnered as well as a personal practice, as is evidenced by tantric gods and goddesses depicted with partners, called *consorts*. Entwined in embrace, they project the male/female balance that is central to tantric practice. Think of some famous people—deities, heroes and heroines, or historical figures—who are linked together. What feelings do they evoke in you? How are those reactions related to your own relationships in life? Make your list, adding to some of the examples I give you here. Have your partner do this exercise, too, then discuss your choices.

Couple's Energy Exercise

Name of Couple:	Qualities This Couple Evokes in You:
Shiva and Shakti	Ultimate ecstasy, perfect balance
Samson and Delilah	Women turned on to men's displays of power and strength
Romeo and Juliet	Tragedy, love thwarted by disapproval
Lancelot and Genevieve	Passion fallen by infidelity
Edward of England and Wallis Simpson	Love so deep that he would give up the throne
Elizabeth Taylor and Richard Burton	Passionate love that can't sustain itself; can't live with or without the person
Other: _____	_____
Other: _____	_____

The Essence of the God/Goddesses Within You

As I've mentioned, certain gods and goddess and their essences will resonate with you, giving you insight into how you are or how you want to be. Review the list of deities, especially those whose names you circled, and consider whether you are like them or want to be like them. Don't be concerned with the details of their stories; because tantra is the transmission of energy, it is only important if you feel their energy.

In the following exercise, write down the names of the deities whose names you circled. Notice how you feel when you read each name; if you feel drawn to that deity in a positive way (excited, energized, happy), place a checkmark in the Positive column. If you feel something negative in your body (tightness, pain, pressure), you might have a negative charge on the qualities he or she embodies; place a checkmark in the Negative column.

Ask yourself, "What am I trying to avoid?" For example, because Kali is the goddess of power, some women might feel attracted to her to express more assertiveness in their life; others might be frightened by that energy. Don't judge what you feel, just notice it. Don't worry whether the deity's sex matches yours. Remember that according to tantra you have both male and female essence within you, and must embody both.

Have your partner do this exercise, too. Discuss the energies stimulated in each of you, as a way to learn more about yourselves, each other, and your relationship.

Your Reaction to the Deities' Energy

	Positive	Negative
Deity: _____	_____	_____
Deity: _____	_____	_____
Deity: _____	_____	_____
Deity: _____	_____	_____
Deity: _____	_____	_____

Using Deities in Your Sex Practice

The gods and goddesses can add great power to your tantric practices. In Chapter 16, "Advanced Tantric Lovemaking Techniques," I'll discuss more advanced ways to draw from their energy.

You can buy a form of the deity as a statue, photograph, mandala, or thangka. Ask at local yoga centers or check your local Yellow Pages for stores specializing in Eastern artifacts, or check the stores within Web sites listed in Appendix B, "Workshops, Web Sites, Teachers, and Tantra Communities."

Festivals and Other God/Goddess Gatherings

All kinds of celebrations honoring deities have existed in every age. The following are some that relate to tantric principles.

> **Dr. Judy's TantrAdvice**
>
> Visualization using pure light, described here to identify with qualities of a deity, has also proven effective in other situations. For example, some cancer patients who have been taught to imagine healing light through their bodies have been shown to produce fewer cancer cells.

Fertility Festivals in Japan

Each spring hundreds of worshippers parade through the streets of small towns, carrying effigies of the phallus through the streets, chanting testimonies to its power and potency. Legend has it that every time a princess laid down with a mate, he woke up the next morning with his penis bitten off. A suitor who was a smithy proved his worth and finally cured the princess by forging a steel phallus that was inserted into her vagina, whereupon steel teeth lodged inside her vagina gripped the rod and were extracted; his prize being her hand in marriage. Local worshippers and hundreds of tourist onlookers (like myself!) attend the charming circus-like parade that has more recently been turned into a street fair (selling phallus-shaped candy) and distributing educational materials about AIDS prevention.

In this annual fertility festival in Japan, worshippers carry effigies of the phallus through the streets.

Burning Man Festival in Nevada

Although it's dusty and 107 degrees, thousands of free spirits journey to the annual Burning Man festival at the end of summer for the week-long experiment in temporary community dedicated to radical self-expression. Participants set up villages and theme camps (like Fertility, Outer Space, and The Seven Ages) in a psychedelic maze of art installations (like the "Boom Boom Womb" or "Impotence Compensation Project") and rest stops. The scene is unique, but some recall their days at Woodstock, sharing food, art, music, and love.

Many tantric devotees come to Burning Man each year because of its kindred spirit to tantric energy, creativity, lovingness and sense of community. A favorite attraction in past years has been the Temple of Ishtar (www.ishtartemple.org), a magical community dedicated to raising awareness, educating, expanding and healing sacred sexuality, sensuality, and relationships.

Goddess Gatherings

During the women's movement of the 1970s, women formed "consciousness raising groups," meeting in homes and talking about men, sex, and how to have orgasms. Similar gatherings of today often are called goddess groups, in which women come together to share their stories, support each other in careers or relationships, and connect with their priestess energies. Often they perform ritualistic ceremonies, lighting candles, invoking feminine spirits, forming drum circles, declaring intentions, and celebrating femininity.

These can be held on a private, small scale with selected invited friends, or they can be large gatherings such as the "Goddess Gather," an annual weekend of workshops and rituals for women to connect with their feminine spirit, held at a nature farm in California. (For more information, e-mail motherbearscott@mindspring.com.)

Temples

A tantric temple is a place where tantric rituals take place. There are several varieties of such temples. In ancient cultures, women were considered priestesses and goddesses because they were the holy creators of life, thought to be sent to Earth from heaven with secret powers as healers. Girls were brought to buildings, called temples, before puberty and taught by older women all the secrets of using sexual energy to heal; and the sacred arts of sex, including love, lust, rituals, magic, and spiritual practice. These temple goddesses also taught younger men how to reach realms of bliss through the pleasures of the female body, rejuvenated older men by practicing their skills of lovemaking with them, and healed warriors with sacred waters. Some tantrikas today form collectives for similar purposes.

The town of Khajuraho, south of New Delhi in India, was the heart of medieval tantrism. The ancient temples here are renowned for their erotic sculptures. Figures in a seemingly infinite variety of combinations and positions adorn the edifices from the base to the top. The reliefs at ascending levels become more refined, as a symbol of the ascension to higher states of consciousness. Many were destroyed in wars, but a large number remain. I can assure you—because I've done it—that visiting them is an awesome and educational experience.

An erotic scene from the temple at Khajuraho.

The Least You Need to Know

➤ Every man and woman is a god or goddess. Consider yourself as having the qualities of divine beings, to embrace the highest level of self-esteem and to confront powerful characteristics you consider positive or negative.

➤ Gods and goddesses that you may relate to come from every era and culture.

➤ Think of lovemaking as a divine act that expresses the sacred union of you and your partner as enlightened beings (god and goddess).

➤ Visiting sacred temples and festivals can inspire you to embrace the divinity within you.

Part 2
Getting Started in Sacred Sex

Now that you're breathing right and sending powerful surges of sexual energy through your body and out to your partner, you're ready to start using that energy. When you can turn up the heat or calm it down at will, you're more in control and therefore more ready to lose control—into bliss.

In this part you'll learn specific practices to amp up your sexual energy—or to bring it down a few notches—at will to prepare you for long-lasting lovemaking. You'll discover how to look at love through totally new eyes and learn techniques that will take you further into sensuality than you ever thought possible. Discover the secrets of the sacrum tap, the Shakti shake, the heart hold, and the muscle locks that unlock your door to sexual pleasure. You'll learn how to break through any blocks you have to embracing bliss, opening the door to a whole new world by setting your stage for love—preparing your room, your mind, and your body as a temple of love.

Chapter 5

Prep Your Body Temple of Love

In This Chapter

➤ Getting to know and learning to love your body

➤ The two colors of tantra

➤ How white tantra helps your tantric sex life

➤ Inner muscle holds that give you better control in sex

➤ How to keep your spine healthy and straight

➤ Eating right the tantric way

Tantric practice asserts that your body is your temple. You must keep it healthy and fit for your journey to bliss. In this chapter I'll introduce you to some principles and routines that help you honor this temple.

I'll also share with you some ways to tone your body to facilitate the important practices that you are undertaking to heighten, channel, and control your sexual energy to reach a higher consciousness.

Your Body as the Bridge to Bliss

When studying tantra, be prepared to experience a thrilling ride: energy soaring up and down your spine, and electrifying every cell in your body from your toes to the top of your head. Your entire body becomes the bridge between the earthly and the spiritual on your road to bliss.

Consider the metaphor of you as a car. This requires remembering about the chakras, or energy centers I described in Chapter 3, "Spinning Your Wheels and Breathing to Ecstasy." Your sex center is your gas tank; your chassis and tires are the first chakra, or base center, helping you hug the road (remember, the first chakra's job is to ground you). Your breath mixes with your sexual energy (as air does with gas in a car) to serve as the fuel injected through your spine (your gas line). The muscle holds (bandhas) described later in this chapter are your spark plugs. Every system in your car (ignition, battery, exhaust, electrical), like every system in your body (circulatory, endocrine, nervous), has to be working for you to cruise down the highway effortlessly—or to gun the motor and speed ahead.

All too often we are not even aware of the body temple we live in. We take it for granted—usually until we have some breakdown (pain), or look in the mirror and get distressed about what we see. Worse, we've abused our body temples with toxic food, lack of sleep (I'm guilty of this one!), overeating, drugs, alcohol, and even sex that we've regretted afterward. Another abuse is self-criticism—but to be ready for tantric love you must turn body hate into body love.

Building Body Love: Through the Looking Glass

A fundamental part of every sex therapy seminar or workshop (I have taught a vast variety of them over the last 25 years!) involves looking at your body and changing any negative attitudes. Often called "homework," I prefer to refer to such exercises as "homeplay," since everything you do to increase pleasure should be play and fun, rather than work. Do this exercise for your whole body and private parts:

1. Stand naked in front of a full-length mirror (a good time to do this is after a bath). Look at every part of you, starting from your feet and moving slowly up to the top of your head (as in Chapter 3, when you moved your energy through the energy centers). If you catch yourself criticizing, stop and say something kind instead; for example, "My breasts are too small" becomes "My breasts are nice and firm"; "My thighs are too bulky" becomes "My legs are so strong." Don't obsess that you are not telling the truth; you are simply shifting your focus and being gentler with yourself.

2. Examine your genitals. Women can sit on the bed and use a hand mirror (and flashlight) because the female genitals are less obvious than men's. Open the lips and notice colors, moistness, shapes.

3. Examine your first chakra (your base center located around your anal area, the symbol of security). An easier position to do this for men and women is to squat. As in the genital exam for women, men can use a mirror and flashlight to see more clearly. Notice colors and skin texture.

Examining, and loving, your body temple.

Describe Your Sexual Parts Inside and Out

Most men have looked at their genitals, because they're so accessible every time they go to the bathroom. In contrast, women have been taught not to look—and even today most females are shy or unsure of what's "down there."

I am always surprised at how little even sophisticated men and women know about their sexual parts. I remember not knowing much when I was young—my mother just gave me books to read, and my confusion lasted until I was well into my 20s. Compare your descriptions of your body to the following figures, which show the major parts of the male and female genitalia.

Both men and women should note the following:

➤ There are actually sets of muscles in the pelvic area, including those around the genitals and around the anal openings, that play an important role in sexual toning and excitement. These are affectionately called the *love muscles;* I'll tell you more about them a little later in this chapter.

Dr. Judy's TantrAdvice

Women have rarely seen inside their vagina at the view their gynecologist sees. You can get a plastic speculum (the instrument the doctor uses for your examination) from a reputable outlet like Eve's Garden (see Appendix C, "Tantric Tools"). Carefully insert it inside your vagina, creating an opening. Position a mirror and flashlight so you can see.

➤ The *sacrum* is actually a triangular area above the tailbone which, when tapped, awakens energy, as I'll describe in Chapter 8, "Practices for Beloveds to Reach Bliss."

➤ The kundalini gland is the seat of blissful energy that lies dormant within the spine until activated by tantric practices. It is often depicted artistically like a coiled serpent.

A closer look at the female anatomy shows ...

➤ The clitoris is more than the bump, knob, or tip that you feel. It actually has a shaft that extends into the body, which is also pleasurable to stimulate.

➤ The urethral opening is in front of, and separate from, the vaginal opening.

➤ There is a sponge-like tissue surrounding the urethra (called the "urethral sponge," consisting of glands, ducts, and blood vessels) that produces fluids emitted through the urethra during high states of arousal. These "love juices," also called female ejaculate, can be triggered from stimulation inside the vagina in the goddess space (also known as the G spot). This process will be described in Chapters 10, "Giving Her the Best Nights Ever," and 17, "Sexual Healing to Set You Free."

A closer look at the male anatomy shows that you can reach (and stimulate) the prostate gland from the outside along the perineum and from the inside through the anal opening, as will be described in Chapter 17.

Tantra Tutorial

Tantric homeplay often includes a genital display for your partner, where the partners "play doctor" for each other, showing each other what they have learned about their bodies. This is not only educational, it helps overcome embarrassment and increases intimacy.

If Your Penis or Yoni Could Talk

Fans who listen to me on the radio tease about hearing me ask callers, "If your penis could talk, what would it say?" The truth is, our bodies do talk to us—and we talk back. Try this exercise and say aloud what your genitals might say to you (such as "Why do you criticize my size?" or "Can't I have a rest?" or "I'd like to be adored").

Go on a Genital Exploration

Take some deep breaths. Center yourself. Now that you've looked at your genitals, touch them with the primary intention to explore. Notice the colors, shapes, and textures. After your exploration with a more objective view, get emotionally involved. Allow yourself to touch your genitals with pleasure in mind.

Watch what happens in the mirror, or just lie back and enjoy the sensations. Focus on the smallest sensations, without any expectations.

RECTUM
KUNDALINI GLAND
SACRUM
PELVIC MUSCLES
TAIL BONE
ANUS
URETHRAL SPONGE
(GODDESS SPACE)

UTERUS
BLADDER
PUBIC BONE
CLITORIS
INNER LIPS
OUTER LIPS
URETHRAL OPENING
VAGINAL OPENING

BLADDER
PUBIC BONE
SHAFT
URETHRA
GLANS
URETHRAL
OPENING

SACRUM
KUNDALINI GLAND
PROSTATE
PELVIC MUSCLES
TAIL BONE
PERINEUM
TESTES

A closer look at the female and male body.

The Two Colors of Tantra: Merging the Sexual and the Physical

There are two types of practices, or colors of tantra, which I'll be telling you more about throughout the book:

1. **White** tantra refers to the practices that are more physical, and related to yoga and other physical fitness.

2. **Red** tantra refers to the practices that are more sexual in nature or that use powerful sexual energy, channeled in a highly spiritual manner.

Dr. Judy's TantrAdvice

Masturbation might bring up old feelings, particularly from early childhood; you might have learned it is "wrong" or "bad." Tell yourself the opposite: Self-pleasuring is healthy and will benefit your love life.

The Yoga Connection

Yoga is the most popular of the white tantra paths. Many tantric masters are also yoga masters who have studied and practiced poses for many years. Yoga helps you focus on your body, still your mind, strengthen and stretch your body, and control your movements. All that can help you achieve ejaculatory control and multiple orgasms, and benefit your overall health as well as the physical experience of the transcendent energy you share with your beloved.

Take a course at a local yoga center or contact any of the resources listed in Appendix B, "Workshops, Web Sites, Teachers, and Tantra Communities," about whether they offer yoga classes. Most tantra workshops will introduce you to simple yoga practices.

Some Simple Yoga Movements

Here is a brief description of a few simple yoga movements in many individual routines. See Chapter 14, "Getting Fit Together for Tantric Sex," for interesting yoga poses your can do with your beloved as part of tantric practice.

➤ **The head lift.** Stand up as straight as possible. Reach your head up to the sky as if a string were pulling it upward from the middle of your crown. Inhale through your nose, pulling your shoulder blades back toward each other. Exhale and press your feet solidly into the ground, as if rooting yourself like a tree. Relax and repeat.

➤ **The cobra pose.** Lie fully extended on the floor on your stomach. Place the hands under the shoulders, arms close to the body with elbows back, and slowly lift the upper body and head in a curve, looking upward.

➤ **The cat pose.** From the cobra pose, bring the head down slowly and rise up on the knees, rounding the back to stretch the spine in the opposite direction from the cobra pose.

➤ **The resting pose.** From the cat pose, lower the chest to the knees and forehead to the ground, keeping the arms outstretched. Breathe naturally.

Blocks to Bliss

Always move slowly, and always have a teacher instruct you on proper breathing, form, and progression of yoga poses for maximum benefits and to protect the spine.

Hold It: These Are Called Bandhas

In certain yoga poses or breathing practices in tantra, you hold a body part a certain way or create muscular contractions to control your energy; these are called *bandhas.* They act like waterway locks in that energy is pooled in a certain area by tightening muscles there, then the energy is released in a stronger force and sent wherever you want it (up or down the spine, or up to the sky).

The three most common holds are ...

➤ **Throat hold.** To do this, inhale and turn your chin down toward your throat, drawing the back of your neck straight; then lift the chin and exhale slowly.

➤ **Belly hold.** Exhale, suck your navel back toward your spine, and pull your belly up toward your throat.

➤ **Pelvis hold.** Tighten your PC (pubococcygeal) and anal sphincter muscles. (I'll discuss more about how to exercise those PC muscles in the next section.)

The bandhas greatly benefit your sex life. Here's how:

➤ The three-step lock, as I call it, incorporates the three most common holds and helps men control their ejaculation without losing their erection. Inhale and do the throat hold. Exhale and do the belly hold. Squeeze the PC (or "love") muscles for the pelvis hold. Repeat.

➤ Pelvis holds help both women and men to strengthen their pelvic muscles, which results in more powerful orgasms.

➤ Muscle holds help men and women condition the entire body, strengthen lower back muscles, and intensify the effects of love muscle exercises to create more intense sensations in self-pleasuring or intercourse.

Tantra Tutorial

Bandhas increase the energy you can cycle within your own body or out to your partner. As you breathe in, do the pelvis hold and imagine drawing energy up from the earth through your body and out to your partner and cycle it back again.

You can do these holds any time—while you're waiting in a movie line or stuck in traffic—for an energy rush. (Once while teaching a class I was saying that no one would notice, but when demonstrating how you can practice in secret, the students laughed at how my skirt was lifting!)

In doing yoga, keep the following important tips in mind:

➤ Always check with a doctor before starting a yoga program or any physical routine.

➤ Warm up before each routine.

➤ Never force your body beyond its limits.

➤ Rest when you feel tired.

➤ Always keep balance (for example, bend forward after you twist or bend backward).

Love Muscle Exercises for Men and Women

Women's pubococcygeal muscles run along the sides of the entrance to the vagina. Strengthening and toning them creates more pleasure in sex for the woman and her partner (and tightens the muscles, especially after childbirth). Locate them by squeezing, as if to hold back urine, and then release as if forcing the urine out. Now purposefully contract them in faster and faster progression for about 30 seconds. Do this several times a day. (You can even insert a finger to help you better focus on gripping with these muscles.)

Men's PC muscles run through the perineum and connect to both the anus and the scrotum. Locate them as for the woman, by squeezing as if holding back the flow of urine, then release as if forcing the urine out. Contract and release 10 times, at an increasingly faster pace, several times a day. This is a powerful method for men to control the timing of their ejaculation.

Ecstasy Essentials

The secret to using the PC muscles to send powerful energy through the body and brain is to coordinate the breath. Inhale through the nose as you pull up the muscles, hold the breath as you contract as many times as you can, and then exhale through the nose.

Contracting and releasing the anal sphincter muscles for the man and woman also increases sexual pleasure. Locate these muscles by squeezing as if to prevent defecating, then bearing down as if forcing yourself to eliminate.

Follow a Conscious Workout

There are many workouts that will tone your body and build your strength. These can complement your tantric sex practices as long as you stay aware while you do them, which means focusing on how the particular exercise is moving your energy and how you are moving your breath. These workouts can include …

➤ Western-style workouts such as weight lifting, aerobics, or specialized routines from your own gym or trainer.

➤ Eastern style practices such as T'ai Chi or the increasingly popular Qigong (pronounced *chee-gong*) are systems of Chinese yoga movements that open the body to allow the flow of life-force energy. Some exotic-sounding movements include T'ai Chi Bo Balancing to build a strong and supple back and Bagua Xun Dao Gong, which stretches and strengthens the legs.

The Spinal Tap

Having a healthy spine is crucial to the practices of tantric sexuality. The spine is the pathway of the breath through the body, from the base (first) chakra through the inner flute to the top of the head (the crown chakra). It brings the sexual energy from the genitals through the body and into the head for transformation and awakening.

Pay attention to your spine! At this very moment, how is it positioned? How is it when you walk, sit, or stand? Your spine is, of course, directly related to your posture. Take the following quiz to see what kind of shape your spine is in:

Your Spinal Condition

Check Yes or No to each of the following questions:

1. Are you slumped over when you stand? ❏ Yes ❏ No
2. Do you slump over when you sit? ❏ Yes ❏ No
3. Do you stand in a crooked position (leaning to one side)? ❏ Yes ❏ No
4. Is your neck protruding forward (instead of sitting on top of your spine)? ❏ Yes ❏ No
5. Are your hips thrust decidedly forward when you walk? ❏ Yes ❏ No
6. Do your feet turn inward or outward when you walk? ❏ Yes ❏ No

If you answered yes to any of these questions, you need to pay more attention to your precious spine and your posture.

Everyone worries about getting that slumped-over look as they age. Not only is this unpleasant aesthetically, it's not good for your breathing, which is necessary to send that crucial breath carrying life energy (called prana) through your body. Pay attention now to keeping your precious spine as clear a channel as possible. If you need help getting your spine in correct alignment, see a doctor or a chiropractor.

Many variations of chiropractic practices help realign the spine for more freely flowing energy; one new trend is called *network spinal analysis* (NSA). California NSA practitioner Lexi Fisher explains

Tantra Tutorial

Life experiences or traumas (physical, emotional, or biochemical) that are left incomplete get stuck and stored up in the spine just as they do in your unconscious, preventing the body from healing or responding freely.

that this gentle form of chiropractic adjustments (developed in 1979 by Dr. Donald Epstein) consists of a series of very light contacts (pressure similar to that you might place on closed eyelids) to areas of the spine along the vertebral column. These contacts re-awaken the body to unresolved experiences and traumatic tension patterns to release them and free up the channel for more energy.

Fisher explains how it works: "Gentle rocking of the vertebrae frees what was stuck there, allowing it to be integrated back into us. As the nervous system becomes more flexible, chronic holding patterns let go as a wave of muscular contractions and pulsation moves through, discharging tension stored there and reorganizing the nervous system. Once the spinal cord becomes more flexible we experience increased ease and more energy flowing throughout our body, as we are not as invested in our old ways of resisting life."

Just as important as how you move your body to achieve the total good health crucial for your tantric practice is what you put into it. That means paying attention to your nutrition.

Food for Thought: You Are What You Eat

Food is the body's fuel, so it is crucial to pay attention to what you eat. Of course, you know that fatty foods are bad for your health, and that eating heavy meals is not conducive to good sex. However, healthy eating practices go beyond this; they must be part of your entire tantric life routine.

A clogged or unclean digestive tract can seriously interrupt the flow of energy. Many tantric devotees do an occasional "cleanse" to purify their body of toxins. Cleanses range from eating only raw foods to juice fasts. Not all approaches are right for everyone. To find the right one for you, get a full medical evaluation and consult a nutrition expert, read books on nutrition—especially those with a tantric perspective—and ask friends and tantric teachers for recommendations.

Blocks to Bliss

Never go on a fast or other radical dietary routine without proper consultation and supervision about what's right for you.

The Least You Need to Know

➤ Your body is a temple of love; pay attention to how you treat it as a sign of how you treat yourself.

➤ Exercise routines such as yoga draw attention to your body, promote health, increase your sexual energy, and prepare you for tantric sex.

➤ Pay particular attention to the position of your spine because it is the channel of life energy through your body.

➤ A healthy eating plan contributes to your general health, which in turn contributes to a healthier relationship.

Chapter 6

Amp Up or Damp Down Your Sexual Energy

In This Chapter

➤ You are in control of your energy

➤ Exercises to calm down your energy

➤ Reducing stress with air yoga

➤ Exercises to amp up your energy

➤ The sacrum tap, chakra thump, and pelvic thrusts to shake up your Shakti energy

➤ How a partner can help

Now that your body is in good shape, you can progress to the next step: controlling your energy by relaxing or intensifying it as part of your tantric practice. It's important that I discuss these two states because they are consistent with the tantric principles of opposites. That is, energy can be still or active; dynamic or in motion. You need to know how to move your energy in both of these directions.

In this chapter you'll learn some exercises to put you in a mellow mood, with your sex energy at a calm, flowing pace, or to amp you up so you're fully energized and hot to trot. Remember that you are in control of your body temple; as long as you have been properly prepared, it will respond to what you ask it to do.

Ways to Calm Down

Life is stressful, so understandably it might be difficult to do some of your tantric practices if you aren't in the right frame of mind. Worrying about work, a health problem, or a relationship can prevent you from directing your energy as you wish.

Here are some ways to calm down and relax your energy:

➤ Control your breath. Take a deep breath in to the count of seven and exhale to a longer count (see how high you can go). Exhaling longer than you inhale relaxes you and decreases your heart rate. Refer to Chapter 3, "Spinning Your Wheels and Breathing to Ecstasy," for more details about using your breath to direct your energy.

➤ Sit still and empty your mind. Let thoughts come and go without focusing on them. Or try meditating on a single word, such as "om," to calm your mind.

➤ Adjust your environment to eliminate distractions such as ringing phones, irritating street noise, or glaring bright lights.

➤ Light candles and soak in a warm bubble bath.

➤ Take a long walk, play with the dog, or toss a ball around with your kids. Just about any physical activity is a stress reducer.

➤ Close your eyes and picture a soothing scene, such as the ocean. Imagine the smell of the salt air and the feel of the sand between your toes.

➤ Soothe yourself with massage. Use long, smooth strokes to calm you while you breath slowly and deeply. Use cream to glide your hands over your skin.

Dr. Judy's TantrAdvice

Notice the level of your energy at any particular time by rating it on a scale from 0 to 10, with 0 being the least energetic and 10 being the most. Watch how the rating changes by activities you purposefully do to raise or lower your energy.

Air Yoga as a Stress Reducer

You likely have a basic idea about yoga, if you don't already practice it—but *air yoga?* What is that? It's a fascinating variation on more traditional yoga that incorporates tantric principles. Developed by Washington, D.C., tantric teacher Joshua Smith, it involves moving the body into traditional yoga poses, then letting your body settle comfortably into positions it feels it wants to move into.

Start by assuming one of the simplest yoga poses, the *tree pose.* Stand with feet shoulder-width apart, knees slightly bent, looking down. Exhale deeply through the mouth, focusing on a spot on the ground, falling deeper and deeper into your body with each exhale. Close your eyes, inhale through the nose, raise your head, and allow your hands to drift upward as if holding a balloon in each hand (until level with your head). As you exhale through the mouth, allow your arms to arch forward, letting the head and body to be guided gently toward the ground. Relax the head, arms, jaw, and shoulders, feeling like a rag doll.

Now move in whatever way your spine and body want to move. This is different from other yoga, Smith explains, because you are not following poses that are defined in a book or established practice, but moving completely in the unknown. "With each exhale in your mouth," Smith instructs, "allow your body to move in a different way. Stay tantrically aware of your breath and you will be carried into a state of transcendent stillness."

Amping Up for Good Loving

Sometimes you really feel too tired for sex or not interested enough, even if part of you really wants to make love or satisfy your partner's desire. The good news is there are many ways tantric sex practices can help you energize your body for lovemaking.

Control Your Breathing

Take a deep breath in to the count of seven and exhale to a shorter count. Inhaling longer than you exhale increases your heart rate. (This is the opposite technique of what I described earlier, to calm down your energy.)

Another breathing technique that can recharge you is the fire breath. Inhale and exhale rapidly through the nose. Let your belly fill up and then deflate with the air.

Practice the Sacrum Tap

Tap on your sacral area (the triangle above the end of your tailbone and below your waist). This is the home of powerful energy (called "kundalini" energy because it is released from the kunda gland located at the base of the spine). Tantra workshops, like those taught by a highly respected organization called Tantrika International (see Appendix B, "Workshops, Web Sites, Teachers, and Tantra Communities"), often include more elaborate variations of this practice. For example, one partner lies down and the other adds motions (running thumbs up the spine, breathing warm air up the spine) to move the energy up the spine after tapping the sacrum.

Blocks to Bliss

Consider your physical condition in any activity that alters your energy, especially since accelerated breathing can make you lightheaded or dizzy. For example, people with heart conditions should be especially careful; consult your doctor.

Taps to awaken energy.

Do the Chakra Thump

Tap on any of your chakras to awaken the energy there. This doesn't mean tap danc-ing with your feet! Rather, it means making rapid repetitive up-and-down tapping motions on the body with the pads of your fingers. You can also make a fist and use the softer sides of your hands. Review the locations of the chakras in Chapter 3.

Practice Streaming

Streaming is a variation of the previous exercises. The giver taps forcefully on either side of the receiver's spine with the fingertips, starting from the sacrum and progress-ing up to the neck. A nice addition: When you get to the shoulders, do a nice mas-sage!

Dance Up an Energy Storm

The benefits of dance as movement, body conditioning, and just having fun are end-less! I'll discuss this more in Chapter 15, "Make It Juicy with Magic and Play," when I share some playful things to do with your partner. Put on some music at home and let yourself sway, bob, shimmy, and shake. Improvise. When I do this, I go from imagining being a ballet dancer to thinking of myself as a Chinese god wielding a sword. Don't worry if you don't have a partner to dance with. Consider taking a dance class, whether modern, jazz, ballroom, swing, or tango (quite popular now).

Get that Pelvis Moving!

Pelvic thrusts are essential to generating sexual energy and pleasure in sex. Doing them is like downing a power bar for your sexual energy. This is the movement men naturally make when they have sex—but usually don't prolong long enough to get the true benefits.

Pelvic thrusts are one of the favored and fun exercises in tantra workshops. It's quite a sight to see a room full of men and women standing or lying on the floor, arching their back and thrusting their pelvis forward. When everyone adds sound to the movement, the energy in the room is nearly enough to lift off!

Pelvic thrusts can be done from a standing position, progressing to the floor through various levels of squatting; or in the opposite direction (starting from a lying down position and getting up). Doing them basically involves thrusting the pelvis forward and backward. It's important to coordinate your breath (exhale through the mouth as you thrust forward and inhale through the nose as you arch backward). Once you get the hang of it you can move your arms to help move your energy. When you do these exercises alone, you can picture yourself thrusting against a partner, having intercourse to help allow yourself to get really sexy and seductive. Or you can do these exercises facing a partner—and feel as if you are already in the sex act!

Pelvic thrusts to build sexual energy.

Fantasize

It's normal and even healthy to have sexual fantasies—fleeting thoughts or extended stories in your mind about past experiences or imagined situations that are arousing. Give yourself permission to have these thoughts without worrying about whether they are bad or wrong. However, keep in mind that tantric practice requires that you always bring your attention back into your body sensations and the present so you fully appreciate your real experience, your partner, and what is going on in the moment.

Let Yourself Go!

An important principle in building sexual energy is to free your thoughts and movements from inhibitions. One technique to do this is called "the dynamic meditation." This is a technique developed by the Indian mystic, Osho, who originated many tantric practices to bring about enlightenment. The first time I did this practice, at the Osho retreat center in Pune, India, I was impressed with how brilliantly and artfully it can help move energy.

The "dynamic meditation" is done in several parts. In the first part, shake your body for up to 15 minutes while breathing in and out forcefully and quickly. Flap your arms (you'll look humorously like a chicken!) to get more energy flowing. Let your voice go and say gibberish. Free your mind and loosen your jaw, and let your limbs fly where they may. Bolts of energy will surge through your body and every cell will feel alive and tingling. Afterward, stop abruptly and go into a state of meditative silence to absorb the energy. After this period of meditation, let yourself become active by dancing and having uninhibited fun. You can purchase a tape of this meditation from Osho International (see Appendix B for contact information).

Do the "Shakti Shake"

Another way to activate your energy is to do the "Shakti Shake." This is a wonderful technique I use in many of my classes and workshops, especially when participants come in feeling tired from their days of classes, studying, or work. The technique is very simple: Put on some music that you can't resist moving to. Start by shaking just your right leg, then your left leg. Keep up with the beat of the music. Get your hips, arms, and hands moving. Rock your shoulders. Let your head go (careful with your neck!). Get your whole body into the action. Notice how alive you feel.

Take Lama Breaths

Lama breathing is one of my favorite ways to amp up. When I give lectures I even have the attendees do it to refresh themselves, even at times in the middle of my speech! It's quite an exhilarating experience—and quite a sight! The monks in Tibet use these movements and find them so effective in warming the body that they can go up in the mountains naked and stay warm. There are an extended series of moves in sequences. Here are two simple techniques that I have adapted for use in my groups with great effectiveness:

➤ Stand straight with knees slightly bent and shoulder-width apart. Inhale and raise your arms straight out to your sides. Exhale, dropping your arms to your sides, blowing the air out and making a bellows-like sound until your arms come to rest at your sides. Notice how you feel. Repeat this three times.

➤ Stand firmly rooted to the ground, legs shoulder-width apart. Inhale and raise one arm, making a fist, up above your head and drop it while exhaling, blowing out the air forcefully, and letting a sound come out. Alternate arms. (Twice might be enough to jazz you up.)

Tantra Tutorial

Spinning—twirling around in a joyful dance movement—is part of energizing ceremonies in Sufism, an Islamic mystical movement that some Westerners follow. Spinning is intended help you connect with the divine (God). If you try it, don't spin so long that you become dizzy and lose your balance, and take care not to bump into anything.

Lama breaths.

Ask Your Partner for Help

Any one of the techniques in this chapter can be done alone or with a partner. Letting your partner know the level of your sexual energy and your willingness to adjust, or to match his or her interest, increases trust and intimacy between you.

For example, Andy knew that his partner Ali had planned a special evening for their anniversary and would want to be especially close and to make love. But he had had an especially bad day at the office, with an important deal that fell through, leaving him feeling fatigued and discouraged. Not wanting to disappoint her, he explained the dilemma. She happily allowed him time alone to calm down by breathing, meditating, and taking a shower, and then helped him shift his mood by giving him a long, relaxing massage.

Moving your energy alone or with a partner prepares you for sharing nights of pleasure, as described in the following chapters.

The Least You Need to Know

➤ You control your energy and decide whether you want to be sexual; don't give up, feeling that you're just too tired and can't do anything about it.

➤ It is possible to calm your energy for tantric sex by controlling your breath, thoughts, and movements.

➤ You can also amp up your energy for sex by particular ways of controlling your breathing, or performing certain exercises or movements that get your body moving.

➤ You can increase or decrease your energy levels with certain movements or activities on your own or with your partner; let your partner know your energy level and what help you would like.

Chapter 7

Setting the Stage for Your Tantric Nights of Pleasure

In This Chapter

➤ Making time for lovemaking

➤ Preparing for your tantric night of pleasure

➤ Bathing rituals

➤ God and goddess attire to spark your desire

➤ Arranging your temple of love and your love altar

➤ What to do and where to go on your tantra date

Consider lovemaking as your "tantric date," a special get-together in two steps: planning and preparing for your night of pleasure, and spending the actual time together. Having sex is not just an act; it is a ritual experience that requires thought and deliberate actions as part of the seduction.

Every action serves a multiple purpose: to quiet your mind, put you in the mood, build anticipation, and honor your partner. Dress up your self and the space where you will make love, paying attention to the smallest details. Attention to details is a sign of honoring each other and your time together; it shows the value you place on each other and on your relationship. Your tantric night of pleasure starts with setting aside time to be together—something many couples neglect.

Making Time Enough for Love

We never have enough time for sex. This is one of the most common complaints I've heard from couples over the years! Of course you're busy with work, family, friends, and a full calendar; but what could be more important than making time for this special kind of loving?

Set aside time for one another to do these practices. Start with an hour on two different occasions during the week. Agree on the specific time and write it in your calendar. This will affirm that your relationship is of primary importance from which other aspects also flow, including your job, family relationships, and your life in general.

"But where's the spontaneity?" complained Donald when I told him to set up such a tantric sex schedule. "Who wants sex to be so organized? That sounds like no fun." Donald's objections are common, especially for men. However, every new exercise or self-improvement effort requires allotting time and expending effort, whether it's yoga, weight lifting, or a weekend workshop. To keep your priorities in order in our busy world, you have to insist on scheduling, at least at first; later you can be more spontaneous. Use the following calendar to check off when you will be together for your tantric sex practices. Start with one hour twice a week and add more time as you advance in your practices.

Ecstasy Essentials

Falling into a passionate embrace—spontaneously, anytime, anyplace—is exciting and certainly adds quick fire to a relationship—but preparing for that special encounter can build a steady burn. Putting time, energy, and care into preparing for your time together makes you both feel special!

The Conscious Cleanup

Surely you know the experience of dressing your best for a special date, or a quick cleanup if you anticipate taking your date back to your place (tossing newspapers in the garbage, hiding piles of papers, throwing clothes in the closet). If you've been together a long time and take each other for granted, it's time to go back to those days of dating when you were making an effort to impress. Consider the following 10 tips for conscious cleanups, both alone and with your partner:

1. Always keep your fingernails clean and neatly clipped. Neatly trimmed, clean nails are not only attractive (dirty nails are most often mentioned as turnoffs by both men and women), they are important for hygiene, because you'll use your fingers to stimulate your partner's skin and pleasure his or her internal organs.

2. Brush your teeth regularly, especially before a romantic interlude with your partner. Like nails, unbrushed teeth are high on the list of turnoffs mentioned by both men and women. Use toothpaste with baking soda for a good cleansing, and swish with mouthwash for an extra feeling of freshness.

Tantric Love Together Time

	6A.M.	7A.M.	8A.M.	9–11A.M.	NOON–2P.M.	3–5P.M.	6P.M.	7P.M.	8P.M.	9P.M.	10P.M.	11P.M.	MIDNIGHT–2A.M.	3–5A.M.
Mon.														
Tues.														
Wed.														
Thurs.														
Fri.														
Sat.														
Sun.														

3. Wash each other's hair. This is particularly good for the man to do for the woman, as it is often the first time he has done such an act for her.

4. Shave him, paying careful attention to being tender on his skin. Trusting her to do this will make her feel proud and pleased.

5. Paint her toenails. Do his nails, too, for something new, as more men are letting themselves enjoy this primping without thinking that it is unmanly.

Tantra Tutorial

In the Arm and Hammer First Impression Study of more than a thousand men and women, top turnoffs included body odor (89 percent), unpleasant personality (86 percent) bad breath (84 percent), discolored or yellow teeth (70 percent), too much perfume (62 percent), and dirty fingernails (60 percent). More than half of those surveyed said fresh breath becomes more important the longer they are in a romantic relationship. People with bad breath were described as unclean, unhealthy, lazy, unattractive, and unsuccessful.

6. Adjust the lighting in the bathroom. Most bathrooms have harsh lighting, especially over the sink. Replace the bulbs with rosy colored ones for a special evening, or bring in a special lamp. Place candles on sink counters, bathtub ledges, and floor to create a sensuous atmosphere.

7. Take turns preparing a bath for each other or share a romantic bath together (more on that in the next section). Check the water temperature. Although a cool bath is stimulating, warm water usually is best for relaxation and to generate feelings of warmth.

8. Play music during your bath. One couple I know mounted stereo speakers in their bathroom! A simpler idea is to bring in a CD player or radio (be careful, of course, that electrical appliances don't fall in the water!).

9. Buy special scented soaps, bath oils, soft brushes, and even bath mitts. Most department stores have large sections for bath items, and stores such as Bed, Bath and Beyond and The Body Shop specialize in all kinds of accoutrements for the bath.

10. Prepare your exit with a mat (to avoid stepping on a cold floor), cozy bathrobe, and large, plush towels. Keep the latter two items separate from what you use everyday, to make the experience special.

The Tantric Bathing Ritual

I'm sure you're familiar with taking a quick shower or swish in a tub after a stressful day to get ready for sex. But when's the last time you languished in the bath with your lover? Languorous, deliberate showering and washing together is an essential part of tantric sex. Time in the tub is for far more than getting clean; it also is to …

➤ Enjoy the experience of being together in the water.

➤ Get in touch with your bodies.

➤ Arouse your sensations.

➤ Build your awareness of each other.

Tantra Tutorial

Bathing is an ancient tradition as a prelude to lovemaking. Ancient Roman and Greek lovers stepped down into large open baths, and in Japanese tradition lovers went from an extremely hot tub to an extremely cold tub to stimulate circulation, a practice continued at Oriental spas.

The most important aspect of tantric bathing is to make washing each other a ritualistic act, done with deliberate attention. Instead of swishing soap quickly over body parts, linger on certain spots. Be creative as you would during a massage. Soapy hands offer a wonderful opportunity to slide over your partner's skin. Use different touches to delight the skin; from long, smooth strokes to circular tracings around areas such as the back and buttocks. Alternate your touch, using the soapy palms of your hand on especially sensitive places and light fingernail scratches on places such as arms and legs.

The beloveds' bathing ritual.

85

Dr. Judy's TantrAdvice

Water striking the skin can be pleasurable. If you don't have the luxury of jets in a hot tub, buy an attachment that can be installed in your tub to circulate the water, or a shower head that emits either diffuse or pelting flows.

Just as you would in massage, start with nonsexual areas to build anticipation for more sexual parts. Trace around the breasts and chest deliberately, and up the inner thighs. Slip hands delicately onto more sexual areas. It can be an entirely new experience for couples to wash each other in these private parts. Clean with an air of innocence—still intending to stimulate your partner—to add an element of teasing and tantalizing.

God and Goddess Dress Up

Remember when playing dress up was fun? Little girls love dressing up as mommy or dressing their dolls, and boys like donning cowboy outfits or GI Joe gear. As we grow up we tend to become conservative and cautious about attire. On your tantra date, let yourself have fun again; play with styles and fabrics, pick clothes you might never imagine wearing, or use that finery in your closet you've been saving for a special occasion.

Of course, you like to think you're loved for exactly who you are rather than what you look like or what you wear. Indeed, your inner being is what really matters in tantric lovemaking, but beautifying your outer being is a statement of respect for yourself and your lover.

Most men get quickly to the stage of being naked in lovemaking, and of course you can choose to be *au naturel*; but tantric sex involves dressing up before you undress. Dressing up to seduce your lover—and to feel good about yourself—is a meditative act to draw attention to your body, to put you in a seductive mood, and for just plain fun. Let yourself be creative, following these suggestions:

➤ Tantric clothes are usually loose fitting and diaphanous, to match the feeling of flowing. Sensuous fabrics such as cut velvets and silk encourage touch. Women can wear flowing dresses, wrapped scarves, or beaded collars, the more revealing the better, to entice and please the eye and invite touch! The tantric man can wear a silk shirt (with top buttons open), silk boxers, or even cotton slacks. Tantric men are not afraid to wear wrapped materials (commonly worn on exotic islands such as Hawaii and Tahiti) called *pareos,* which look like skirts but are actually quite masculine.

➤ Make sure these clothes are special, not the same things you wear every day, working around the house, or just hanging out.

➤ Clothes can be loungewear or outerwear, as long as you feel good in them and they delight your partner.

God and goddess dress up.

➤ Wear jewelry that draws more attention than what you would normally wear in public. Be dramatic, letting a string of pearls dangle into your cleavage. Try extra-long dangling earrings, or a thin belt strung around your belly. Extra spark can come from ankle bracelets or toe rings. Some tantric men let themselves go, wearing a bracelet or necklace (as men did in ancient Roman or Egyptian times) to add extra sparkle and to surprise their partner.

➤ Experiment with new styles of clothing you haven't thought of wearing before. Pick attire for your tantra date that gives you an opportunity to explore new parts of yourself and new fantasies.

➤ Use color. The traditional tantric colors are red and purple. Refer to Chapter 3, "Spinning Your Wheels and Breathing to Ecstasy," to review the colors associated with different chakras, and choose colors of clothing to stimulate and accentuate certain energy centers. Wear orange underwear to awaken the sex center, a yellow scarf around your waist to boost your power, a necklace with a turquoise stone at your throat to help you express yourself, or a purple shirt to inspire you to achieve a more spiritual state of mind and union.

You can undress alluringly for your partner, even putting on a strip show. Or undress each other slowly and seductively, or even rip each other's clothes off in a fit of passion.

Your Ideal Romantic Setting

Lights! Camera! Action! Think of a movie set for the most romantic or exciting love scene you can imagine. What does the set look like? Fill in the following chart for yourself and with your partner. Do you have the same ideal lovemaking space? Talk about your different ideas of a perfect setting for lovemaking. Take turns describing your scenes fully and enjoy your partner's scene, allowing yourself to imagine yourselves being there.

Describe how the most romantic scene would look, if you were directing a love scene in a movie. For example, under Place, your ideal scene might be outdoors in a field of lilies, whereas your partner's might be indoors in a bedroom with a crackling fireplace. Under Era, you might choose ancient Rome as being most exciting or romantic; your partner might choose seventeenth-century France.

Our Ideal Love Scene

	What I Like:	**What My Partner Likes:**
Place:	_____	_____
Lighting:	_____	_____
Furniture:	_____	_____
Style:	_____	_____
Era:	_____	_____

Other characteristics (specify): _____

_____

_____

Prepare Your Sacred Lovemaking Space

Think of the most elegant temples, cathedrals, and synagogues you have ever been in. Remember your awe at the stained glass windows, elaborate ceiling paintings, marble floors, gilded wood carvings, gold satin, or red velvet drapery. Think of your lovemaking space with the same reverence and care as such temples.

Dressing up your lovemaking space follows the same principle as dressing yourself up before a special date. Think of going to a special event: Just as you'd put on your best finery, dress up your room. Be mindful of stimulating all the senses, following these tips:

➤ Light candles all around the room. Put dimmers on your lights, replace harsh lighting with softer fixtures, or put colored bulbs in lamps. If you have overhead lights, place lamps strategically. Drape scarves over lampshades with lights that are too bright (a favorite tantric trick). Think of yourself on TV or in a movie, where lighting creates flattering views of the people's faces and the environment.

➤ Add scent. Put fresh flowers in the room, light incense, or spray aromatic room oils. (Don't overdo it, and, of course, be attentive to any allergies you or your partner have.)

➤ Dress up your bed. Put on a new coverlet, drape it with colored materials purchased specially for these occasions, and add soft pillows as decoration and to support body parts.

➤ Keep love toys handy, including massage oils, feather boas, and silk scarves to run over your partner's body to awaken sensations.

➤ Have sacraments nearby that stimulate your taste buds and to toast your lovemaking. These can include anything from chocolate-covered strawberries to the traditional chilled glasses of champagne.

➤ Neaten up. Store messy piles of papers in a closet, stash exercise equipment under the bed, cover distracting items such as stacks of videos with scarves or attractive swatches of material.

Dr. Judy's TantrAdvice

Don't inhibit lovemaking by fearing that your fancy satin sheets will be ruined by oils or body fluids. Buy them for that purpose, replace them when necessary, or put towels down for protection. Use silk sheets for sensuality or put on flannel sheets because they are warm, absorbent, and feel comfortable on the skin.

Change Your Setting

Be creative in your lovemaking. Make love in different places inside and outside the home, blessing each area with your love. Flowers will bloom and trees will grow taller where you come together with blessed intention and spiritual union.

However, making love in the same setting and keeping your love altar in the same place are also good ideas, as your lovemaking creates an energy vortex that builds and intensifies your union when you return to that space. Cellular memory and mental associations are triggers, so that even if you are not in the mood, entering that space can get you there.

Blocks to Bliss

One tantra teacher I know recommends not always making love in your bed, saying it can trigger physical reactions and mental associations with sleep and the release of melatonin that induces drowsiness. In addition, a too-soft mattress or waterbed does not provide as much friction of body parts pressing against one another as a floor (padded, of course).

Music to Make Love By

Music stirs the soul. Research has proven that certain sounds and tempos directly affect our breathing and heart rate, which in turn affects our mood. For these reasons music will play a very important role in your tantric date. Choose music you and your partner enjoy, whether it is classical, operatic, or even rock-and-roll. Most important, select music consciously to create the mood you desire. I'll go into more detail about this and give you suggestions about what kind of music to play in Chapter 18, "Sex, Song, and Videotape." Check out that chapter when it's time to stack your CD changer for your date.

Building an Altar

An altar is a space on a ledge, table, or on the floor where you place sacred objects symbolic of your prayers and respect for spirits. Just as in a religious institution, looking at these objects inspires you to a higher state of consciousness. Be on the lookout for sacred objects to decorate your house that trigger spiritual feelings when you look at them. Collect the objects and design this space together, as an experience that brings you close together and a testimonial to your togetherness. Approach this altar before your lovemaking and say a prayer together—silently or aloud—to bless the items and your upcoming union.

Ecstasy Essentials

As is done in ancient Native American traditions, light sticks of sage (available at health food stores) to purify the air with its pungent aroma. Move it around the room, into each corner, and around your body.

Items on your altar might include ...

➤ Photos of yourselves that you cherish, or photos of revered religious leaders or tantric masters.

➤ Objects from your life together that are especially meaningful (shells from a trip to Fiji, the class ring he gave you, the crystal she bought in a small shop in the mountains).

➤ Items representing the elements: earth (a special stone), fire (candles), water (a bowl), air (a feather) and spirit (crystal).

➤ Flowers, especially fresh flowers.

➤ Special gifts that you've given each other.

➤ Sacred objects such as statues of Shiva and Shakti in embrace, or the bell and *dorje* (symbolic of the male and female spirit).

Honoring Rituals to Sanctify Your Space

Love rituals involving movements and dedications help create a safe space and a sanctified area in which to surrender to each other. Here you can achieve transformation and trance-like states that lead to ecstasy. The following are some ways to sanctify your special space:

➤ Walk around the space in each of the four corners, saying a prayer at each corner. Make up your own prayer, such as: "I dedicate this experience to you, my beloved, may it fulfill all your heart's desire." Or recite a prayer that comes from your ancient people. Maria Yraceburu is an American Indian descendant in touch with her spiritual heritage, described in her book *Legends and Prophecies of the Quero Apache* (Inner Traditions International/Bear Books, 2002). Here is her suggestion for a chant:

> We come from the Earth Mother, We come from the Sky Father,
> We come here to be all that we can be,
> The legacy unfolds here in life,
> Moving like soft warm rain, Our love ascends
> Cascading to Earth. Spirit's saving grace.
> Daaiina, and so it is.

➤ Walk around the space in each of the four corners, blessing it, saying a prayer to make it safe, or invoking and inviting the spirits of the four directions of the universe, and any other spirits you would like to bless and protect you in your lovemaking (good guides, holy spirits, or ancestors). For example, walk to the north corner, ring a bell, and say, "We invite spirits of the north to send their blessing and protective energy to our lovemaking." Say something similar at the south, east, and west corners.

➤ Give each other a gift as an offering of your love and devotion, and to sanctify the space as holy and honoring. This can be a small gift that does not have to cost a great deal of money. Make it something thoughtful that you can use immediately in your lovemaking ceremony, such as a small stone, a CD of his favorite music, a scarf, or scented oil.

Giving gifts of love.

Quiet the Mind

Settle down into your space after bathing and honoring the space rituals, and quiet the mind to allow your energies to mingle. Sit in the yab yum position, as described in Chapter 2, "The Basics: Yes, Yin Yang, Yoni, and Yab Yum." Do eye gazing and breathing techniques as described in Chapters 3, "Spinning Your Wheels and Breathing to Ecstasy," and 8, "Practices for Beloveds to Reach Bliss." Chant to synchronize your energy and quiet your mind. Follow the repetitive mantras of a particular CD, do traditional ones (such as simply repeating "om" or "aum"), or make up your own.

Set Your Intention Together

All too often couples jump into bed—and sex—silently. But since tantric sex is a dedication and not a mindless act, sit opposite each other and set an intention for your lovemaking. Sexual and love energy is powerful energy—say what you would like to manifest in this lovemaking session, and it will be more likely to come true as you let your energy expand and merge. Take turns, speaking from your heart, allowing whatever needs to be said to come up. Ask for anything from your partner or from divinities, including personal happiness and world peace.

Tantra Tales

Barry's intention in making love with his girlfriend Beth was: "I intend for this time together to bring us to a better understanding of each other, to cleanse our hearts from the anger of last week, and to blend our bodies so that we feel higher states of pleasure than we ever have before." Beth said, "My intention is for us to go deeper in our love than we have ever gone before; for me to feel better about my body; and for the love energy that we generate to spread out to heal the children in other parts of the world who are suffering, and the men and women who are the victims of cruel unloving acts from others, and to inspire all those who do not yet know the joys of these practices." Alex had a similarly touching blessing for his beloved, adding a dedication to her health, but also a humorous request: "... and may you have that Mercedes Benz car you drool over!"

Going Out on Your Tantra Date

The tantra date refers to your lovemaking ritual in a private space, usually at home. However, the prelude to this date can certainly include activities you do on a regular date, in which you actually go somewhere to do something—before coming home for lovemaking. Excitement can build when you are out somewhere together. What are the most exciting things you can do together that will increase your feelings of togetherness and build your anticipation for private time together?

Review the following list and check off activities you would most enjoy. Add to the list. Write down pleasurable activities you can think of, ask your partner to do the same, and compare your lists. Did you come up with similar activities? Read your list to each other and discuss what you would most enjoy about each one. Go over them one at a time, slowly, enjoying the description of what you would do. Notice how you feel when you imagine the activity. Where is the pleasure—or resistance—to these activities? What fears do each of you have about doing what each of you chose?

Activities List

Activity	I Like:	My Partner Likes:
Have a romantic dinner	_____	_____
Walk in the park	_____	_____
See a movie	_____	_____
Go dancing	_____	_____
Ride bicycles	_____	_____
Visit friends	_____	_____
Attend a concert	_____	_____
Work out together	_____	_____
Other:	_____	_____
Other:	_____	_____
Other:	_____	_____

The Least You Need to Know

➤ Even if you have a full calendar of work, family obligations, and other commitments, it's important for you and your partner to make time for love.

➤ Prepare for lovemaking to make your encounter special by pampering yourself and setting up your ideal love scene (your bedroom or wherever you choose to make love), paying attention to appeal to all the senses.

➤ Create a sensuous bathing ritual not just for cleaning but for adding to your sensual pleasure.

➤ Dress up for a special occasion, selecting apparel that flatters your shape and seduces, and adornments that draw attention.

➤ Sanctify your body and your space with ritualistic purifying and prayers and set your intentions that honor the special event you will make of your union.

Chapter 8

Well, practice makes perfect...

Practices for Beloveds to Reach Bliss

In This Chapter

➤ How to reach the state of bliss

➤ Simple methods to synchronize your energy

➤ Spicing up your senses and stimulating your partner

➤ Finding your tantric love triggers

➤ Learning "sex in the flow lane"

➤ Rituals that make lovemaking special

Now that you've set the stage for your tantric connection, what are you to do? A natural answer would be to do what comes naturally. But since tantra is a ritualistic practice, there are some activities and ceremonies you can do together to facilitate your pleasure and help you reach those higher realms of bliss. This chapter introduces you to some of those practices.

What Is Bliss?

Have you ever been so happy you almost couldn't believe it? Been so attuned to everything around you and smiled so hard that your face hurt? Felt a bright white light enveloping you and maybe even transporting you to another dimension?

Blocks to Bliss

Many people actually resist bliss, living with the limiting belief that "It can never be this good!" or fears that they will lose that feeling of happiness. I invite you to give yourself permission now for it to be that good! Believe that you deserve it!

That's the state of bliss—deeper than delight; juicier than joyful. You're enraptured and have the feeling that all is perfect. "Bliss" is the highest happiness. In a word, "heaven," says Bodhi Avinasha, master teacher of spiritual transformation and author of *Jewel in the Lotus* and *Living in Bliss* (Tantrika International, 2002). "Bliss means feeling so good that every cell in your body feels alive," says tantra teacher Laurie Handlers, who leads workshops titled "Being in Bliss."

How do you get to that magical state of bliss? By being present in the moment, breathing, channeling your energy, feeling your love, and practicing the techniques I'm sharing with you in this book. Bodhi Avinasha has developed this *dynamic bliss formula:* simultaneous activation and integration of mind, body, and soul. The magical process involves activating the body and stilling the mind; then channeling sexual energy through the body to reach higher states of consciousness. "With this formula, you go from survival to service, from pleasure to creativity, from control to surrender," says Bodhi. It's brilliant, and it works.

Synchronizing Your Energy

Because life is so stressful and you can't always expect that you and your beloved will be in the same mood, it is very important before beginning any tantric practice that you do as much as possible to be on the same wavelength. The magic of tantra is that you can start out in a different space and place, figuratively speaking and through certain practices, you can get into the same groove.

One way to synchronize your energy is by breathing together. Review the breathing practices I described in detail in Chapter 3, "Spinning Your Wheels and Breathing to Ecstasy." You'll recall that the breath guides your energy in various ways that you want it to go.

You can do these breaths in different positions to achieve interesting new sensations. For example, sit back to back while you do the breaths (instead of facing each other) and feel your partner's chest, sides, and back expanding through the contact with your back. You can feel this easily if you both have taken a full breath so that your chest and back expand. As you breathe, make up a sound to chant together (use "om" or any sound both of you like). Adding a sound to breathing together intensifies your connection to each other.

Look into My Eyes: Eye Gazing

Eye gazing is a basic tantric sex practice, widely taught by tantra teachers of all schools of thought. It's a fundamental practice that leads to intense experiences when you do it right. It sounds so simple—looking at each other—but in fact, think about how difficult it can be to actually look into anyone's eyes for any amount of time. Fears of intimacy can make it even more uncomfortable to look into a lover's eyes deeply for an extended period of time. How do you feel when a lover looks deeply and directly in your eyes? You might be delighted, but you might also feel vulnerable, self-conscious, or embarrassed. These feelings are normal!

Eye gazing in tantric sex practice means looking deeply into your partner's eyes, to see behind the obvious (eye color, eyelashes, expression) into his or her soul. It can be challenging and take practice.

Eye gazing with deep breathing and energy connection.

You should do eye gazing in most of the exercises I tell you about throughout this book because …

➤ It stills your mind and focuses your attention on what you are doing rather than on distracting thoughts, to keep you present and in the moment.

➤ It gives your partner a good feeling that you're totally paying attention and are present for him or her.

➤ It enables you to confront your fears of deep connection with your beloved.

➤ It transforms your relationship to each other by getting beyond mental distractions and physical judgments to enter each other's soul.

Eye gazing is the favorite sexual practice of the husband and wife tantra teaching team of Mark Michaels and Patricia Johnson. "When people first fall in love, they often spend extended periods gazing into each other's eyes," says Michaels. "In perfecting eye gazing you are consciously re-creating the experience of falling in love."

Ecstasy Essentials

Teachers Michaels and Johnson recommend starting with the classical practice of *Tratak,* in which you fix your gaze on a candle flame for several minutes, usually just before bed. This helps you develop the concentration necessary to exchange intense gazes with your partner.

To do eye gazing, stand facing your partner in a relaxed and open posture and gaze softly into each other's eyes for at least three minutes. (You can also do eye gazing while sitting in yab yum or any comfortable position as long as your energy centers are aligned.) Look predominantly into each other's left (receiving) eye. Remember it's not a staring contest; keep your eyes relaxed and blink if you have to. Come back to gazing if you get distracted. Instead of focusing on the outward act of looking, be receptive so you can melt deeper and deeper into the union with your beloved. "Recognize and appreciate the beauty and joy that you find in your partner's eyes," advises Johnson.

Notice whatever feelings come up (fear, embarrassment, attraction, love). Keep breathing. Notice your body's reactions (lips tightening, squinting, coughing, shifting). Eventually you will be able to keep more still.

The Heart Hold

This exercise sends love energy through your hands and into each other's heart. Place your right hand over your partner's heart. At the same time, your partner places his right hand over your heart. Imagine sending out your love energy through your heart down your arm and out your right hand into your partner. You have several options for where you can put your left hand to run the energy between you:

➤ Over your partner's right hand, pressing it over your heart.

➤ On your partner's middle back, directly in back of where his or her heart is.

➤ On your genitals or on each other's genitals.

Experiment with different places, to experience heart energy cycling through your body in various ways. On each occasion, go slowly, breathe, and feel the energy actually passing between and through you.

The heart hold sends love energy through your hearts.

The Partner Passion Pod

Being encircled by your lover's arms feels secure, comforting, and even exciting. Tantric practice encourages connecting between partners in all types of positions and situations. In this exercise, approach each other slowly while eye gazing and let your bodies float into each other and embrace in any way that seems comfortable. As you embrace, do the synchronizing breath while slowly inhaling and exhaling. As you breathe, feel your bodies melting into one another. Stay in this position as long as you like. When you separate, move apart slowly, still maintaining eye contact since abrupt separations should never occur in tantric connections. Look at each other and notice how different you look. After such a connection, you might look as relaxed and happy as you do after a massage.

Stimulating the Senses

All the senses are honored in tantric lovemaking. That means all the organs involved with these senses are also centers of the body. Here are some examples of exercises you can do with your partner to create bliss between you that activates each of the senses:

➤ **Mouth and face**   Trace around your beloved's mouth with your fingertips and pull the lips apart gently. The lips are related to the genitals, according to Eastern tradition, and licking and sucking them can stimulate the sexual organs. Press your lips to your partner's and make motions. Extend your touch to the area around the mouth and to the cheeks and face. Blindfold your partner and feed him or her various tasty morsels with different textures (try strawberries, chocolate-covered cherries, a spoonful of ice cream, a slice of crunchy cucumber). Tantalize your partner as you do this. (Later this feeding will get more playful in Chapter 15, "Make It Juicy with Magic and Play.")

Sensuous touch.

➤ **Eyes**   The eyes truly are the window to the soul. At the beginning of this chapter I mentioned the importance of eye gazing as fundamental to all tantric connecting. Go a step further by touching your partner's eyes gently around the eye sockets and across the lids, making circles at the corners and tracing out to the temples. Let your gaze roam from each other's eyes down to other parts with wonder and appreciation.

➤ **Nose**   The nose is cherished in tantric practice, since along with the mouth it is the entrance for the vital breath that is the life force (called *prana*). Besides, its function (scent) plays a vital role in attraction! Stimulate your partner's sense of smell by blindfolding him or her and passing various scents (scented oils, oranges, wine) under his or her nose. Sniff various parts of each other's body in a natural, uninhibited way, as animals do, as if scouting each other out. Use your nose as you would your fingers to stimulate each other and see what new sensations you can create.

➤ **Hands**   Touch has been proven to have healing effects, and the role of massage is paramount in tantra. As I've mentioned, it is an excellent idea to take a massage class, read a book, or watch a video about tantric massage to hone your skills.

Here's an exercise I use in my workshops to teach participants how to enjoy sensations through touch. Taking turns as giver and receiver, close your eyes and hold your partner's hand. Feel the energy of the hand you're touching and that of your own hand, so you can identify the different sensations of touching and being touched. Breathe deeply, sending energy through your hand, and explore your partner's hand. Feel the different textures (bony parts, soft palm, sharp nails). Massage, using different strokes and pressures, with the intention of making your partner feel good. Give each other feedback about the different sensations of touching and being touched.

➤ **Ears**   Too often neglected, this part of the body can be very erotic. Press your thumbs into the openings of the ears, pressing around the inner skin. Stretch and tug at the earlobes (they can take pressure)and around the outer ear. Whisper sweet nothings into your partner's ear. Sing a song; it doesn't matter whether you can really sing, just let yourself improvise to express yourself into your partner's ear.

Ecstasy Essentials

Consider aromatherapy and the use of essential oils in your individual and partner practices. Research has shown that such scents actually have particular effects on the brain, facilitating certain mood states.

Dr. Judy's TantrAdvice

While you and your partner are both in the shower, soap up, turn your backs to each other, and rub your back and backside against each other. Bump up against each other's sacrum, to stir up energy.

As I mentioned, music is so important in your tantric practice. (I'll discuss this in more detail in Chapter 18, "Sex, Song, and Videotape"), so improvise making music together. That means you don't have to play someone else's CD; instead, use anything around the house on which to keep a beat, or get some simple percussion instruments (drums, rattles, bells, chimes) from a music store. (As a musician, this is one practice I particularly enjoy!)

101

Call It Sacred: Finding Your Tantric Love Triggers

Consider your relationship as sacred, meaning that you hold it in the highest esteem, reflect on it with awe, and treat it with the utmost respect. To infuse your love with this quality, preface any descriptions of your relationship with the word "sacred." Infuse this sacredness with words or symbols that are special to the two of you and evoke your tantric union (I call these *tantric triggers*). One of my personal tantric triggers is the depiction of the dragon and the phoenix, two magical beings and auspicious symbols in China often paired together as statues, etched on sidewalks, or printed on wedding invitations, as shown in the following illustration.

The auspicious pairing of the phoenix and dragon.

Sex in the Flow Lane

Tantric sex requires an awareness of every sensation—but so often we're so busy "doing" that we don't really *feel* how we're moving. Personal coach Greg Ehmka developed a technique he calls *Sexyhan* (I call it "sex in the flow lane"), in which you don't move any body part until your body feels the motion from within. Ehmka describes this technique in his book *Money, Sex, Power and You: Transforming Your Ego,* and many tantra teachers, including myself, use a variation of the process in their workshops. It is quite wonderful to run a workshop where everyone starts moving in slow motion and gets the experience of this sensation of allowing experience to happen instead of forcing it!

Ehmka, who lives in a tantric community in Austria, recommends doing this exercise on your own for 20 minutes and then with a partner. Start by sitting or standing together with your eyes closed, making low sounds and being still until you get motivated to move (called *inner guidance*). As impulses come, you can touch each other gently, curl up together, or over time get more vigorous even to the point of screaming—as long as it's not a preconceived or automatic motion. "After this practice, measure on a scale of 0 to 10 how joyfully empowered you feel," says Emhka, "I guarantee the more you do it, the higher will be your rating."

Advanced Body Exploration

There are endless secrets hidden in your body temple, to be uncovered though your tantric practices, either alone or with your partner. Don't be afraid to show yourself. Even if you have been making love for years together, or doing tantric practices, your partner's genitals might still be a mystery. Here are some exercises that go a step further than the body explorations and physical sharing that I have mentioned in previous chapters.

Her "Yoni Show" for Him

This exercise is an ultimate act of trust and intimacy. It's also very exciting—physically and energetically—to allow your partner to truly see you inside. Most women are embarrassed about how they look in their most sacred space: their vaginas.

In this exercise the woman is given tremendous encouragement to display her most private, sacred temple for her beloved. It must be preceded by many of the rituals described in Chapter 7, "Setting the Stage for Your Tantric Nights of Pleasure," so that she is extremely relaxed and feels adored by his bathing and massaging her. She then either disrobes or he lovingly disrobes her. As I've emphasized, he must ask permission to see her. At her own pace she reveals her most private parts, using her fingers to direct his attention and open her lips more.

Some couples worry that this exercise will be too clinical—like a medical examination—but actually, if you have prepared together using tantric breathing, it is inevitable that the mood and spirit will be one of loving rather than objectivity. If you feel objective, do not criticize yourself. Realize that this is a way of controlling any fears or self-consciousness. Breathe deeper and let these feelings transmute into more calm, connected ones.

This exercise could evolve to another activity; for example, a demonstration of how she likes to be pleasured, or more free-flowing play leading to a tantric sexual interaction. However, there should never be a goal, as the purpose of the exercise is for her to be relaxed.

Tantra Tales

When Matt and Julie did this exercise, she was excited for him to truly see her but extremely frightened and embarrassed. With his reassurance, she could continue, slowly opening her thighs. "I needed to hear him say that he really wanted to see," she said. Once he did, she was more reassured.

His "Love Arrow Show" for Her

In tantric sex, lovers always take turns at different activities, usually with the woman going first. After her show of her sacred gates to heaven to him, it's his turn to show her his lingam (the "jade stalk" that can enter her gates of heaven). As with other exercises, remember not to have any expectations or make any demands, but to simply enjoy the experience with a spirit of curiosity and adoration. As mentioned for her yoni show, his love arrow show is best preceded by many of the rituals described in Chapter 7.

Making Sacred Water Magic

Water serves many purposes in tantric sex practices—it's cleansing, healing, playful, and a turn-on. I've already mentioned in other chapters many ways you can pleasure each other in the bath or shower. For example, you can do many of the breathing exercises, eye lock, and heart hold. Sit in the bathtub in yab yum position with genitals close together. Breathe slowly and rock your pelvis toward each other on your exhale. Do this for a few minutes.

There are also some interesting techniques some tantric experts use to awaken powerful energies in water. For example, California tantra teachers Steve and Lokita Carter are experts in a bodywork technique called *Watsu Water Shiatsu*, in which the receiver is cradled, stretched, and slowly moved in warm water, interspersed with intervals of stillness. The resulting experience can be a wonderful combination of feeling loved and peaceful. But powerful emotional releases can also happen (I know from experience!).

While working with an expert is certainly helpful to work through any strong emotions that arise, couples can do a more elementary variation of this technique together. Next time you have the chance to be in a pool of warm, still water (a moving sea or cold ocean won't work since you have to be relaxed) you can try this exercise that the Carters recommend. (As in every exercise throughout this book, always greet each other first with loving words and compliments.) Take turns, in water about waist deep. For example, the man stands in the water and helps the woman lean backward in the water. He gently sways her from side to side, holding her by the ribcage or hips, keeping her nose out of the water and pressing her sex center (yoni) to his genitals or belly. (It's a nice addition to put a water pillow under her head, leaving his hands free to gently stroke her chest, belly, and sex center.) Change places. When you're done, thank each other for this special time.

Staying in Bliss: The Afterplay

What if neither of you wants to fall into that post-sex syndrome in which he falls asleep and she lies there unfulfilled? Tantra teacher Robert Frey has a favorite tantric solution for this dilemma, which he calls the *afterplay*, to keep you in bliss.

After ejaculating, says Frey, keep the lingam in the yoni and sit up in the yab yum position. Take a deep breath in and picture drawing that powerful energy of the ejaculation up the spine, like heat rising. Then picture a golden light or mist coming down the spine as you exhale.

Frey suggests doing this for up to a half an hour—and promises that if you do, you could build into a profound full-body orgasmic state for both of you. "Both the man and the woman may have several additional orgasms, simply from being completely turned on by the power of the circulating energy," he explains. In this way, afterplay means there really isn't any "after," because bliss just keeps on coming.

The Least You Need to Know

➤ Bliss is an ecstatic feeling of connection with a loving energy that expands inwardly and outwardly.

➤ Simple exercises can create intense pleasure and deep connection; for example, looking deeply into each other's eyes, sending energy through each other's hearts.

➤ Stimulate all your senses for a truly all-consuming experience; explore tastes, smells, sights, sounds, and touches.

➤ Each of us has particular thoughts, sounds, or symbols that can trigger sensuous feelings; know what these "love triggers" are for yourself and for your partner.

➤ The most blissful sexual experiences can happen when you do not force any actions, but rather when you are still and allow the urges to move to come from within (what I call "sex in the flow lane").

➤ Instead of abruptly ending your lovemaking, stay in bliss by taking deliberate actions to stay connected.

Chapter 9

Breaking Through Blocks to Bliss

In This Chapter

➤ How issues from the past can interfere with your practice of tantric sex—and with your life in general

➤ The importance of making time together

➤ Releasing intense emotions

➤ Getting past desperation, obsession, and anxieties

➤ Balancing your male and female energies

➤ Lifestyle practices that keep you healthy

On any new path of self-discovery, self-improvement, or spirituality, you can make exciting discoveries about yourself and the world around you. However, as you make changes in yourself, your relationships and your lifestyle, blocks can arise from resistance, conflicts, or anxieties. These blocks can come from unresolved problems in your past, partnerships, or even your upbringing. You need to be free of these blocks so you can experience ecstasy not only in love but in all areas of your life.

There are many therapeutic techniques that offer help. I use a wide variety and combination of these in my workshops, and with private patients as well as in my work giving advice on radio, TV, and the Internet. In this chapter I'll address some tools and techniques that will be especially helpful in solving conflicts and clearing emotional blocks so that you'll be free to explore the tantric sex path.

When Big Emotions Burst Forth

Sexuality is a powerful force, and these tantric sex practices generate intense sexual arousal! As a result, it makes sense that you could confront some strong previously suppressed issues. It can be scary when upsetting feelings emerge unexpectedly, but it's important to allow them to come up and resolve them. Instead of repressing problems or traumas, welcome the opportunity to work through them. Trust that their appearance means that you are ready to deal with them. To ease your fear, seek the help of a trained person; ideally a tantric master also schooled in psychotherapeutic and clinical techniques.

To release blocks caused by unresolved issues in your past, some tantra teachers include what's called *emotional release* in their workshops. Deep-seeded emotions stored in the body can be freed through particular patterns of breathing and movement. A partner can also act as a witness and guide. It's amazing to be in a workshop, such as the ones held by those of us trained in the techniques of Tantrika International (see Appendix B, "Workshops, Web Sites, Teachers, and Tantra Communities"), in which a roomful of people are lying on the floor, doing pelvic rocking, breathing, and making sounds, when suddenly a large number of people connect with intense past experiences. Some people might be joyful and laughing, while others express explosive or angry outbursts when they remember a past experience that made them feel that way.

Not all emotional releases are loud or connect with pain; I've had many that are calm and blissful. One of my emotional releases was so powerful that I began to see colors radiating from my body, leading to a feeling of jubilance. Some lead to astounding, physically obvious transformations. When facilitating one woman in an emotional release, I witnessed her transform from looking sad and haggard to looking joyful and 20 years younger!

Transformation as a result of an emotional release process.

Making Time for Each Other

I often hear couples complain that they have no time for sex. Everybody is too busy and other priorities can push quality tantric time together to the back burner, so it's important to find practices you can realistically do together to keep the energy flowing between you. Here are some simple practices you can do that don't require much time but that create an intimate connection in your relationship.

Blocks to Bliss

Critics of emotional release, such as tantra teachers Mark Michaels and Patricia Johnson, maintain that emotional release exercises focus on potential pain, which they say can become a self-fulfilling prophecy. They assert that tantric practices themselves are healing, and deeper work is best left to professional therapists.

Couple's Morning Blessing

Tantra teacher Robert Frey suggests doing this daily morning practice with your partner before getting dressed for your day. Begin by sitting on your knees facing each other. Bow to each other with hands in prayer pose. Take 10 deep belly breaths in unison, the first five with eyes closed, and the second five making eye contact with your partner. Take turns saying the following blessing to each other, with a breath between sentences and three breaths with eye contact between turns (writing these words on a 3 × 5 index card can be helpful). Feel free to improvise and make up your own words for this blessing:

> I recognize you as an important ally for me, and I am grateful that you are in my life. I feel blessed to be co-creating with you. My life is enriched by knowing you. I want you to feel fulfilled, victorious, happy, and at peace today. I wish for you love, wisdom, creativity, and a flowing, meaningful experience today. I love you.

After you have both said the blessing, take three more breaths while maintaining eye contact and end with a bow, hug, and kiss. Further conversation is optional; usually the best choice is simply to get up and move on with other activities, with your beloved in your heart.

The Ten-Minute Connect

In his workshops and book on conscious loving, Charles Muir poses a solution to couples who don't connect due to lack of time or interest—a simple exercise called the "10-minute connect." I have often heard Charles emphasize how couples should do this connect even if they don't feel like it because it keeps the love flowing. He's right!

A loving 10-minute connect.

Here's how to do the 10-minute connect, along with two other simple exercises you can do to connect with your partner:

➤ **The 10-minute connect**   The couple takes 10 minutes at some point in the day, preferably at the beginning or end, to lie quietly together, just feeling each other's energy. This can be in a spoons position, with synchronized breathing.

➤ **The 10-minute sharing**   Take 10 minutes to talk about what happened in your day, how you feel, anything that is on your mind.

➤ **The 10-minute acknowledgment**   Take 10 minutes to tell each other what you most appreciate about each other. Recognition makes us feel alive and loved.

The sharing and acknowledging connects can be done in addition to the silent 10-minute connect, or at another time in the day whenever you can both give each other your complete attention.

Diffusing Your Anger

It's inevitable that at times you and a partner will get angry at each other, but instead of storing that anger or confronting it head on, tantra offers another option. The *lion's play* is an exercise that California tantra team Steve and Lokita Carter find highly effective for couples who have tension between them. Put your hands together and roar loudly like a lion, and push on each other's hands with equal strength. It might sound silly, but try it! After a few minutes even the most skeptical of you will probably start laughing. Keep it up until you and your partner are both laughing and watch your anger dissolve.

The lion's play exercise can help diffuse anger.

Overcoming Feelings of Separation

Tantra is about connecting; therefore, when you are in pain or feel a block impeding the progress of your practices, you are probably experiencing some degree of separation. You could be feeling separated from your own self, from your beloved, from your work, from your family, or from the world in general; indeed you might know that terrible feeling of being isolated or not belonging. Tantric practices heal this separation by opening your heart.

Think of the ways you create a feeling of being separate from others: judging yourself, judging others, or having unrealistic expectations. In my classes and workshops I lead people through experiences of separateness and connectedness by facing each other and saying "I feel separate from you when I …"; then saying "I feel connected to you when I …." This gets you in touch with how you create those feelings, and empowers you to choose which situation to create.

Dr. Judy's TantrAdvice

Any time you protest that you don't have the love you want in a relationship, consider how you might be creating the blocks yourself. Perhaps you are not ready to receive the love you say you want.

Balancing Your Male and Female Energies

In Chapter 2, "The Basics: Yes, Yin Yang, Yoni, and Yab Yum," I explained that uniting male and female energies is key to tantric practice. Sometimes blocks come from the inability to balance these energies, which throws you off balance and causes tension or incompatibility between you and your partner.

The Sexual Relations Review

As a therapist for over two decades, I certainly know how past relationships affect present ones. Painful pairings keep us panicked about their repetition. In my previous books, *The Complete Idiot's Guide to Dating* and *The Complete Idiot's Guide to a Healthy Relationship* (see Appendix C, "Tantric Tools"), I presented many exercises to get free from "the ghosts of the past." Do those exercises to see how patterns in your past relationships affect your present ones.

The following exercise is based on the tantric principle that imbalances in male and female energies in relationships can cause incompatibilities that you might not even be aware of. For this exercise, consider "male" and "female" to be whatever comes to your mind that defines those qualities. Use the following table to review past important relationships and see which partner has demonstrated more male or female energy, or whether these have been balanced. Rate the degree of male or female energy on the scale by putting a mark on the line closest to the description. Include what your parents' relationship was like, and several relationships that have been important to you, even if they have not been overtly sexual. Note in the space provided what happened in the relationship (we broke up, I was dissatisfied, he left me, I left him, we fought, and so forth).

Notice whether you are repeating your parents' pattern (for example, if you are a woman and rated your mother and yourself as extremely "female" and your father and your partner as extremely "male"). Also notice from the chart whether you consistently pick partners with similar energy, and whether they are similar or opposite to the energy you bring to the relationship. Knowing your pattern in important relationships gives you more freedom to choose to change it, either by changing yourself, or by choosing another type of partner next time. Notice your emotional reaction to the relationships. Were you happy about or annoyed by the female or male characteristics of a person?

Tantra Tales

Juliette found Damian sweet and attentive during their first dates. But after a while his high voice and tentative manner annoyed her. When he looked at her like a hurt puppy or begged her to come to bed she would snap at him. She found herself longing for her ex-boyfriend who had a much deeper voice and was more strong-willed. She couldn't put her finger on the problem until she realized from doing the Partner Sexual Review that Damian was being too "female" (or yin) for her taste, while she rated two ex-boyfriends higher on the "male" scale. In her therapy sessions with me, Juliette realized she had to become more balanced in her own male and female energies to attract a man who was similarly balanced.

The Sex Relations Review: Getting the Yin and Yang of It

Person	Degree of Male or Female Energy				
	A great deal of female energy	Balanced male and female energy	Some male energy	Some female energy	A great deal of male energy
	├──┼──┼──┼──┼──┼──┼──┼──┤				
My mother:	├──┼──┼──┼──┼──┼──┼──┼──┤				
My father:	├──┼──┼──┼──┼──┼──┼──┼──┤				
Any other significant parental figure: (fill in): _____	├──┼──┼──┼──┼──┼──┼──┼──┤				
My partner 1 (fill in): _____	├──┼──┼──┼──┼──┼──┼──┼──┤				
Me with partner 1:	├──┼──┼──┼──┼──┼──┼──┼──┤				
What happened in the relationship? (describe):	_____				
My partner 2 (fill in): _____	├──┼──┼──┼──┼──┼──┼──┼──┤				
Me with partner 2:	├──┼──┼──┼──┼──┼──┼──┼──┤				
What happened in the relationship? (describe):	_____				
My partner 3 (fill in): _____	├──┼──┼──┼──┼──┼──┼──┼──┤				
Me with partner 3:	├──┼──┼──┼──┼──┼──┼──┼──┤				
What happened in the relationship? (describe):	_____				

Seven Ways to Balance Sexual Energy

Once you become aware of your male and female energy from doing the Sexual Relations Review, how do you balance them (as in Juliette's case)? All the tantric practices mentioned in this book help you to do that. Be patient; this achievement takes time. Meanwhile, here are several simple ways to balance those energies:

➤ **Nostril breathing**   You can control the balance of your male or female energy by choosing which nostril to block or open. To stimulate more male (yang) energy (active, analytical, assertive), block your left nostril and breathe only through your right nostril. To stimulate more feminine (yin) energy (receptive, passive, nurturing), block your right nostril and breathe through your left nostril. You can also turn your head to the left to be more in your male energy; this assists in breathing through your right nostril. Turn to the right to activate more female energy.

➤ **Alternate nostril breathing**   This is a common exercise in yoga classes. Sit quietly. Put your right index finger on your third eye and rest your thumb and middle finger on your nostrils. Exhale forcefully and then close one nostril with your finger and inhale through the other nostril to the count of seven. Then close that nostril while releasing the other nostril and breathe through the open nostril to the count of seven. Without pausing, continue alternately closing and opening the nostrils as you breathe. In more advanced practice, you would contract the PC muscles (see Chapter 5, "Prep Your Body Temple of Love") to create more force in the breath.

➤ **Use different sounds**   Chant "om" to stimulate more male energy and "aum" for more female energy. Then chant the two sounds alternately for several minutes until you feel the sounds are merging.

➤ **Focus on symbols of male or female**   The Star of David, commonly identified as a symbol of the Jewish religion, is actually a mediation design, with the two intersecting triangles symbolizing the male and female, mind and body. The points on the Star of David also symbolize the sex organs, with the penis and vagina at the upper and lower tips, the breasts at either end of the top line, and the testicles at either end of the lower line.

The Star of David.

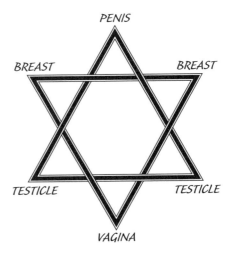

➤ **Walk a mile in his or her shoes**   In my workshops I often invite the class to purposefully walk around the room as if they were a stereotypic male and then walk purposefully like a stereotypic female. (This often leads to most amused re-actions and amusing demonstrations!)

➤ **Focus on colors**   Because male energy is cool, logical blue, and female energy is emotional, passionate red, surround yourself with either color. Mentally focus on red or blue, look at an item colored red or blue, or purposefully put on red or blue clothing.

➤ **Move your body**   To draw in more male energy, sweep your hands out from your sides over your head, into the sky; looking up, imagine calling in the en-ergy from the sky. For more female energy, bend down slightly and scoop the energy up from mother earth and into your heart. In a variation of this, use just the right arm to sweep the sky and the left hand to sweep the earth while keep-ing the other hand on whatever energy center you want to empower.

Frustration Over Who's on Top

Many relationships are about control and battles of control. In tantric terms the cen-ter for control is in the third chakra (the area below the belly). To resolve control bat-tles in your relationship, do exercises related to this center. Pick exercises in this book and hold your hand on your power center as you do the exercise. For example, you could do eye gazing with your partner and put your left hand on your power center to receive more power. Breathe. Then bring your right hand up and out to your part-ner as a symbolic gesture that you are expressing your power and right to be heard.

Getting Past Desperation and Attachment

Part of any spiritual path is to reach a state in which you are not attached to anyone or anything. You might know this feeling of desperation or clinging to a partner. For Janine, it pushed all past lovers away from her. She admitted to me, "They all said I was too needy." One way to ease this feeling of desperation is to understand it. Review in your mind about your past with your parents to see whether they aban-doned you (in which case you are still panicked over being left) or suffocated you (so you felt used). These dynamics can make you resist intimacy out of fear of repeating abandonment or suffocation.

Besides understanding, the following two tantric practices might help:

➤ **Breathe deeply**   When you feel needy, before you do or say something that grasps at someone, take a deep breath, letting the sound come out loudly as you exhale. Let the energy go through your body and out of you.

➤ **Ground yourself** Feel yourself rooted to the floor. Stand with feet comfortably apart and bend your knees slightly. Bounce up and down (be careful not to put pressure on your knees!), taking deep breaths that go into your first chakra, the center that symbolizes security. Feel rooted to the ground like a tree. Doing this helps ground you so you feel more secure, safe, and more your own person.

When you are breathing deeply and feeling grounded, you won't grasp at a partner.

Dr. Judy's TantrAdvice

Try this favorite breathing variation of mine: Put your thumbs in your ears and your fingers on the top of your head. Listen to the sound of your breathing. (This is one of the wonders I discovered while scuba diving. It accomplishes a womblike relaxation.)

Purging Panic and Obsessions

Fears and anxieties that can lead to panic attacks, and repetitive distracting thoughts that become obsessions, are not only distressing but take you out of the moment—yet, as I've discussed throughout this book, all tantric practices require you to be present in the moment. To overcome this, you need to create being present. To achieve this, use the two techniques in the previous section to get past desperation and attachment. Other breathing techniques are helpful, like exhaling for a longer time than inhaling.

Focus on what is present in the moment. Ask yourself, "What is present now?" "And now?" "And now?" When you catch yourself fretting about the past or worrying about the future, keep asking, "What is present now?"

Tantra Tutorial

Rebirthing is an advanced (and controversial) technique that can help people cleanse the pain during their birth by reliving the experience. People play certain roles (for example, the mother) to facilitate the process and to offer support and structure. In some exercises, the love partner is present. Because the process involves regression and birthing, some practitioners submerge the receiver underwater. Rebirthing should be done only under the supervision of people trained in this process because it can bring powerful emotions to the surface that must be processed and worked through.

More Ways to Clear Blocks

In addition to you mind, blocks can be cleared through working on your physical body! One way is to clear blocks physically is through exercise and the practices described in Chapters 5 and 15. You might already know the experience of being able to clear your mind and work out your problems with physical exercise.

Blocks can also be cleared through working on your nutrition. What are your eating habits? There is convincing evidence that food affects our moods. Could you be eating foods that are creating trouble (too much sugar, not enough protein)? Also, evaluate whether you have any food allergies. Investigate eating plans that could be more healthy for you. Ask friends, read about nutrition, or consult tantra teachers and other tantra students you meet about what they do.

I have mentioned that some tantric practitioners do a cleanse as part of their health routine, in which they drink only juice for a period of time or follow other eating plans to clear their digestive system. Removing toxins from your system in this or other ways can also help unblock emotions.

> **Blocks to Bliss**
>
> Uncovering emotions should always be taken seriously. Although any loving person can assist and witness, it is important to be cautious. Consult a qualified therapist if you feel you have any distress that persists a few weeks or to answer your questions.

The Least You Need to Know

➤ Blocks to reaching states of bliss can come from feeling separated from others, storing up anger, and obsessive thoughts—all of which can be eliminated through processes like emotional clearing and tantric breathing techniques.

➤ Misunderstandings and tension between you and a partner can be eased by resolving to spend even short amounts of time together to exchange acknowledgements and blessings.

➤ Simple breathing and meditative techniques can help you balance male and female energy in yourself and in your relationship that cause incompatibilities.

➤ Although many blocks to bliss can be eliminated, it is important to seek professional help when problems are persistent or deep seeded.

Part 3

Making Major Progress on the Path to Ecstasy

Now that you know all the basic steps toward bliss and have cleared away roadblocks on your journey to joy, you're ready for the "best nights ever"—truly!

Get set for great experiences in this part, as you learn step by step exactly what to do to treat your partner to unforgettable nights of pleasure. Best of all, you'll learn how you can make it last as long as you want using effective practices that lead you to extended lovemaking and more orgasms, and better than that—much more love. This requires a shift in your ideas about sex and orgasm, though; so get ready for some new ways to look at lovemaking. And get fit in the process, as I show you some wonderful workout routines that will make your journey with your partner more fun and keep you physically and spiritually in tune.

Chapter 10

Giving Her the Best Nights Ever

In This Chapter

➤ Preparing to please your goddess

➤ What to do on the first of her nights of pleasure

➤ What to do on the second and third pleasure nights, and beyond

➤ What to say and which specific pleasure techniques to use

➤ The possibility of love liquid flow

➤ Giving her what she really wants and needs

It's time for the culmination of all the work you have done in the previous part of this book: his and her nights of pleasure, when the partner promises to be totally present to please the beloved. It's delicious and ever so much fun—and yes, a little scary; but I'll guide you through the steps so that you're bound to have an amazing time and look forward to the next.

The goddess gets her turn first, consistent with ancient worship of the goddess and the Taoist tradition of the male "consort" as servant to his goddess, considering her satisfaction ahead of his own. In this chapter I speak directly to the man as giver, but of course the woman will want to read closely to see what's in store for her as receiver. In the next chapter she'll be the one orchestrating his night of pleasure. For now, men, it's your turn to please your goddess.

The Value of Taking Turns at Pleasure

Taking turns at pleasing and being pleased might sound programmed, but the technique has proven successful in many sex therapies. I've recommended it for years, as it is highly effective; particularly because so many women worry, "When is my turn up?" and "Have I taken too much time?" and because many men fret, "Have I performed well?" and "Have I really pleased her?" Taking turns is crucial in some tantric lovemaking practices to allow full focus on either giving or receiving without worrying about taking too much time, being selfish, or your partner getting tired.

Ultimately, when the energy of lovemaking is truly flowing, the partners are so intertwined that it's hard to distinguish who is giving and who is receiving. Body parts and souls merge into one and into universal consciousness. The receiver and giver blend into one.

Choose one night when she will be the total receiver and you will be the full-on giver, attending to her every need and delight. Choose another night when it is your turn to receive all of her undivided attention.

Ecstasy Essentials

Of course, your pleasure time together does not have to be nighttime. It can be any time of day—morning, afternoon, or evening. Whatever suits your schedule!

What Do Women Really Want?

What do women want? It's the question the famed psychoanalyst Freud asked, and that men have been asking for ages. When you're a tantric man, you really *know*. Even if you have any doubts, you won't after this chapter, which shows you exactly how to please your woman. In short, women want caring, attention, and love. The tantric man is committed to giving that.

How can you make sure this night is different from all other nights? Let's go over the five basic steps to prepare you to receive your beautiful goddess and then to please her.

Step 1: Set Your Intention

"Winging it" on a date can get some good results, but you're better off if you deliberately plan a good time. Write your intention here:

What I want to happen tonight: _____

_____

Go back over your intention and make sure it has some encouraging, positive statements in it, such as "I want to make her feel good." Make your intention even more positive: "I want her to have the most memorable evening ever."

Step 2: Remind Yourself That This Is Her Night

This is one of the most fulfilling aspects of tantric practices. It means that you are totally devoted to your goddess on this night. It's not about your tension at the office, your aching back, and your aroused erection; in fact, clear your mind of those worries. Notice how you feel (irritable, nervous, excited, confident) and what physical state you are in (tired, energized) so that you can focus on your role—being there to please her.

Step 3: Be Prepared to Serve Your Goddess

For some men this is the first time they have considered this concept: serving the woman 100 percent. She will not bring you the newspaper, put your socks in the laundry, or lick your lingam. It's not easy to be totally selfless, but it's worth it to make this night work and to earn your own—and her—deepest appreciation.

Tantra Tutorial

Men who are used to concentrating on themselves have to remember that they'll have their turn on "his night," when he'll be the focus. This is described in Chapter 11, "Giving Him the Best Nights Ever."

Step 4: Face Your Fears

"What will she expect of me?" "What if I can't take this much intensity of feeling?" "What if this means I have to be like this or even better next time and I can't live up to it?" "What if I don't do it right?" These all are natural feelings that you need to recognize and face now, so you can be clear of them as you go deeper in your loving connections and sexual pleasuring. Being clear now will allow you both to enjoy the evenings and look forward to more. In true tantric style, let fears come up, feel any reactions (tight chest, weak knees), and breathe through them. They will pass and the anxiety will transmute into energy, which leads to being turned on. What a wonderful twist!

Step 5: Decide How You Will Call On Her

Notice I use the phrase "call on," a dating term from the 1930s, to purposefully evoke the gentleman style (as gentlemen "came calling"); it works well for this first night of pleasure.

Blocks to Bliss

Some men might be thinking, "When do we get to the sex?" Hold on, that's why you're on this path: to relish all the delicious buildup, especially since that's what the goddess wants!

Here are some ideas:

➤ Call her at work and tell her to meet you somewhere first. Pick a romantic spot, or someplace where you know she'll have fun (a concert, play).

➤ Arrange for her to do something that treats her first (like getting a manicure or a massage at a spa).

➤ Tell her to meet you at home (where you will already have prepared a love nest).

Fill out the following, to help you prepare for her night of pleasure; then go over your list and picture doing the steps in your mind:

Preparing for Her Pleasure Night

Where you will first meet (for dinner, a show): _____

Where you will end up (in your bedroom, at a hotel): _____

How you will invite and entice her: _____

What you will say: _____

What you will wear: _____

How the room will be set up: _____

Boudoir Basics

Women are bound to be impressed with a man who has put some effort into preparations, especially in the house, making the setting look romantic. Here are some tips to set the stage for romance:

➤ Turn both the bathroom and the bedroom into a sensuous seduction scene. Use scents (jasmine, rose, ylang-ylang), soft lighting (candles in purple shades to invoke female energy or blue shades to enhance size), and flowers (rose for female genitals; hibiscus for fulfillment).

➤ Choose the music you are going to play. It's usually a good idea to pick something sensuous and slow for this first evening (see the suggestions in Chapter 18, "Sex, Song, and Videotape").

➤ Set out sensuous food and drink to surprise her during your pleasuring (chocolate kisses, fresh fruit slices, sparkling water).

Night of Pleasure 1: Promises to the Goddess in the Pleasure Palace

Greet her at the door dressed in your god attire (silk pajamas, silk shirt and slacks), freshly shaved and bathed. During the evening use words of endearment and reaffirm your enthusiasm; for example:

➤ "This is *your* night."

➤ "I am totally here for you, at your service, devoted to your pleasure."

➤ "Take all the time you need."

➤ "Be sure to tell me exactly what you want."

➤ "I am enjoying tonight so much."

➤ "It gives me such pleasure to be able to give to you fully."

➤ "You don't have to do anything for me tonight."

Dr. Judy's TantrAdvice

Women need to be reminded that they can make requests and that their partner *is* enjoying the role of giver. Keeping asking questions such as "What can I do to make you feel good tonight?"

Tantra Tales

In Charles and Caroline Muir's weekend workshops on Conscious Loving, his and her nights are central to the couple's pleasure. The sharing after their nights of giving is heartwarming and inspiring. Many men report delight in serving their goddess. One man said, "I was so proud to make her so happy"; another, "I never knew it could feel so good to give."

Relaxing Her

Everyone needs to be relaxed before sex; in tantric practice, every step of the way is sex. Remember that tantric lovemaking is about moving energy through the breath, and being present in the body and in the moment. Here are several ways to help her relax to achieve these goals:

➤ Invite her to express her feelings. Encourage her to say whatever is on her mind. She will be ecstatic at that suggestion alone! Invite her to vent about whatever may be bothering her from her day to clear her mind so you can concentrate fully on the good feelings between you. Venting feelings inevitably leads to a release, which produces warm feelings toward the person who witnessed the purge.

➤ Bathe her. Prepare a bath with scented bath oils. Pay particular attention to washing her feet, an ancient tradition that shows respect and service. Bathing also is meant for purification.

➤ Give her a massage. Once her mind is at peace, she is more ready to be touched. Ask permission to massage her. Don't worry that you are not a professional masseuse, or that you don't know anything about proper techniques. This is about a gift of love through your loving touch; as long as your hands communicate love, the techniques are not important.

Massaging the goddess.

In giving her a massage, keep these techniques in mind:

➤ Always use a *nondemand touch,* which means you are not expecting your touch to lead to intercourse. Touch just for her pleasure of being touched and your pleasure in touching.

➤ Never take your hands off the body when you massage; always maintain some physical contact to keep the person feeling safe and secure.

➤ Focus your attention on your touching, without allowing your mind to get distracted into worries, fears, or plans.

➤ Be confident about what you are doing. Don't fret that you are not touching her right; ask for feedback right away so you are reassured that she is pleased.

➤ Close your eyes, connect with your feelings, and tune in to her; let your fingers do what you feel her body is asking for.

➤ Encourage emotions and be prepared for their release. Encourage her to make sounds and move in any way that feels comfortable.

➤ Pay attention to often-neglected sensuous areas such as the palm, side of the little finger, and base of the spine.

➤ Ask her what part she would like you to pay specific attention to. Linger on that part.

➤ Send your love through your hands and all parts of you.

➤ Move her energy by focusing your attention to where you feel she needs it (to her heart to be more open, to the power center around the midsection to empower her, to her base chakra at the base of her spine for more security and grounding).

As I've emphasized, using a loving touch is all that matters in massage, but getting some training in techniques can add something extra. Buy books or videos on erotic and tantric massage, such as those from expert Kenneth Ray Stubbs (see Appendix C, "Tantric Tools"), or take a couples' massage course together.

Night of Pleasure 2: Getting Closer

When something is pleasurable, why not repeat it? On a successive night that you identify as her night, you can repeat the previous steps. Add something extra as a surprise, such as a small gift, new massage stroke, different music, or new outfit that you wear. With each date you can get more intense about pleasuring her sex center and her sacred space. Remember to do the following:

➤ Hold your hand on her sex center (yoni) and ask permission to enter her sacred space.

➤ If you and your goddess are comfortable with it, use flowery words to label this area ("your love cave," "your flower garden," "your secret love space").

➤ Do the *Double Love Blast*. I use this term because he sends and she receives love from both her sex and heart centers—just what women want: sex with love! Send your love through your hand and into her "sacred cave" (a tantric term for vagina), and through your breath into her heart.

➤ Ask to examine her body all over. Be enthusiastic ("I'm enjoying this") and complimentary ("You look so beautiful").

➤ Use different strokes to touch her sexual area inside and out.

➤ Keep looking in her eyes and encouraging her to look at you. Breathe together to harmonize your energy.

Sending love energy from her sex center and his heart into her heart.

➤ Add oral pleasure. A woman who has gotten over her shame or embarrassment about her genitals can experience tremendous excitement from your lips and mouth on her genitalia. She will feel truly adored and pleased. Be sure to tell her how much you enjoy doing this. Include "polishing the pearl" (a tantric term for oral stimulation of the clitoris), and exploring her sacred cave. Ask her what kind of stimulation she likes.

Sending pleasure by polishing her pearl and pleasing her sacred space into her heart center for total love connection.

The tantra man who can bring a woman to heights of oral pleasure is rightfully pleased with himself. As one man told me, "I'm even happier knowing I can please her than when I get satisfied first. Women think we're all selfish but we're not!"

➤ Encourage her to pleasure herself. Before one of her nights, encourage her to pleasure herself; then, on one of your dates, ask her to show you what she does so you know exactly how to please her. Likely she will concentrate on her clitoris, using motions you should study carefully so that you can repeat them. Reassure her how much men enjoy watching a woman do this.

> **Ecstasy Essentials**
>
> Learn everything you can about the clitoris, as it is an important trigger for a woman's pleasure. Read *The Clitoral Truth* by Rebecca Chalker (Seven Stories Press, 2000) to ease into the conversation about exploring exactly where this pleasure button is, how far it extends into a woman's body, and how it becomes erect (like a lingam) when excited.

The Resolution Phase

In tantric sex, the resolution phase, or cool-down period, is meant to continue the intimacy. Keep in mind that women usually need more of a cooling-down period after intense lovemaking than men. Of course, you both could be tired and want to sleep; this is fine. But she might want to spend some time dwelling in the moments of pleasure, talking about how she feels or about what happened, and certainly would want you to be awake enough to listen and share. Be sensitive to her needs on these special nights and resist the desire to fall asleep. (Over time you can better coordinate your timing in this phase, because you will have learned to control your ejaculation and both of you will be able to continue cycling your energy.)

Some tips to accomplish this phase in ongoing delight:

➤ Assume the *spoons position,* in which one of you nestles into the chest of the other, so you are essentially back to front.

➤ Continue the synchronized breath so you are breathing in and out at the same time, staying in tune.

➤ Lightly tap on each other's energy center—not enough to generate a great deal of energy, as you both want to relax now, but enough to keep you both awake and drinking in the delights of your experience.

Night of Pleasure 3: When Love and Love Liquid Flow

Honoring the goddess takes on a special meaning on the night that she is ready to allow you to explore her sacred space freely. Always start with giving her a loving massage and repeat the steps in the instructions for the first two nights. Ask permission to pleasure her and to enter her sacred space. Using your finger, enter her yoni gently, guided by her response. Use your middle finger to make a "come hither" motion to stimulate the sacred space on the front wall of the vagina, one third of the way up (commonly called the G spot, but actually an area, also called the goddess space and sacred sector). The tissue might become a little rougher to the feel and expand, yielding more lubrication. If she responds with pleasure, you can become more vigorous. As her excitement mounts, call out encouragement and quicken your motion.

*How to pleasure the
goddess space.*

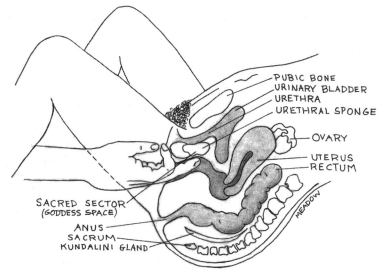

FINGER IN YONI ON SACRED SECTOR

Always wait for her invitation. Do not enter her until she asks you to by words or actions. Then enter slowly, feeling each exquisite sensation. Move to her rhythm. Keep reminding her to breathe. Keep reassuring her that you are enjoying yourself, that she has all the time she needs, and that you appreciate her.

Remember to avoid having expectations about how she will respond. Some men feel challenged to "make" a woman have a female ejaculation. Take the pressure off her, just as you don't want any pressure to perform! While any woman can ejaculate, not all do, partly because the sensation immediately before often feels like the urge to urinate, which confuses women and makes them stop what they are doing. It's also not as easy as men's ejaculation, because women (except those practiced in this art!) take longer to get exited. Additionally, women really do have more emotional prerequisites than men for letting go in orgasm.

Tantra Tutorial

Some sex therapists are skeptical about female ejaculate. However, researchers such as Gary Schubach prove the earlier now-famous research of Whipple and Perry about the existence of the G spot (see www.DoctorG.com). Schubach's studies of female emission from stimulation of the area he calls the *G crest* show it is a mixture of fluid from urethral glands and ducts, and the bladder (although definitely not urine). The fluid seeps from the urethral sponge tissue surrounding the urethra and exits the body from the urethral opening.

The One Thing Women Need Most

In all my work with couples over the years and teaching women to have orgasm, the one thing women mention as being most important to them is trust. A woman needs to be able to trust that you care about her and that you love her. Obviously it would be best if you really do love her—and then profess your love openly, honestly, and passionately.

The One Thing Women Want Most

Yes, it's still about that four-letter word: love. Show your love abundantly at all times, but especially on her night. Granted more women are becoming "liberated," willing to choose a sexual connection without intense emotion, but when it gets down to it, women want to love and be loved. Fortunately, more men are willing to reveal that they want this, too; on his night he can get that—and more.

The Least You Need to Know

➤ A very rewarding and pleasurable tantric practice is for couples to alternate nights devoted to each other.

➤ Prepare your night of pleasure for her beforehand by making the room and yourself look special. Come up with your own ideas and ask her what she wants.

➤ Pleasing her usually includes relaxing her with a massage and appreciating both her body and her soul.

➤ Always start by harmonizing your energies and connecting at the heart level before you progress to more sexual actions. A solid foundation of trust, loving, and sharing will open her—and you—to pleasure.

➤ As you progress in pleasuring her sexually and more intimately, ask her permission and continue to send your love energy into her heart.

➤ Include oral pleasuring and pleasuring her sacred space, encouraging her to allow the fullest extent of expression, including the possibility of a female ejaculation.

Chapter 11

Giving Him the Best Nights Ever

In This Chapter

➤ The beginning of many nights of pleasure for him

➤ Helping him surrender to pleasure

➤ What to do on the second and third nights, and beyond

➤ What to say and which specific pleasure techniques to use

➤ Moving energy to his heart to create more love

➤ Lingam strokes to send him into bliss

She had her night in the previous chapter; now it's his turn! In this chapter I'll guide you through several nights of pleasure for him. Of course, you can use the exercises in this book to inspire you to design your own night of pleasure. I encourage you to use your imagination—after all, tantra is about you expressing your inner self! Although I speak directly to the woman in this chapter, since she is the giver, the man will want to read about the delights in store for him as receiver. (Even though you both did this exercise for "her night," there will still be surprises for you.)

Remember, you are goddess to his god; Shakti to his Shiva. You are the embodiment of all eternal beauty of women, the source of all nourishment, the essential other half to complete his path to bliss. He is the embodiment of all that is eternal strength in man, the source of light, an essential completion of your being on your path to bliss. He is Zeus to your Hera, Lancelot to your Geneviere, Romeo to your Juliet (but no tragedy, please!).

Night 1: Taking Your Man into Tantric Bliss

The first evening of pleasing your man will be only the beginning of many nights of pleasure. Keep in mind that this night is different from the other nights you have spent together. This night will incorporate the specific tantric rituals you have been learning about in this book, including your preparation and what to do during the actual time between you.

Blocks to Bliss

Of course you might be nervous during this evening, doing something new, and worrying about getting it right. Don't be! In time you will become more comfortable. It's only important that you are devoted to adding a new dimension to your lovemaking and intimacy.

Preparing Him for Pleasure

Decide on some surprises for your man, such as where you will meet and how he will get there. Make it original and special. For example, tell him to meet you at a restaurant that you know has a romantic atmosphere. Call him and tell him where to be. Be mysterious. Be yourself, or pretend to be a secret admirer. Dress in a way that you know will excite him.

Gather the items you'll need for his night of pleasure so you are prepared (see Chapter 7, "Setting the Stage for Your Tantric Nights of Pleasure"). This includes music, sacraments (wine, special drinks or foods), and clothing. Prepare the pleasure den as much as possible beforehand by arranging the furniture, adjusting the lighting, placing candles in the bathroom, and making any other preparations.

Fill out the following checklist—just as he did for your night of pleasure in the previous chapter—to prepare for his pleasure night. Go over your list and picture doing the steps in your mind:

Preparing for His Night Checklist

Where you will first meet (for dinner, a show): ⸺⸺⸺⸺⸺⸺

Where you will end up (in your bedroom, at a hotel): ⸺⸺⸺⸺⸺

How you will invite and entice him: ⸺⸺⸺⸺⸺⸺

What you will say: ⸺⸺⸺⸺⸺⸺⸺⸺

What you will wear: ⸺⸺⸺⸺⸺⸺⸺⸺

How the room will be set up: ⸺⸺⸺⸺⸺⸺

Tantra Tales

Although Patrice and Hank lived in New York for years, they had never taken a horse-drawn carriage ride through Central Park, one of the tourist attractions, and a romantic experience. For his pleasure night, Patrice called Hank at the end of his work day and said, "I'm waiting outside for you; come downstairs." When he arrived on the street, Patrice was in the horse-drawn carriage, waiting to whisk him away. As they cuddled under the blanket in the cool air, Patrice promised him the evening was for him—and the tantric pleasures that she had prepared for him.

Leading Him to the Tantric Love Temple

Once you've been out on the town, or whatever place your god enjoys, you are ready to go back to the tantric love temple to begin the rituals of pleasure. Your tantric love temple is whatever place you have decided you can have private time to enjoy your tantric love ritual. Of course, you need to spend some time and energy on the preparations.

Preparing Him for His Night of Love

Once your man is in your sacred space, the next stage of your pleasuring begins.

Step 1: Put Him at Ease

Make him comfortable by seating him in a soft reclining chair or laying him on a couch while you go prepare his bath and yourself. Put on music he enjoys to ease his mind; then dress in your goddess clothes. It is always a good idea to dress separately to create surprise when you see each other, just as a bride and groom dress separately before their wedding. Come out in your goddess clothes and pose before him, allowing him to appreciate your beauty.

Dr. Judy's TantrAdvice

If you are at his house or another place, prepare your *goddess bag:* a traveling bag with your goddess clothes and all the accoutrements you will need for his night, including special music, candles, and foods.

135

You can also ask him to prepare himself in his clothes while you wait. Do this even if you will be disrobing him either for his bath or for lovemaking. His dress-up makes him feel the evening is special, and delights you when you see him.

Step 2: Bathe Him

As I've pointed out earlier, bathing is an important part of the tantric love ritual. Escort your Shiva god into the bath with your most seductive smile. Tilt your head, expose a thigh, drop a strap off your shoulder. Undress him, admiring every part of his body.

Proceed with the bath:

➤ Suggest that he shave and then watch as he does, or do it for him, if he agrees (carefully, of course!).

➤ Wash each part of his body including his feet and hair (if he agrees); this is especially erotic.

➤ Tantalize him by washing other parts before you get to his genitals. Run soapy hands up and around his lingam and scrotum area, and the cheeks of his buttocks and gently around his first chakra (anal area).

➤ Make appreciative remarks about his body parts as you are bathing them.

➤ When you're done, wrap him in a soft towel or bathrobe and walk him into the bedroom or other room designated as your love temple.

Step 3: Enter the Love Temple

Lay him down on the bed, mat, or whatever you decide will be your love nest. Give him a few minutes to relax in the space and get comfortable.

Step 4: Promise Him Pleasure

Tell him a few exciting promises about how the evening will go. Although men are not always verbal—often responding to just action—tantric lovemaking stimulates all the senses, which includes offering verbal statements about your love, what you want to do, and reassurances. Men also often like to be in control, so giving him some cues about what is happening and what will happen will probably make him feel more relaxed. Say just enough to put him at ease but not too much; that would be a distraction or engage his mind. The idea of tantric sex is to feel in the body and quiet the mind.

Use the following four R's as guidelines:

➤ **Reassure him** Assure him that he does not have to perform or do anything to please you. "You don't have to do anything to please me. I'm here totally to please you tonight"; "This night is totally for you." As the pleasuring progresses, add statements such as "You don't have to have an erection or get excited, just enjoy the feelings in your body."

➤ **Relax him**   Say, "I'm going to massage you to relax you and you just have to lay there and enjoy the sensations. You can tell me what to do that you would particularly like."

➤ **Relieve him**   Constantly tell him that you are enjoying what you are doing, so he does not worry.

➤ **Reward him**   Men (just as women) love to be acknowledged, so tell him how delighted you are with him as a person. Compliment who he is and tell him what you particularly like about his body.

Now that he feels relaxed and appreciated, you can begin more physical pleasuring.

The Tantric Shiva Massage, a Time to Surrender

A massage should always be part of a pleasure night. Nothing is more relaxing, or makes a partner feel more open emotionally. Spend at least half an hour doing this. Here are the key steps and points to remember about giving your Shiva a tantrically superlative massage:

➤ Begin by laying him comfortably on his back on a flat but padded surface. Run your hands smoothly over his body, then rest them along the top of his spine and the base of his spine (this connecting the entire spine). What do you feel? Is he warm or cold in one of those spots? Cooler places may need more of your love energy to warm them up.

➤ Warm his skin with lots of oil. Use your body as much as your hands, rubbing your breasts from his mouth down his belly. Tell him, "You feel so good." Rub his back and legs and turn him over to pleasure his chest.

➤ Keep looking into his eyes and encourage him to make sounds of pleasure.

➤ Open his heart. Run your hands from his sex center (lingam) to his heart, transmuting his sexual arousal energy into loving feelings. This is what you want from him—and what he wants for himself! Send your love through your hands. Always be conscious and respectful that you are moving energy in the massage, bring his energy from his sex center up into his heart.

Tantra Tales

Be aware that as your man lies on his back (in a traditionally "female" receiving position), he may feel vulnerable. Reassure him that these feelings are natural, and expect him to resist. Kelly found all kinds of excuses ("I'm tired," "that's enough") but Joelly insisted they continue. As she rubbed his stomach, he began to cry, feeling never before opened in this way or so loved.

Using massage to draw his sex energy into his heart.

Languishing Over His Lingam

After you have massaged his entire body, you are ready to begin concentrating on his lingam. Most men delight in being touched there. After a body massage, he might be so excited when you touch his lingam that he feels the urge to ejaculate. In that case, use the stop-start technique (see Chapter 12, "Make Lovemaking Last … and Last … and Last") and transmute the energy, so he gets a chance to dwell in the pleasure of this part of the massage.

At this point reassurance is very important; reassure him he doesn't need to get an erection, only to lay back and enjoy it. There are more than three dozen strokes you can choose from. All of the massage strokes that are relevant to the body massage can be applied to the lingam massage. Keep in mind the different degrees of pressure, firmness of your touch, and different touches: from smooth strokes to light, feathery touches and from presses and squeezes to light scratches.

When pleasuring his lingam, tune in to his energy and the degree of touch he wants at any particular moment. Vary your touches to surprise him and heighten the stimulation. Remember that in tantric lovemaking you are not trying to turn him on, get him hard, or make him come, you are playing with and moving his energy. Be attentive, respectful, and aware of the power of this massage act as part of your union.

Consider these lingam love strokes:

➤ Start by delicately feathering the lingam by lightly brushing your fingers up the shaft and around the tip.

➤ Do a traditional up-and-down motion, gripping the lingam fairly firmly (ask him what pressure feels good for him).

➤ Move your hand up and down the lingam with your fingers working their way up in a motion like a spider's legs.

➤ Work your hand up and down the lingam, pulsing your hand as you move it up a notch.

➤ Hold your hands with palms stretched out, press the lingam between your hands, and twist the lingam inside your hands as you move your hands up from base to tip as if kneading dough. This stroke is called *rolling thunder*.

Loving the lingam with rolling thunder *along the shaft.*

➤ Grip his lingam with one hand at the base—this helps him keep his erection. With your other hand, start at the base and run your hand up the shaft and over the top of his lingam, stopping to caress the head in a circular motion, and then run your hand down the shaft again.

➤ Hold the lingam between your hands and gently "toss" it from one hand to another.

Dr. Judy's TantrAdvice

Many men want women to be more assertive in how they caress their lingam. Ask what degree of firmness he likes. Shift from more yin (light, gentle) touches to more yang (strong, firm) ones, and vice versa.

The Second Pleasure Night

Repeat all the steps you've learned so far, but add some variation. Wear a different goddess outfit. Put on different music (see Chapter 18, "Sex, Song, and Videotape," or Appendix C, "Tantric Tools," for some ideas). Make love in a different room or place, or decorate the room and bed differently.

A Variation on Massage

For his second night, repeat the strokes and techniques he liked in the last massage you gave him, then surprise him with new approaches or touches. Some more advanced massage techniques include:

Dr. Judy's TantrAdvice

Always remind him to breathe; when he gets excited he might hold his breath (just as women tend to do). This holding can be helpful only if it is done in the context of a tantric breathing practice in which he is consciously moving his breath to move his energy. Encourage him to make sounds as a way to ensure that he continues breathing.

➤ Don't just use your fingers; use your palm, heel of your hand, your breasts, even your feet.

➤ Insert his lingam between your breasts and press your breasts lightly together. Move them up and down and side to side.

➤ Brush your hair lightly against his body parts.

➤ Use longer strokes that start at the top or bottom of his body and end at his lingam, then trace back to the extremities.

Include More Lingam Strokes When Pleasuring

Here are some advanced strokes to try for pleasuring your partner. Use lotion on both hands to make the movements glide more smoothly and the sensations more pleasurable. Some lotions become too sticky or will irritate the penis, so experiment with different kinds. Vaseline will feel good for him; just be sure not to insert the lingam in the yoni unless this is wiped off because it is not healthy for the chemistry of the vagina.

➤ **Corkscrew**   Hold the lingam firmly at the base while the other hand slides from the base to the tip with a twisting motion. Change hands and continue the motion. Ask him how tight a grip he likes of your hands, and how vigorously he would like you to rotate your hands.

➤ **Heady trip**   Hold the base of the lingam firmly as you caress the tip by making circles. Alternate this caress with pulling the head up and twisting it gently.

➤ **Polishing the helmet**   Move one hand up and down the shaft, as you cradle the head in the center of the palm of your other hand and move that hand in a circular motion.

➤ **Palming the crown**   Hold the shaft firmly with one hand and rotate the tip with the palm of the other. Move the hands so they change position.

➤ **The lingam mudras**   Press two fingers lightly on two different parts of the lingam, scrotum, *perineum* (the space between the scrotum and anus), and anal opening. This runs powerful energy through his pleasure spots.

Loving the lingam by holding the base and caressing the tip.

Pleasing His God Spots

In popular jargon the woman has the infamous G spot—that spot inside the vagina that is super-sensitive. Similarly, the man has sensitive G spots, hot spots or *god areas.* On night 2—focus on his two external hot spots:

➤ The frenulum, which is the knob-like protrusion on the underside of the penis where the tip meets the shaft.

➤ The perineum, located between the testicles and the anal opening.

On night 3 you can get to his internal god area. This can be done only when he is more relaxed and prepared to get more intimate, because this type of stimulation will raise many more feelings in him, possibly even resistance and fear. (I'll discuss these concerns in detail in Chapter 17, "Sexual Healing to Set You Free.")

Building His Sexual Charge

To drive your man wild in tantric sex, build a sexual charge starting in his sex center (lingam) and then assist him in sending this energy throughout his body. The techniques to do this have been described in earlier chapters in this book, but to review them follow these steps:

➤ Sit together in yab yum position, or whatever position feels comfortable for you. Do the synchronizing breath for five breaths and then the alternating breath for five breaths, to get yourselves in tune.

141

➤ Do your own PC pumps (bandhas) as described in Chapter 5, "Prep Your Body Temple of Love," to build a sexual charge in your yoni, so that when you cycle your energy into his body, you will be sending intense sexual energy into his body.

➤ Do five cycles of breath between you from your sex center through your power and heart center and into his heart, and down through his power center and into his sex center. Be conscious about how powerful this energy is.

➤ Do five fire breaths together, inhaling and exhaling vigorously through the nose.

➤ Ask him to do his PC pumps, squeezing his PC muscles on the inhale to build the intensity of the energy, and letting go on the exhale, drawing the energy up his body. Do this five times.

The Secret to Moving His Energy

As you are pleasuring him, concentrate on directing his energy to connect the sexual charge from his genital area to other body parts, particularly his heart (to create more love). Choose which part of him you feel needs energy or that you want to energize. For example, if you feel he needs to be more sensitive at that moment, you can help move his energy to his heart center. If you feel he needs to speak something at that time, you can move his sexual energy to his throat center.

While stimulating his lingam with your right hand, move your left hand up the center of his body to his other energy centers. Send your breath into his lingam through your right hand and trace the breath with your imagination as it goes up his body into the chakra you have chosen, then out your left hand and into your body again. Exhale as you send the energy into his body and inhale as you draw it into your body to be recharged, creating a cycle. With these chakra connects, you can actually move the energy up by sweeping your hands up his body. Adjust your own position from sitting between his legs to sitting at his left (receiving) side, so you can reach his energy centers easily.

➤ Move your hand to his power center and gently hold your hand there. Keep your other hand on his lingam. Encourage him to feel any feelings he might have, including any sensations of power.

➤ Move your hand to his throat center and gently hold your hand there. Keep your other hand on his lingam. Encourage him to feel any feelings that he might have, including his ability to communicate and say what he wants.

➤ Move your hand to his brow center (third eye) and gently hold your hand there. Keep your other hand on his lingam. Encourage him to feel any feelings he might have or see any visions that may come.

➤ Move your hand to the top of his head and gently hold your hand there. Keep your other hand on his lingam. Encourage him to have any feelings or sensations.

Be aware that as you touch these places on his body, he might feel flashes, bolts of light, or electricity. This is because you are acting as a conductor of powerful energy, facilitating its travel from one place to the other. Experiment with different touches and ask him what he likes.

The Third Night of Pleasure

On each successive night of pleasure for him, repeat some of the previous techniques. While you are pleasing his lingam, don't forget other areas of pleasure:

➤ Stroke his inner thighs.

➤ Stretch his legs apart and squeeze the muscles that connect the thigh with the genital area (the ones that seem to pop out when you stretch his legs). This feels exceptionally good.

➤ Start at his belly button and "walk" your fingers down his body into his pubic area, pressing his sensitive god spot located in the perineal area (as described earlier in this chapter). Repeat the same steps in reverse.

➤ Pay attention to his testicles (be gentle) at the same time as the lingam.

Entering His Sacred Space

Now you're ready to enter his sacred space—the anal opening that most men panic over. They usually have never been touched there or fear the homosexuality they believe it implies. When he seems extremely relaxed, ask him, "May I enter you?" Remember, always ask permission!

If he says no, go back to doing something he was enjoying. If he wants you to continue, rest your finger at his opening. Encourage him to breathe, allowing whatever feelings come up. Cover the area and your finger with lots of oil. Hold your finger steady, and let him push against you showing his readiness. Entering slowly, he can tense his anal muscles and release them against your finger. Remember to go very slowly. Allow him to guide the degree, speed, and depth with which you stimulate him. Rest your finger inside in a still fashion.

Exploring and Exciting His God Spot

Once he is more comfortable with being entered in his sacred space, read his signals about when to be more vigorous and experimental with how you please him there.

➤ Add manual pleasure with your other hand to his lingam and scrotal area while you are pleasing his sacred space.

➤ Add oral pleasure to his lingam and scrotal area while you are pleasing his sacred space.

➤ Move the energy with your other hand to his other energy centers as described previously for night 2.

143

➤ Let your fingers explore his sacred space by varying the depth and type of touch. Let your fingers sweep inside his sacred space, imagining a clock inside and sweeping from 10 o'clock to 2 o'clock.

➤ Press your palm against his perineum (external G spot) and anal opening to add pleasure. Use your other hand to stroke his lingam up and down. With the tip of your thumb gently and rhythmically stroke the frenulum, the sensitive underside at the tip.

*Pressing a male G spot
for pleasure.*

As you do these advanced stimulation techniques, remember to transmute the energy, always drawing it up to his higher energy centers. Lightly "hum" into an area, or blow warm breath onto it. The warmth of your breath and your love will surely warm his heart besides making him excited all over.

The Least You Need to Know

➤ On his nights of pleasure, let him know that you are totally his servant; you are there to please him, and he does not have to do anything in return.

➤ Prepare yourself (what you will wear, say, do) and your space for lovemaking, then be spontaneous and create new delights.

➤ Build the types of stimulation in several steps so that he is able to receive pleasure comfortably and without fears or anxiety.

➤ Build his sexual energy by pleasuring his lingam, and then direct that energy to other energy centers, particularly his heart, to build more love between you.

Chapter 12

Make Lovemaking Last ... and Last ... and Last

In This Chapter

➤ How tantric sex makes men—and sex—last longer

➤ What's your reaction to quickie sex?

➤ Myths and facts about lasting longer

➤ The pros and cons of delaying ejaculation

➤ Sexual Kung Fu and other secrets of delaying ejaculation

➤ What the woman can do to help the man delay

Wouldn't it be nice if you and your partner could have those long lovemaking sessions of your romantic fantasies? Suppose he could be alert and pleasuring her for hours ... wouldn't she be delighted? And best of all, what if he could last as long as he wants instead of having such a quick sexual high and then falling asleep? More and more men have the same desire for long lovemaking and more pleasurable orgasms for both of you.

The great news is that this height—and extended length—of his pleasure (which gives her pleasure, too) is entirely possible through the secrets and practices of tantric sex. Yes, men can make love for hours, once they know what to do; this chapter will tell you how. Best of all, it's not a difficult effort for him but a real pleasure for both of you.

How Long Is He Supposed to Last?

Several dimensions have been used to determine how soon is too soon for a man to reach his peak, or how long he should last before ejaculating. Consider the following:

➤ Famous 1950s sex researcher Alfred Kinsey thought "too soon" was lasting only two minutes.

➤ Statistics show that about 75 percent of men last between four and seven minutes.

➤ Because a woman needs about fifteen minutes to reach an excitement level that takes a man only three minutes to reach, he would need to delay himself five times the male average.

➤ The timing is based on the man's ability to control his excitement level, not an actual amount of time.

➤ Is the man (or his partner) upset about his performance? Is his partner satisfied at least half the time? If the answers to these questions are no and yes, respectively, there's no reason to worry.

Here's the tantric take on how long a man should last: Both the man and his partner should be satisfied—and they will be, when he learns control. Essentially it doesn't matter how long you have sex, as long as you are channeling energy between you in a mutually satisfying way. But if you want to last longer, you can—and there are more joys in store for you if you do so. Acquiring the skills found in this chapter will boost your self-esteem sky high and delight your partner—and you can choose to come whenever you please!

Tantra Tutorial

Traditional Taoist belief demands semen retention, claiming that spilling sperm other than for having children weakens the man's health and even provokes anger toward women. Releases are allowed once every three days in spring, twice a month in summer and autumn, and not at all in winter, and only 5,000 in a lifetime. But please don't let that you scare you!

When It's All Over Too Fast

It's a complaint so many women have, as one woman appearing with me on TV said, "An egg takes three minutes, why does my husband?" She was referring to the disappointment women feel when the sex act lasts only about three minutes. When the man reaches orgasm so quickly and the woman is left unsatisfied it has an effect on both partners that can be hurtful to the relationship.

Her Reaction to Three-Minute Sex

Remember that women have a different natural sexual response cycle than men—she needs more time physically to get to the same level of pleasure. Women are also stereotypically more emotional about sex—they want lovemaking to last longer because they want the intimacy, communication, and closeness, both in foreplay and afterplay (concepts not necessarily consistent with tantric sex, because all of lovemaking is the main act!). If the buildup and cool down are both cut short as it is when the man reaches his peak in three minutes and then withdraws, and falls asleep, the woman can have many reactions that are not healthy for her or the relationship.

The following list will help you evaluate your reactions to the length of time spent lovemaking. Pick what best describes how you feel by putting a checkmark next to that item in the Yes column; then think of another possible way you can react and fill it in the column under the Instead I Can Feel This Way column. The idea is for you to have an alternative way of reacting. Read over your reactions and what you have written as new affirmations.

Her Reaction to How Long Lovemaking Lasts

Do I Feel …	Yes	Instead I Can Feel This Way
Frustrated, unfulfilled, resentful?	❏	_____
Angry toward my partner?	❏	_____
Disinterested (withdraw from sex)?	❏	_____
Responsible (like I don't turn him on)?	❏	_____
Less confident (lose self-esteem)?	❏	_____
Abandoned and unloved?	❏	_____
Like I'm too fat?	❏	_____
Like I'm not attractive?	❏	_____
Like he's probably having an affair?	❏	_____
He's selfish?	❏	_____
Other: _____		
Other: _____		

His Reaction to Three-Minute Sex

Some men and their partners are okay with a short sexual experience. Some women may not like sex much and are relieved to get it over with. This sadly cuts off her potential for pleasure, and reveals deeper problems that likely stem from childhood or earlier sexual experiences. However, if you know your partner wants to make love last longer and you're willing to find out how to do this, be reassured that this is possible. Changes in a relationship happen most effectively when both people are motivated.

Even if men defend, rationalize, or joke about "quickies," they are often unhappy about not lasting longer. They might have fears, inhibitions, and past hurts that get in the way (I'll talk more about those and how to help heal them in Chapter 17, "Sexual Healing to Set You Free"). The man who comes too quickly wonders to himself "What's wrong with me?" He feels cheated out of a better experience, just as his partner does. Worse yet, he feels out of control, as his body seems to take over, leading him quickly from excitement to ejaculation.

Now it's the man's turn to fill out the following checklist, this time focusing on *his* reactions to the length of time spent lovemaking. Pick what best describes how you feel by putting a checkmark next to that item in the Yes column; then think of another possible way you can react and fill it under the Instead I Can Feel This Way column.

His Reactions to Lovemaking Timing

Do I Feel …	Yes	Instead I Can Feel This Way
Like I'm a bad lover?	❏	_____
Selfish?	❏	_____
Disgusted with myself?	❏	_____
Frustrated and angry?	❏	_____
Depressed?	❏	_____
Anxious, like my partner will lose interest in me?	❏	_____
I'm to blame?	❏	_____
My partner is to blame?	❏	_____
Like I want to block it out (try not to think about it)?	❏	_____
Disinterested (withdraw from sex)?	❏	_____
Other:		_____
Other:		_____

Review your list. Come up with alternate ways you can handle these reactions. For example, instead of deciding you're a bad lover, be hopeful that you can do something about it. Instead of refusing sex again, purposefully decide to try the exciting and effective techniques I'll discuss here. There is no reason to suffer disappointment in sex any longer!

Compare what each of you said in your lists. Talk with your partner about your answers to better understand those reactions. Review what you both wrote in the column about how you could react more positively.

Why Men Come So Fast

You can't always blame him for being a "three-minute man." Men essentially train themselves to respond quickly. This stems from childhood, when a young man learns to masturbate quickly, so he won't get caught by someone walking in on him in the bathroom or his bedroom. If he was looking at sexy magazines or an X-rated video in the family VCR, he's even more in a rush—so his "naughty" act won't be discovered. This get-done-quick routine perpetuates even our computer age, when he could get caught checking out sexy Web sites.

Another reason men peak fast—faster than women—is that they *can*. Messages in the male brain go quickly to the sexual organs, and sperm is released quickly with the contractions of the musculature. Once these behavior patterns are established, the man has to be motivated to do the practices that will help him last longer. It takes effort and a change in beliefs. These include overcoming myths such as the following:

➤ **Controlling ejaculation is not possible.** Wrong. It is possible!

➤ **Holding back ejaculation is dangerous.** Wrong. You won't explode or "blow a gasket."

➤ **If he lasts a long time, he won't be able to repeat the good performance.** Wrong. Of course, he will!

➤ **It's not pleasurable for the man to hold back.** Wrong. The answer to "Can I still have pleasure?" is a resounding "Yes!"

No Expectations, Please!

Expectations are the absolute ruination of a man's ability to enjoy sex. If the man thinks he has to last long, his body will be sure to sabotage him and he will ejaculate quickly. Emotionally he will also cut himself off from the pleasure, out of pressure and resentment about how he is supposed to behave. Men typically expect that they have to get it up quick and keep it up. The more a man expects he has to have an erection, the harder it will be to have one; the more he thinks he has to last forever, the quicker he will come.

Tantra Tales

Mick found one night of pleasure so fulfilling, he shocked himself by admitting "I didn't even have to ejaculate at all!" It happened when he was performing oral sex on Noreen and she was sending energy down her body and out her clitoris. The energy was so strong, he felt it shoot throughout his body. He wondered, "How can I feel so good without ejaculating as I feel when I do ejaculate?" He described to Noreen, "I felt bolts of electricity going through my head." Without realizing it, Mick was receiving Noreen's energy and allowing the energy to cycle through him and go into his crown chakra (the reason he felt the bolts in his head). The experience was so powerful, he did not need to ejaculate!

Ejaculation and Orgasm Are Different

The relationship between ejaculation and orgasm is crucial to how long a man lasts in sex. Read the following two statements and circle whether you think they are true or false:

Dr. Judy's TantrAdvice

There is a place in tantric sex for a "quickie," as long as the couple stays conscious of what they are doing. Have a quickie if you have no more time before work, or get the urge before a dinner engagement, as long as you both feel connected and honored.

➤ True or false? A man can ejaculate without experiencing an orgasm.

➤ True or false? A man can have an orgasm without ejaculating.

Both are true. Understanding that ejaculation and orgasm are two separate functions is crucial to the delight of tantric sex. A man can delay ejaculation or not ejaculate at all, but still achieve orgasm—and not just one orgasm, but many. Men can have multiple orgasms, just like women. To understand this, one has to understand the physiology of the man's body.

The mechanism of ejaculation, like an erection reflex, is triggered from the spinal cord (the sympathetic nervous system). The penis responds to stimulation by sending a message to the lumbar portion of the spinal cord (the ejaculatory center) through the nerves. This triggers contractions of muscles in the internal genital organs. Although, it all sounds so automatic, the timing of the process can actually be controlled consciously.

The Stages of the Male Sexual Response Cycle

The traditional model of the male sexual response is composed of four stages:

➤ Excitement (increase in muscle tension and sex flush)

➤ Plateau (vasocongestion, pronounced muscle tension, increased respiration)

➤ Orgasm (reduced muscle control, increased heart rate, involuntary pelvic thrusting)

➤ Resolution (reduced muscle tension within five minutes, loss of vasocongestion, heart rate and blood pressure return to normal)

Other theories have added concepts such as desire, but none has taken energy into account. In my model, the initial stage is one of attraction in which energy is being stimulated. With continued interaction, the sensations build and are felt in various parts of the body and mind. Tension rises in response to the energy. The energy mounts and surges through the body, causing more general physical and emotional alert. Using the tantric transmutations properly (using breath to direct the energy) causes an overall sensation of both relaxation and excitement. In the next cycle, energy can go to either higher or lower levels, depending on how the person and partner play with the energy. The resolution phase is less abrupt than in traditional models, as the energy can be moved into many surges.

Traditional Control Tactics

Traditional ways to help a man overcome premature ejaculation have included the following techniques:

➤ **Stop-start** This technique was popularized by the famous sex therapist and research team of Masters and Johnson more than 40 years ago, but is still effective. The man stimulates himself to the point where he feels he will ejaculate and then stops the stimulation. When he feels more in control, he starts stimulation again.

➤ **Squeeze** When he feels the urge to ejaculate, he applies pressure on the shaft of the lingam, where the shaft connects to the head, with the thumb on the top and the forefinger and middle finger on the underside, on either side of the bump that is sensitive (the frenulum). When the urge subsides, he resumes stimulation.

➤ **The testicle tug** At the point of no return the man pulls his testicles down (gently) to inhibit the ejaculation. This method is tricky and potentially dangerous (don't pull too hard!), so try the others first, please.

The man can do these techniques on his own or his partner can help. It's best if he learns on his own what works best for him and then teaches her. Give her precise cues (sounds, movements) about what to do.

Ecstasy Essentials

One traditional technique to find the point of no return is the *ladder,* in which during masturbation the man pays attention to his level of excitement as if going up and down steps on a ladder, to pinpoint which step comes close to ejaculation (as if on a split screen in his mind). He imagines climbing a ladder, looking ahead, and not falling off the top. While he (or his partner) does whatever is stimulating, he switches his attention from the sensation to another part of his body and asks, "Where am I now on the ladder?" When he is close to the top, he stops stimulating until he goes back a few steps to the bottom of the ladder, where he waits until he is calmer and then starts again.

Certain aids to delay ejaculation that are not compatible with tantric practices (which requires being tuned in to every sensation) include lotions that desensitize sensations in the lingam, devices to trap blood in the penis, or purposefully distracting thoughts (like of baseball scores or other nonsensual subjects).

Blocks to Bliss

Some critics charge that continual high pressure on the perineum can damage nerves and blood vessels crucial to sexual functioning, and warn that *injaculation* (causing the semen to flow back into the bladder) can force bacteria into the bladder, causing an infection.

"Sealing the Penis," or Sexual Kung Fu

The spot located halfway between the anal opening and the base of the scrotum—called the *in-between spot* or "million dollar spot"—can be pressed to inhibit the flow of semen out of the penis. Look for its location on the perineum as shown in the diagram of the man's body in Chapter 5, "Prep Your Body Temple of Love." To find it, feel for a slight indentation where your finger seems to press into a softer area, and press this spot at the moment when you feel the sensation that you are about to ejaculate. Putting two fingers behind your index finger (for more support) is called the *finger lock*. Variations of this practice are called *sealing the penis*, or *sexual Kung Fu* in Chinese.

Tantric Sex Versus Other Methods of Prolonging Lovemaking

Of course, you can delay ejaculation through these traditional sex therapy methods—sex therapists have been teaching certain ejaculation delay methods for decades, since Masters and Johnson popularized them more than 40 years ago. The stop-start and squeeze techniques are effective; however, they can be even *more* effective when you add techniques of tantric sexuality while carrying them out. The secret: encouraging the man to focus on, direct, and channel his sexual energy.

Conscious awareness of sexual energy when performing any of the traditional methods of ejaculatory control is important in tantric practice, and makes the man and his partner more attuned to his body's needs and responses. In tantric practice, techniques for ejaculatory control include breathing exercises and other specific actions, which I'll describe a little later in this chapter.

The following table summarizes the several differences between traditional sex therapy techniques for premature ejaculation and tantric sex techniques.

Traditional Sex Therapy Versus Tantric Sex

	Traditional Sex Therapy	Tantric Sex
Technique	Uses mind control, such as identifying grades of excitement and imagining steps on a ladder adder to measure excitement level.	Insists on awareness of energy and directing energy.
Recommended positions	Advises the man not to be on top, but rather the woman be on top, so he can relax.	The man can be on top to move energy more freely; preferred position is yab yum with female in male's lap.
Communicating with the partner	He gives her feedback.	Their energetic connection helps her sense where he is in the sexual response cycle.
Measuring success rates	Squeeze or stop-start training is 90 percent effective within 10 weeks.	Considers measurement contrary to the experience of energy.

There are also similarities between traditional sex therapy techniques and tantric sex techniques. Both …

➤ Emphasize relaxation.

➤ Focus on enjoying sensations in all parts of the body (called *sensate focus* in traditional sex therapy).

➤ Recommend practices for the limp lingam, such as *stuffing* in traditional sex therapy (the woman inserts the nonerect penis in her vaginal opening, and tightens her muscles to hold it there). This is similar to second chakra connecting or *kareeza,* in which the man is inside the woman feeling their energy co-mingling but unconcerned with how erect he is, since energy can be transmitted regardless of the erection.

The Transmutation Breath

This is the tantric variation of the stop-start—but a lot more fun! As soon as the man feels the urge to ejaculate, he draws up the energy from his lingam through his spine, up his chakras, flooding his heart. He can do this on his own or with a partner. The circuits can vary, according to what you have practiced. She can move her hand from his lingam to his heart, sweeping the energy to his heart, or she can charge it even more with her own sexual energy, by holding one hand on her yoni and sweeping the other hand from his lingam into his heart and then into her yoni and out again, in a continuous cycle.

Moving his own energy from his lingam to his heart.

As soon as she (or he) feels he is at the point of no return, she can say, "Breathe, sweetheart," or "Let's breathe together," or "Imagine my love going into your lingam and your heart and your love coming out to me."

Helping him move sexual energy to his heart.

Tips on How She Can Help

It can be threatening for a man to ask his partner to help him control his ejaculation, but a partner can be very helpful. Here's what you both can do:

➤ He can teach her about how ejaculation and male orgasm work, and what it feels like for men—specifically for him.

➤ Spend time together "playing doctor" and examining his body. Get over any embarrassment or shame about how you look or what you want. The man should let her get close. Sit down on the bed with plenty of light so you can both see.

➤ Show her how you respond. Yes, that means pleasuring yourself in front of her. Men and women will have differing reaction to this—some are excited, others are embarrassed. As in all tantric practice, allow yourself to feel these feelings. Sometimes talking about them aloud can help you process them so they will clear.

➤ The man should give his partner cues and feedback in movements and sounds, even if he thinks she already knows. Needs can change over time, so don't make your partner guess.

Ecstasy Essentials

The more a man thrusts vigorously, the more likely he is to feel the urge to come. A good solution: While keeping the lingam in the yoni, sit up in yab yum and breathe together. The change in position will quiet down the energy but still keep it flowing.

Dr. Judy's TantrAdvice

Remember the tantric sex rule, "Always ask permission." This applies equally when she is approaching him, especially because we assume that men would agree to anything about sex. Ask if he wants to move his sexual energy rather than assuming he does and telling him to breath, or rushing to touch his body on places that aid such delay.

➤ She should be enthusiastic about discoveries and appreciative of his courage in revealing himself.

➤ She should encourage him that it is possible for him to have control.

➤ Stay with each other energetically. This helps her know the level of his excitement and when he might be reaching his point of no return.

➤ Never criticize if he ejaculates, even if she has not reached her peak.

➤ Be careful not to pressure him to come or not to come. Always be sensitive to his needs and where his energy is at.

If He Ejaculates Before She Is Ready

If you are practicing the techniques I have been describing, it is more likely that you will be harmonizing your energy so well that you are able to be at the same point at the same time often. This makes it more likely that you will reach that experience that many couples want—simultaneous orgasm. However, don't despair if there are times when you are out of tune in your energies, or if he ejaculates before she is ready.

If that happens, avoid all the traps you filled out in the earlier checklists in this chapter, such as criticizing, feeling like a failure, or that you are not right for each other. Remember that there is always another time for lovemaking, and that not each experience is going to be the ultimate—even though you are attempting these new techniques. If things don't go exactly as you wished or planned, rely on another principle of tantric sex: whatever happens at that time is right to happen; just respect where the energy goes.

The Least You Need to Know

➤ A man's ejaculation is a physical act that is separate from the emotional experience of orgasm, a distinction that makes it possible for men to delay his ejaculation but still have pleasure.

➤ Delaying ejaculation is a matter of choice; such acts in tantric sex practice can lead to extended periods and intensity of pleasure.

➤ A man can use several methods to delay ejaculation or teach his partner to help him do this, so that he can last as long as he wants and ejaculate when he wants to.

➤ Being sensitive to your energy, and purposefully directing it within yourself or cycling it through your partner is one of the most exciting and satisfying ways to make lovemaking last as long as you want.

Chapter 13

A New View of Love, Sex, and Orgasm: The Big TTO

In This Chapter

➤ How to approach love, sex, and orgasm in a new way

➤ New patterns of sexual arousal

➤ New orgasms possible through tantric sex, including the TTO

➤ Uncovering secret places of excitement

➤ Connecting sound to movement to raise sexual energy

I've been talking about tantric sex throughout this book, but notice the emphasis is always on sex energy to empower love. This is a new view of love. Tantra also requires a new view of sex. Sex is no longer simply an act, nor is it a performance; instead, it is a spiritual transformation. Consistent with this, the *tantric transformation orgasm (TTO)* is even better than that "Big O" you've been striving for.

In this chapter you'll learn about the different kinds of cosmic experiences, including orgasm, that you can have in tantric sex. You'll also learn some exercises to spark your desire and move toward those higher states. As if I weren't already challenging you to shift your perspective about relationships, here's yet another step I invite you to take: a new view of sex and orgasm.

What's Love Got to Do with It?

The answer is, everything! In my many lectures about sex to diverse groups, even when discussing the latest techniques or the hottest new trends, I always mention that the underlying message is really about how the sex act itself generates love—for yourself, your partner, and even the world.

Tantra Tutorial

Tantric sex energy is harnessed into a force for love. Women have always bemoaned using sex to get love; ironically, tantric sex energy is an adaptation on that theme: Sexual energy is used to inspire, create, and expand love.

Although this book is about tantric sex, it really is about harnessing sexual energy to empower your love for yourself and everything around you. Consider yourself as the beloved—reflected in everything. Tantra teachers Charles Muir and his wife Caroline express this concept perfectly as *conscious love* (the title of their popular workshops and book, *Tantra: The Art of Conscious Loving;* see Appendix B, "Workshops, Web Sites, Teachers, and Tantra Communities"). This means making love with keen awareness about what you are doing—and learning to honor each other as beloveds. Tantric sex allows an expanded view of what sex is, the nature of the sexual response cycles, and what's possible in orgasm.

A New View of Orgasm and the Sexual Response Cycle

I remember the early days of sex therapy (only a quarter of a century ago!) when sex experts argued that there were two types of female orgasm: the clitoral and the vaginal, originating from stimulation of those two parts of the women's genitalia. Over time, professionals came to recognize a third type, called *blended,* because although a woman's orgasm is triggered by stimulation of the clitoris, the sensation can also be extended into deeper internal areas or can start deeper and spread to other genital areas.

Traditional views of orgasm for men were even more limited: the one quick release. More modern views revealed that the processes of ejaculation and orgasm in men are in fact separate, as I described in the previous chapter. Orgasm for men is the psychological experience of pleasure, much like for women; ejaculation is the release of sperm. This opens many possibilities of sexual response and pleasure for men. The practices of tantric sex reveal even more thrills for both sexes.

Over time, we are increasingly aware that there are more types of orgasms, based on the locations, timing, and intensity of the experience. This is true for men as well as women.

Not only are there many types of orgasm, but I have postulated that there are several directions of expression of the energy: *outward* and *inward.* Both are powerful, can lead to states of bliss, and can be expressed alone or with a partner. They are different in that …

➤ The outward orgasm can be wild and uninhibited, as you let out emotions or scream and move vigorously.

➤ The inward orgasm can be quiet and subtle; however, it can release as much energy and reveal as much feeling as a more active response. Thoughts are powerful enough to trigger these responses. Imagine inhaling a ball of energy from your sexual organs, up through your body, and back down again. You can experience quiet inward orgasms as explosions that take place subtly.

Traditional views of sex also posed four progressive cycles: excitement, plateau, orgasm, and resolution. However, the results of tantric practice prove different: You can fluctuate within these stages and stay in these stages for extended periods of time. In fact, the sky's the limit as far as how high you can go.

Notice the three couples in the following figure. The couple on the bottom line are building their sexual energy gradually. The middle couple are generating more sexual energy and building more quickly. The couple on the top are having strong spurts of sexual energy, and then resting (or rather *nesting,* as you see the birds in the figure doing!).

The figures are based on tantric practices of couples in lovemaking that are described later in this chapter. By transmuting their sexual energy during their lovemaking, at different intervals and times they blast off or come down to earth, as they want—together!

Dr. Judy's TantrAdvice

Remember that everyone is individual in his or her intensity and variety and self-expression. Appreciate your individuality and allow responses to emerge from all parts of your body.

Most couples think they have to keep at it to increase the intensity of their arousal. You can add more charge by relaxing into a "sexual quiet place" and then doing a fire breath (quick nostril breathing in and out) for even more intense buildup. I recommend alternating your energy in these ways—the process sustains arousal and also brings you to higher states of pleasure, multiple orgasms, and an expanded sense of well-being so that you can control your sexuality and yourself!

I am always asked about how to have the best orgasms (and have spent years teaching women how to so this), so here's a look at the different kinds of wonderful orgasmic experiences possible with tantric sex.

Couples riding different tantric waves to bliss.

The Cosmorgasm

The *cosmorgasm* is the orgasm that extends out into the universe, or the cosmos. It happens when you alone or the two of you build your energy within yourself, and then when you are fully charged and grounded, extend your energy out the top of your head, through your crown chakra, into the air and sky above.

Blocks to Bliss

Whenever you send energy out your crown chakra for cosmic orgasms connecting beyond your physical body, you have to be sure you are not "throwing it away" or "losing yourself." You must cycle the energy fully, and ground it first within yourself.

The Mega-Orgasm

The *mega-orgasm,* like the Energizer Bunny, keeps going and going and going. It continues in an upward direction, showing increasing excitement, with small valleys where you linger in the good feeling, but then spurt again to an even higher level of excitement and pleasure. Follow the birds in the previous figure to see how the couple on the top line are having a mega-orgasm; they keep going upward for a long time, taking a few rests.

The Clearing Orgasm

The *clearing* orgasm is unleashed from a big release of emotions rather than direct sexual contact—and can be just as powerful. This big release of tension can clear out stuck emotions. Because of this, the release can sound painful, with screams and wails. These reactions might frighten a partner (and will be described more in Chapter 17, "Sexual Healing to Set You Free"), but such releases should be welcomed as a sign of freeing the soul, body, and mind. After such an orgasm, you can feel spent, exhausted, and drained; however, the experience is worth it because of the pleasure it brings—and the pleasure it frees you to experience.

Reaching Multiple and Simultaneous Orgasms

The secret to multiple orgasms lies in controlling the level of your excitement through your breath and cycling your sexual energy. This is similar to what I described in the previous chapter on how men can control their release to make lovemaking last longer. When you get to one of your peaks, you both can do a transmutation breath (drawing the energy up from your genitals) at the same time. Remind each other by saying it aloud, "Let's breathe now!" Do this twice and even three times, building your excitement.

Ecstasy Essentials

Hollywood's classic portrayal of a woman's orgasm was Meg Ryan's noisy imitation in the movie *When Harry Met Sally.* My favorite is the scene in the film *Cocoon,* in which Tawhnee Welch (playing an alien) transmits powerful orgasmic energy across a pool to Steve Gutenberg.

Tantra Tutorial

According to ancient Eastern tradition, the male is expected to bring the woman to nine levels of orgasm. Progressively, the woman sighs and breathes heavily; offers tongue kissing; grasps the man with her muscles; has vaginal secretions and spasms; feels the urge to bite; undulates like a snake; grabs the man furtively; desires to bite more vigorously; surrenders and collapses. Modern views and some tantra teachers point out that the biting response is not necessary and might occur in cases in which women have more unresolved aggression.

The Tantric Wave

The *tantric orgasm* is an undulation that is shaped like a wave. The body flows like a dolphin moves through water, in smooth motions up and down; in natural curves that keep coming and coming.

The tantric wave of bliss.

The Stock Market Orgasm

Banking on a quippy analogy of the sexual response cycle and cycles in the stock market (men's erections go down when the Dow dips!), California sexologist Ava Cadell created a new lovemaking system. It combines sexual techniques such as erotic talk, oral sex, G spot stimulation, and intercourse (in various positions) for men; combined with sensual techniques such as synchronized breathing, body massage, love toys, and the "Venus Butterfly" for women. She calls it the *stock market orgasm* (also the title of her book, Peters Publishing, 1999) because there are seven peaks of sexual excitement, and then seven dips of sensuality maintaining a level of arousal for both partners.

Ecstasy Essentials

Valley orgasms do not refer to valley girls, but to continuous orgasms that extend through the time in between your peaks.

The profit that couples get from their investment is multiple orgasms for both people, once he learns how to separate his orgasm from ejaculation. Says Cadell, "The best lovers are those who are long-term investors rather than those who are addicted to quickies."

How to Have the Big TTO

The Big TTO—tantric transformative orgasm—comes from cycling sexual energy, using all the exercises I've told you about up to now (and more to come in later chapters). Since the time I developed this technique, I have taught it to many men and women, with great results. The process includes the ways to amp up or damp down your energy (as described in Chapter 6), breathing patterns (as in Chapter 3), and many other techniques I am teaching you about in this book, including ways to play and have fun (because I think loving should be about fun!). All of these help you respond freely and connect with love and a beloved.

Taking Sex Drive to a New Level

A pervasive problem for couples today is complaints about sex drive; this ceases to be a problem when you follow the tantric path. It's all about building peaks of sexual excitement, but not leaving it there. Once you got the energy going, the practices invite you to move it. This process is called *transmuting* the sexual energy (a process I refer to often in this book, and one I teach extensively in the workshops I run because it is especially effective in connecting love energy to sex).

The following exercises show you how to do that. You can do any of these exercises by yourself or with a partner. When you do them with a partner, it's a good idea to face each other, sit knee to knee or in the more intimate classic yab yum position, with one of you in the other's lap.

The Shiva Shakti Mudra

One of my favorite exercises is called the *Shiva Shakti mudra.* It connects energy from the earth and sky, bringing it inward to the heart area, then directing it outward to a partner or to the world. You can also add words to the exercise.

Here's how it's done. Stand with feet shoulder width apart and knees slightly bent. Take several deep breaths. On the inhale sweep your arms up from the earth, scooping up energy from Mother Earth, and bring the energy into your heart area. Feel the warmth, security, and love of earth energy going in to your heart. Exhale. Inhale again, this time reaching up to the sky and gathering energy from Father Sky. Sweep your arms down, crossing your hands over each other as you pass your face and into your heart area. Feel the energy of enlightenment and vision going in to your heart. This exercise is called Shiva Shakti mudra because it connects the Mother Earth/female Shakti energy with the Father Sky/male Shiva energy. It's a good exercise to do when you are tired, to give you more energy in general.

Variations on the Shiva Shakti Mudra

To do this with a partner, stand facing each other. After bringing the energy into your heart as described in the previous exercise above, exhale and extend your arms and hands out toward each other. On the next round the two of you can extend your arms and hands out to your sides, sending your collected love energy out to others or to the world in general.

The Shiva Shakti mudra: bringing strength and vision into your love, getting help from the earth and sky.

Make up your own dedication and say words about your blessings while doing this exercise. For example, say, "I bring all the love of Mother Earth up into my heart and send it out to you my beloved, and I bring down from the sky all the inspiration and vision and vastness of the universal love and send it into you, my beloved." When extending your arms out sideways, you can make a dedication, "I send all collected love energy out to the world, to heal all those who are suffering or who are not as fortunate to feel the love we have, so that they may share in our bliss."

Connecting the Sexual Energy to Other Energy Centers

Through the breath, sound, and movements, you can send sexual energy to other parts of the body to empower them. Here are some exercises to do that.

Using Movements to Send Sexual Energy

Put on music with a powerful drumbeat and sway your hips to the music. Start with side-to-side movements, then forward and backward, and then circular motions.

Using Sound to Transmute Music Energy

Remember that all sounds are associated with different energy centers, or chakras. You can send your pooled sexual energy to different energy centers by chanting the sound of the sexual center and then connecting it to the sound of any of the other chakras. In the following exercise, breathe in through your nose and on the exhale, open your mouth and let the sound come out. Allow the breath to pool in your belly and then exhale like a bellows, to get the maximum energy from the sound.

➤ **The ooo-ahhh exercise: Opening the heart**
This is another favorite exercise, both to do and to teach. "Ahhh" is the sound of the heart center. Connecting the sex and heart center is one of the primary techniques of tantra. Use it to prepare yourselves for love-making. Build the energy in the sex center and feel it bolting through your body as you thrust the pelvis forward, saying "ooo" (sounding like the "ou" in the word "you" but with a more rounded mouth). On the in-hale, arch your back as you say "ahhh." The chest will thrust forward, the action itself opening the heart center. In addition, the "ahhh" sound itself opens the heart. Do this repeatedly; as the flow of these two sounds and the movements build they will take you on their own ride after a while, without any effort on your part.

Tantra Tutorial

The ooo-ahhh exercise is particularly important for men, who often separate sex and love. Chanting these two sounds brings sexual energy up to the heart center, making a man more open to feeling his love energy, and more able to create an emotional connection with his partner. It is magical how doing this exercise can open—and melt—a man's heart.

The ooo-ahhh exercise.

➤ **The ooo-ehhh exercise: Freeing the throat**   Do this exercise the same way you would the previous one, but use the words "ooo-ehhh." Sending sex energy to the throat chakra is also a major part of tantric sex, so you can express yourself freely. Too many women—and men, too—are inhibited about speaking up at all;

Dr. Judy's TantrAdvice

The sex and throat centers are closely connected; once you open the throat to make noises in sex, you'll be surprised how much more responsive you are sexually. I'll say more about this in Chapter 18, "Sex, Song, and Videotape."

particularly about making sounds during sex. I have heard so many men complain that women lie too quietly during sex and how they wish women would "talk dirty" (use raunchy words), which many women consider unrefined or demeaning. Yet free expression during an erotic encounter is essential for ecstatic freedom of sex.

➤ **The ooo-uhhh exercise: Grounding more security**   Do this exercise the same way you would the ooo-ahhh exercise, but use the words "ooo-uhhh." Move energy generated by pelvic thrusts from your sex center into your base chakra or anal area. As you emit the sound "uhhh," feel yourself getting more and more rooted into the ground like a tree. This *grounding* stops distracting thoughts and worries that invariably intrude in your intimate interaction.

Sound healer Karin Schelde teaches workshops on freeing up the voice. "Every sound and every part of the body has a vibrational energy that has tremendous healing capacity," says Schelde. "We just need to know that it's safe to be heard." In Schelde's "sound meditations," participants make sounds to express, and release, whatever feelings they have without judgment. "Let the feelings flow through you like a river," she instructs, "to free your expression to heal but also to experience joy."

Tantra Tutorial

Researchers at the recent World Congress of Sexology in Paris presented photographs of what was happening inside the vagina during intercourse, and corresponding measurements of excitement levels. The results showed that in different positions in intercourse, the penis touched various areas of the women's internal genitalia, all of which registered signs of stimulation. Other research shows these physical indications of excitement can occur even if the woman herself does not express the same level of excitement as the measures indicate.

Where Do You Feel the Big O? Alphabet Orgasms

More modern views of orgasm have expanded not only the types of orgasm, but also the places that those delicious sensations occur. There are spots to cover many letters of the alphabet used as shortcuts for the names of these responses.

The G Spot

The G spot is actually an area on the front wall of the vagina, one third of the way up. Although stimulating, at first some women feel discomfort in the form of numbness, pain, or the urge to urinate. However, many women feel intense pleasure and can even release female ejaculate.

The X Spot

This spot is deep in the vagina around the cervix. Although it does not have many nerves, when stimulated it can tug on the internal walls and cause radiating sensations. Taoist views of the orgasm pose that the tip of the penis and the cervical area both correspond to the heart, making it understandable that this area would be pleasurable to the woman. However, it is also easily stimulated manually, with the man inserting several fingers and encircling the cervix at the end of the vaginal canal.

The AFE Zone

The *anterior fornix erogenous* (*AFE*) *zone* is the area from the end of the vaginal canal downward about two thirds to the opening. As with other areas, some women might find this pleasurable; others do not.

The PFE Zone

The *posterior fornix zone* (*PFZ*) is similar to that described in the previous section, but on the opposite wall.

Tantra Tutorial

The most recent extensive research on a woman's G spot, or sacred area, is by Gary Schubach. He posts information on his Web site at www.DoctorG.com.

Blocks to Bliss

Some women find that stimulating the cervical area is painful, especially during their menstrual and hormonal cycles.

169

Tantra Tales

After learning tantric sex, Nancy found, "I can have an orgasm in my wrist! The energy just explodes whenever Michael touches me, wherever he touches me. It's like my body is on fire. I can send the breath anywhere in my body, almost on demand, and make those cells come alive. As soon as he touches me there, it's like the light goes on and he can feel the heat, too.

The Anywhere-in-Your-Body Orgasm

This is probably the best news of all: By practicing tantric sex, every cell in the body can be orgasmic. The orgasm does not just happen in the genitals; you can send it anywhere in the body and make it accessible within seconds.

The Least You Need to Know

➤ Practicing tantric sex requires a new view of sex in which sex is a transmission of energy between the couple.

➤ Orgasm, like sex in general, can be a new type of experience through tantric practice, in which energy that is pooled in the sex center is sent, through the breath, to other parts of the body.

➤ There are many places on the body and inside the woman's genitalia that can be experienced as orgasmic.

➤ Through tantric practices any couple can achieve these high states of sexual ecstasy in addition to a mixture of physical, emotional, and spiritual bliss. For example, connecting sound to movements helps direct energy and heightens sensation.

Chapter 14

Getting Fit Together for Tantric Sex

In This Chapter

➤ How exercising together can pump love muscles

➤ Yoga poses to do together

➤ Workouts that also work your sex energy

➤ How emotional issues are worked through in workouts

In Chapter 5, "Prep Your Body Temple of Love," I told you about the important role that being physically fit plays in pleasurable sex. Your body is your temple of love, and now you're ready to share it with your partner.

Review the steps in Chapter 5 and do them with your partner. In this chapter you'll learn more physical routines and movements you can do together to honor your body temples—and to have some fun!

The Importance of Physical Activity Together

Research proves exercise is an aphrodisiac. In one national survey, 8 out of 10 exercisers credited their workouts with boosting self-confidence, 4 in 10 felt more sexual arousal, and 3 in 10 made love more often. Physical activity is energizing (important for sex), forces you to focus on the body (heightening sensual awareness), builds strength and endurance (for sexual positions and staying power), and releases pleasure chemicals in the brain.

Working out with your lover has immediate payoffs. Your adrenaline is already pumping and you're already feeling better about yourself. Chemicals will flow in your body, such as the love chemical endorphin and the cuddle chemical oxytocin, prepping you for pleasure in love and sex.

Blocks to Bliss

Relationships in which one partner is physically active and the other is not can lead to trouble. In a California study of relationships where one partner jogged, the inactive spouses often became jealous of the runner's independence and attractiveness to others.

The Love Muscle Exercises for the Man and the Woman

Just as I talked earlier in this book about the importance of contracting and exercising your pelvic muscles on your own, you can also do this together. Sit facing each other, look deeply into each other's eyes, and breathe in and out rapidly through your nose (as in the fire breath; see Chapter 3, "Spinning Your Wheels and Breathing to Ecstasy").

Hold your breath and pulse your pelvic muscles 10 times. Relax the muscles and do the fire breath again. Repeat several times. Remember that you both have more than one set of pelvic muscles; one set is around your urethral opening and another set is around your anal opening. As you do this together, don't worry about technique until you get the hang of it; then you can inhale at the same time, hold your breath, and pulse your muscles in unison.

Pulsing PC muscles while you're breathing together does a lot to turn you on to each other. It synchronizes your energy more powerfully than just breathing together, and sends supercharged sexual energy up your spine, which you then can cycle into each other. Deliberately knowing that you are doing this in the same momentum makes you feel very connected to each other, adding intimacy to your excitement.

Partner Pelvic Thrusts

Pelvic motions are the most powerful generator of sexual energy. I've already emphasized that they are important exercises to do on your own; now you're ready to do them with a partner. Put on some music that gets your blood going. Stand side to side or better yet, facing each other. (Later you can let loose and move around any way you want.) You can start from a standing position, gradually thrusting at lower heights until you're thrusting while lying down on your back on the bed or floor (knees up); or start on the floor (knees up) and progress to a standing position. Follow your mood; ending up lying down can leave you in a good position for more intimate contact, while ending up standing could make you want to move around for more active play.

Sounds simple, doesn't it? Just thrust your pelvis forward and backward. But that might not be so easy, considering that for many of us, our pelvis is stiff! Stand with feet shoulder width apart, sacrum tucked in. Thrust forward and backward in a steady motion, picking up speed. The trick for the best effect is to keep your upper body straight and isolate the hips. Feel the energy surge through your body and send it out to your partner. Use your hands to guide the energy out to your partner by making a sweeping motion into his or her pelvis and then up into the heart.

Ecstasy Essentials

Add sound to intensify your energy and excitement. In unison, say "ooo" as you thrust forward, and "ahhh" as you arch back.

I Could Have Danced All Night

Dancing is a wonderful workout that exercises all kinds of muscles and frees your spirit in the process. It's a powerful way to activate your entire body and move sexual energy through your body—even to the point of sensing orgasmic highs for both men and women. That makes the activity a perfect warm-up for when you want to get more interactive. Use your motions together in dance to express your attraction and desire. I'll explain more about different kinds of dances you can do to express and experience your pleasure together in Chapter 15, "Make It Juicy with Magic and Play."

Pace your dance for your desired heart rate, doing slow sensuous movements and building to faster, more free-flowing motions. Let yourself go into a frenzy, allowing your limbs to fly where they will.

An Eight-Step White Tantra Twosome Routine

As I mentioned earlier in this book, white tantra refers to personal practices, including yoga poses, that connect to the chakras, or energy centers. Each time you make a pose, it is meant to stimulate one or several of the energy centers, and the emotions or issues associated with those centers.

Follow along as I describe a wonderful tantric yoga routine for couples, and you'll see what I mean. This practice was designed by New York tantra teacher Carla Tarantola as a result of her practice with her beloved, John. It was so effective, she decided to include it in tantra classes she teaches around the country. "Most couples finish their day too exhausted from work or taking care of the kids to enjoy sex," says Tarantola, "but if they do these physical poses together, they can flood themselves with such a river of sexual energy that they won't even remember they were too tired for sex."

These twosome yoga poses benefit your relationship by …

➤ Establishing deep trust because you depend on each other for the movements.

➤ Creating balance because you really have to physically balance on each other and adjust to the other person's weight to get into and out of the poses.

➤ Requiring and reflecting genuine cooperation because you have to figure out how to get in and out of the poses together.

➤ Providing an example of how you communicate through your bodies, which is a metaphor for how well you can communicate emotionally.

➤ Giving you a chance to support each other in developing the physical strength and resolving any emotional issues associated with these chakras.

➤ Giving you a chance to laugh and have fun together!

The following sections describe the suggested poses, all demonstrated by Tarantola and her beloved, John.

Couple Connect

Start your session by being fully present to one another. Sit facing each other and looking in each other's eyes. With knees bent out, place feet comfortably in front of you with his feet on the outside of hers. Encircle each other by stretching out your arms to hold on to your partner comfortably on the sides or under the shoulder. Inhale and exhale together to synchronize your energies. Do this for about seven breaths, or longer if you like.

Couple connect.

Circling Couple Celebration

Stay on the floor opposite each other. Stretch your legs out as far as possible with feet touching or overlapped at the ankles (as comfortable). Hold hands as one partner leans toward the other and the other leans backward. Reverse this. Do alternating breaths (breathe in as your partner breathes out). Make circles moving to the left together, stretching your right side, and then the opposite side. Reverse directions. Make smaller and larger circles. Be spontaneous, guessing which way each of you wants to go, and have fun! Feel more looseness in your base and sex chakras, which will help you in sex.

Tantra Tutorial

Adjust every position to accommodate your sizes and ability; never strain. Remain in each position for as long as you want or as long as you feel comfortable.

Circling couple celebration.

Squat-to-Stand Support

Help each other into a squat position still grasping each other's wrists. Bounce gently, feeling your lower energy centers getting stimulated. Lift up to a standing position slowly, playing as you balance each other. Lower down and rise again, synchronizing your breath to inhale as you rise up and exhaling as you lower. (Be careful not to strain your knees while doing these movements.)

Squat-to-stand support.

Partner Pelvis Press

Stand close together facing each other, pressing against each other's pelvis for balance as you lean back and lift your arms toward the sky, looking upward. This opens your heart center, but because your pelvis is the seat of power, by pressing your pelvis together you are giving each other strength (from the pelvic energy center) to love. On the exhale, make noises, making the sound come from your pelvis, heart, and throat.

"If I lean too close to my partner, he could fall back, but if I don't lean back enough, he will fall on top of me," explains Tarantola. "Because we are responsible to not let each other fall, we have to balance male and female energy in the way required in tantric sex."

Dangling Duos

Bring your hands together from the pelvis press and step apart gradually, guiding each other to droop downward and hang like a tree (being careful to go slowly and lowering the spine one vertebrae at a time). Relax your neck and shoulders and allow your head to hang loosely.

Partner pelvis press.

Dangling duos.

The Couple Cobras

Lie fully extended on your stomach with heads touching. With hands under the shoulders, slowly lift the upper body, opening the heart to each other and stretching the head and neck upward and curving backward, opening the throat chakra. This will enable you to speak honestly to each other. Lower down and rise up again, inhaling and exhaling at the same pace.

Couple cobra.

Lovers Table

This is a wonderful experience! One partner kneels on all fours, keeping his back straight and creating a table over which the partner can lean backward and drape his or her own body with outstretched arms, opening all chakras and feeling trust in the partner. Reverse places if your weight allows.

Lovers table.

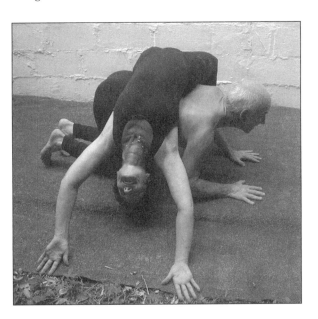

Couple Cuddle

This is the typical resting pose in yoga, but with one partner cradled over the other. Breathe together and feel the energy, connection, trust, and love. Change places.

Couple cuddle.

All of these balance postures relate to relationship skills, explains Tarantola. Notice whether you have trouble with any of the poses (not just physically), that might indicate you are afraid to open your heart, speak up, or trust.

Bedroom Bodybuilding

As a yoga teacher and former professional athlete, Rundy Duphiney worked out every day until his constant cross-country trips from California to Ohio to see his lover Lisa interrupted his fitness routine. He panicked until he realized that making love with his beloved was a workout in itself. Currently also a sex coach, Duphiney developed a sex workout routine to help himself and other men stay physically fit while also creating new highs with a lover. The routine works all the major muscle groups (even several at a time) to build stamina and strength essential for great sex. Some of the exercises include these:

➤ Stand face to face in the shower or bedroom. Warm up by looking into each other's eyes while rolling your head from shoulder to shoulder, and stretching your upper body by leaning in one direction and the other.

➤ You and your partner rotate your arms and hips in synchrony while facing each other, as if looking in a mirror.

➤ Once you're both feeling excited, she can turn her back and lean over as he guides her pelvis into and away from his body. This creates thrusting for her that works out her hips and develops strength in her thighs, and resistance for him to work out his stomach, arms, gluts, thighs, hips, and quads.

➤ In the partner push-up he lies on his back, lifting his hips in the air, thereby working his lower back and abs while she leans over him, supporting herself with straight arms and hands on the bed, lowering and raising her body as if doing push-ups over him. This can also be done in reverse positions, with the man on top doing the push-ups over her.

Push-ups on your partner.

➤ With the man on his back, knees up, the woman squats on top, facing him. He lifts his upper body and grabs her buttocks from underneath, pulling her forward and backward on his wand of light. This has the effect of doing bicep curls, working his biceps, forearms, chest and shoulders.

➤ Sit up in yab yum position. Grasp each other's wrists and with his lingam still inside her yoni, lean slowly backward together and pull each other up again to sitting position, creating a back pull for several repetitions.

The body stores a distinct memory of the movements, explains Duphiney. "So after you've done this love routine," he says, "I guarantee you'll never be able to work out in the gym again without picturing your partner in the same positions of pleasure.

Tantra Tales

Francisco and his girlfriend Nicole had already been doing the pelvic thrusts and partner push-ups before realizing their favorite sex positions doubled as fitness moves. "Thinking about how I'm getting in shape during sex makes me move my muscles more," explained Francisco. "So my body looks buffed and I act like a stud, making Nicole twice as turned on to me." Purposefully exercising during sex can benefit the woman equally. Nicole said, "Francisco and I always loved my legs high in the air and the push-up position, but thinking of them now as formal exercises is a double payoff, because we both need the bodywork. Now I know I'll also do better pelvic thrusts in Pilates class, thinking of his delighting lingam going in and out of me!"

Yogaboxing

"She's the most powerful and persistent woman I ever met," Joshua Smith told me about his girlfriend, "so I could never say no to her. I'd give in until I got so mad that I wasn't speaking my mind that I'd escape to my own house, avoid sex with her, and think about having an affair." The handsome, outwardly confident 36-year-old Washington businessman is not unlike an increasingly number of men today who, although strong themselves, when faced with an "assertive" woman, become intimidated and withdraw sexually and emotionally rather than confront the partner and assert themselves.

So Smith decided to strike out his feelings—at his punching bag. As he released his anger, he had a brilliant brainstorm. A long-time practitioner of marital arts, T'ai Chi, trance dance, aerobics, and yoga, Smith came up with a new workout that he now offers to others in a workshop. He calls it *Yogaboxing,* a synthesis of yoga and boxing that Smith claims clears anger but also brings sexual energy into the heart to renew love.

A highlight of the hour-long routine is the yes/no exercise, in which participants face each other and shout a series of commands that are refusals ("no," "get out," "hear me now") and then affirmations ("yes," "yes I can") while extending fists in marital arts motions. The steps sound like those in self-defense classes, but Smith claims his routine proves the approach can be as effective for intimate relationships as for attacks from strangers.

It worked for him. "After doing the exercise myself over and over," Smith explains, "I realized that rather than staying angry with Laurie, making her wrong, and sabotaging our relationship and sex life, I could give myself permission to refuse her requests, ask for what I needed, and expect her to honor that. The result is that I feel better about myself and even more turned on and passionate toward her."

The first thing Smith did was confront his girlfriend and say, "I need some time to myself and after that I can listen to you." She protested at first but then went along.

Tantra Tutorial

A psychological developmental benefit in Smith's "Yogaboxing" is called "setting your boundaries"—saying what you will or will not do, which proves to yourself and others that you are in control of your life. (This overcomes childhood problems in which Smith and men like him have grown up sensing yet fearing the extent of their own power, and learning to express that power without fear of being destructive.) The physical benefits involve the combination of gentler yoga movements with more vigorous boxing, which infuses the muscles with oxygen-rich cells, stimulates the endocrine glands, and aligns the neck and spine; all of which helps retard aging without putting undue stress on the body.

The workout starts with stretches that reach upward, as Smith instructs his group to imagine reaching for their strength and stretching to speak up. Many exercises are done in pairs, to simulate confronting a real partner, such as the *stop sign* and the *tug of war,* in which each holds an end of a handkerchief, saying "yes" and "no" alternately. After each exercise, the partners share how they felt, and whether they were able to act as strongly as they wanted. Who pulls the handkerchief harder? Whose voice is more convincing? The participants are invited to associate the exercise with experiences in their relationships in which they have disagreed about even small things, such as what movie to see or where to go to dinner.

Yogaboxing tug of war.

The movements and verbalizations in Yogaboxing establish a powerful connection between your sense of power and your throat, allowing energy for self-expression to flow more easily to the sexual area. "After this workout," Smith promises, "a guy can get really turned on because he knows he can speak up to a woman, so he feels safer being more vulnerable—the very combination of qualities that women really like."

Yogaboxing seems to be working for others as well, with women as well as men flooding Smith's Washington classes (www.butterflyworkshops.com). So next time you're mad as hell and won't go near her, grab a handkerchief and engage her in a tug of war, and let the victor enjoy the spoils of sex thereafter.

The Least You Need to Know

➤ Working out together activates more sexual energy between you, which sparks your attraction for each other and empowers your union for more pleasure.

➤ Yoga poses that you do on your own can be adapted to do with a partner.

➤ Facing your partner, you can do love muscle exercises, pelvic thrusts, dances, and more complicated white tantra routines.

➤ Exercises that may seem merely physical can actually have deep emotional components that trigger emotional issues and can deepen your relationship by creating opportunities to establish balance, trust, communication, and support.

Part 4

Going Deeper: More Love and Better Sex Than You Ever Imagined

By now you've progressed beautifully on your path to loving passion and you're ready to add more advanced practices, experience more delight in giving and receiving love, and integrate this more deeply into expanding your consciousness. As you become better at moving your energy in new and exciting ways, love becomes more fulfilling and sex more magical.

In this part it's time to really let go and explore your body, mind, and soul. Learn different kinds of erotic dances to entice your mate, and discover new erogenous zones and positions. As you expand into exploring how to move your energy, stronger feelings can emerge, so I'll reveal some effective ways to heal any past sexual pain, releasing you to have more intense orgasms and greater overall bliss.

Chapter 15

Make It Juicy with Magic and Play

In This Chapter

➤ The importance of play in good sex

➤ Dancing for each other

➤ How food can spark passion

➤ Toys, gifts, and games to please each other

➤ Making sex magic

➤ Tantric events that encourage joyful joinings

Are you having fun yet? Remember that tantric sex is built on a principle of pleasure. I am an absolute believer that you should enjoy loving—and your life! If something feels not quite right, please stop and change the energy so you are experiencing, and sharing, pleasure (unless you're purposefully using the experience to heal, as I will discuss in Chapter 17, "Sexual Healing to Set You Free").

All tantric workshops include time for play. One of the most enjoyable aspects for me in the workshops that I lead is creating new and exciting experiences for the participants. I love when the whole room is energized and having a good time! In this chapter you'll learn some ideas for playtime that you can share with a partner. More important, let your spirit soar and come up with fun ideas that spontaneously occur to you. There are infinite ways to play together; part of the joy is to discover those ways.

The Spirit of Play

Remember being a child—with no fears or inhibitions about what to do to entertain and amuse yourself? Sadly, we develop so many fears as we grow up, usually as a result of negative experiences, punishments, and messages telling us "don't do this" and "be careful about that." Tune in to the spirit of yourself as a child. What would you do on your own or with a partner? Give yourself the permission to be that sweet, trusting, uninhibited playful, charming child.

How Much Juice Is There?

How juicy are you? "I feel the juice between us." "This experience is really juicy." When you say these words, can you feel the succulence? Referring to someone in tantra as "juicy" means that person is being uninhibited, expressing true sensuality, and allowing himself or herself to be turned on and excited. His or her energy is flowing in an excited, sensuous way. Women also are called juicy when they are lubricating, reflecting their excitement—and they're especially juicy when they have that female ejaculation, emitting a flow of love liquid (also called *amrita*).

Dr. Judy's TantrAdvice

Although being called juicy is a big compliment, as with other terms, make sure a woman or man likes being identified this way.

The Importance of Play in Sex

The value of play is endless, both physically and emotionally. Research has even shown that happier people have stronger immune systems and that couples in a happy union live longer than those who are not so content. It has even been proven that smiling lifts your spirits, and that a cheerier mood leads to better physical health.

Affirmations About Joyful Sexual Union

When you consciously decide what you want, it is more likely you will get it. Speaking out loud what you want, or writing it down on a piece of paper is even more helpful. Read the following affirmations aloud and breathe deeply while you say them, to fix them in your being. Imagine yourself in a sexual union while feeling these emotions and states:

➤ I deserve to have joy in my sex life.

➤ I enjoy every moment of pleasure.

➤ I feel good about myself.

➤ My beloved cheers me on in lovemaking.

➤ I have fun in sex.

➤ I give off an inner and outer glow.

➤ I delight in myself and my beloved.

Notice these affirmations are written in present tense so that they feel more real and create the sense of being "present" that is typical of tantra.

Laugh Your Way to Better Health

It is well known that laughter improves the immune system and therefore makes you healthier. It also has infinite benefits from an emotional point of view. Laugh aloud now and see how it changes your mood. Laughter opens you to more love—the goal of tantra.

One of spiritual mystic Osho's favorite courses is "Mystic Rose," in which participants spend three hours a day for a week in a room laughing (at nothing in particular, just laughing). In fact, the experience becomes contagious, so that even if you don't feel initially like laughing, someone else's laughter inspires you to laugh, too.

Dancing for Each Other

Dance is a revered part of the art of love according to ancient Indian texts on the subject. How right they were! Dancing moves strong surges of sexual energy within you and toward your partner. Let your body speak your love by taking turns dancing for each other. Dim the lights. Decide who will dance first, and who will be the audience. The dancer gets to put on his or her favorite music— it could be a salsa, jazz, or even heavy metal. Dress for the occasion in an outfit that makes you feel sexy and that your partner will find sexy, too. Here's the challenge: You have to put aside your self-consciousness.

Ecstasy Essentials

One tantra practitioner tells a humorous (made-up) story that scientists have found that all problems can be solved by opening the clown chakra, located in the belly. All you have to do is intentionally give a big belly laugh and you are cleansed of your troubles and ready for joy with your partner!

I promise if you just take a deep breath and start doing it, and keep your eyes on your partner's enjoyment of your display, your self-consciousness will go away. Let any fearful thoughts ("I look silly" or "I can't dance") come up and then drown them in your mind by concentrating on the music and looking into your partner's eyes. Feel the music in your body and let your body move with it. Now switch and let your partner choose music and put on a sexy outfit to dance for you.

Dancing for each other.

Guys might need extra encouragement to do this, because usually they have convinced themselves they can't dance. Give him extra reassurance. Help him prepare before you do this practice by going out dancing; he should let her lead and copy her moves, getting close and grinding his groin to her rhythm.

California tantrika Francesca Gentille teaches couples sacred dancing. "Lead your partner's attention with your hands," she advises. "Move them in front of your heart area to stimulate your partner's concentration on the heart and therefore your loving feelings. Or, to turn up the heat, rub your hips and thighs."

Tantrika Marci Javril, a dancer herself, suggests a woman can benefit from watching a stripper perform. Go to a club with him, if you're comfortable with that idea, or watch it on videotape, emulating her moves to be just as provocative.

Mirror, Mirror

Dancing together is an activity you can do in the privacy of your own home. Just put on some erotic, sensual music that moves you and let your bodies flow to the rhythm. Moving together in a free-flow improvisational dance will lead to more stimulation, better

Tantra Tales

Lori was tapping away on her computer until late in the night when Lance turned her chair around, and began to slither in a winding motion, putting on a dancing show for her. Lori was embarrassed at first, but was soon delighted at his display. "It seemed like something a woman would do for a man, and here he was doing it for me—and I really liked it."

orgasms, and higher states of ecstasy together. Mirror each other's motions to synchronize your mood, erase any sense of separation, and turn you on to each other.

Mirroring each other's movements.

Men should watch how a woman channels intense sensual energy through her body, follow her and then take the lead. Bend her and let her melt in your arms—good practice for what you want to happen when your genitals are locked in a similar dance. Gaze into each other's eyes and breathe together as you gyrate; when you're ready to reach higher states of ecstasy, fall on the floor or couch on top of each other and continue the action.

The Hand Dance

In this exercise to do with your partner, put up your hands and let them "dance" together. Let one partner be the leader first and the other follow the steps and then switch roles. See how it feels to be the leader or follower. Which feels more natural? If you felt more comfortable being the leader, purposefully be the follower again. If you were more comfortable being the follower, force yourself to be the leader and direct your partner's actions.

Using Your Body Parts

Stand back to back and dance against your partner's back. Play the same leader/follower game as in the previous exercise. Try using different body parts to connect:

your hips, your elbows, whatever you like. Have fun choosing which one, or switch from one to the other. Get your whole body into the action!

Belly Dancing

You might think you could never do those belly rolls and graceful hand motions that belly dancers do, but what if you tried it? Even if you can't dance at all, you have to give it a try to be a true tantrika (men can try it, too). The secret lies in moving the pelvis (the key to tantric energy which is what makes tantric sex practice and belly dancing so compatible).

"Belly dancing is an ecstatic celebration of feminine power, creativity, and sexual energy," says Christina Sophia, a tantrika who teaches a form she calls *sacred-erotic belly-dance* (www.tantradance.com). "The sensual, snaky actions mimic orgasm and the breath as a powerful force moving through the body, with the muscular movements grounding to the earth and the spinning hands reaching to the sky, connecting earth and sky, mother and father, male and female. Also, the pelvic motions mimic the birthing process, connecting you to the source of all life. The benefits are extensive, including increasing your flexibility, and muscular and internal awareness of your torso and pelvic regions. It is also a joyful form of exercise and creative expression that you can do on your own, by looking in the mirror to appreciate your body and gracefulness, or to enjoy with a partner. The body awareness and spontaneous creative inspiration will result in blissful and expansive tantric lovemaking."

Tantra Tutorial

Belly-dancing beginners learn a variety of pelvic and rib cage movements, creating geometric designs (circles, diamonds, triangles, figure eights, undulations); correct posture; steps (to the side, front, back); and arm, hand, and head movements. To find belly dancing classes, check local community centers, telephone directories under Dance Instruction, or see Appendix B, "Workshops, Web Sites, Teachers, and Tantra Communities."

Sophia's beloved and tantra co-teacher, William Florian, says belly dancing brought more aliveness and arousal into their sex. "Men need to learn to move that way," says Florian, who also provides original singing at their weekend workshops. "Once they do this, their erections get stronger, they can last longer, and please their women more." Sophia says that gradually men are taking up belly dancing. "It's a way to re-experience their sensuality, reclaim their feminine side, and enjoy a creative, joyful outlet for their energy. The snaky, muscular movements are grounding into more power, not emasculating. Think of powerful arms reaching up to the sky to connect with spiritual energy."

Ecstatic Dance

A premier dance instructor, musician, and teacher who runs workshops around the world, Gabrielle Roth teaches students a moving meditation and workout she calls *ecstatic dance*. It consists of five essential rhythms: flowing (a fluid circular motion), staccato (stops and starts), chaos (wild and free), lyrical (trancelike), and stillness (inner movement). Dancing to these rhythms takes you through stages of sexual arousal. Music is an essential element to create these progressive moods; use Roth's customized CDs or create one of your own.

The Temple Dance

The temple dance starts with a ritual bath, or an erotic version of an ancient Balinese trance dance. As in ancient times, instead of following certain steps, you channel your energy according to what your partner needs. In this way, your dance is not only for pleasure, it's also for healing.

Sit facing your partner and look into his or her eyes. Watch his or her body language and movement. Observe everything about your partner and sense what he or she is feeling and desiring. Then sway to the mood and the desire you sense. Let your self-consciousness fade away. Allow yourself to change your movements when you sense a change in your partner's mood.

Next take more of the initiative, and purposefully entice and seduce your partner with your movements and undulations. Raise his or her energy and interest. At first, tantalize from a distance, then move closer. As you feel tingling and waves of energy flowing through you, transmit those to your partner through your movements, glances, and gestures. Let the dance go where it will, perhaps leading to a massage or more, then switch places and let your partner dance for you!

Feasting on Your Love

I have long recommended a healthy way for couples to use food to spark passion. In a *sensuous supper,* every aspect—what, how, where, and when you eat—awakens all your senses. The experience follows the curve of sex from foreplay (shopping and cooking together, serving each other), to a peak (consuming), to lingering in afterplay (cleaning up).

Tantric lovemaking takes the use of food for pleasure or heightening sensuality to a new level, where you also become the table! A highlight of tantra seminars called "Being in Bliss" and "Ecstasy," run by Butterfly Workshops, is the *Gate feast* (meaning "to go beyond" in Sanskrit). In this erotic banquet you prepare seven courses of foods that are visually appealing, taste good, and can be easily eaten from various body parts (such as salmon mousse, juicy fruits, and ice cream).

Make abundant portions to create the sense that you can have it all, says workshop leader Laurie Handlers. Use no utensils and feed your lover with your hands or mouth, or offer up courses on any part of your body for your partner to feast on. The experience invariably leaves everyone laughing, loving each other, and wanting to taste more.

The erotic Gate feast.

"If you go slowly and savor the experience of giving and receiving pleasure in each sample and swallow," explains Handlers, "you go into a dreamy state, making you feel sexy."

Ecstasy Essentials

To use food as a turn-on for sex (called *sitiphilia)*, choose foods with pleasing smells, suggestive shapes (cucumbers, artichokes), colors (red tomatoes symbolic of her ripeness), and stimulating textures (peaches that remind him of her skin).

Games Lovers Play

Tantric sex celebrates games. After all, that's what kids do, and they embody the spirit of joy and delight. The word "game" has taken on a derogatory connotation, as often it is used to refer to single men and women playing games with each other, to trap them into relationships. (I have always advised in my dating workshops that you should never play games!) Redefine the word to have a positive meaning, to represent release, freedom, and joy. Here are some tantric games you and your partner can enjoy together:

➤ **Make up a story by taking turns to add different themes and events.** Let the story go in any direction it takes, without censoring yourselves or worrying about what it means. You can speak into a tape recorder or write the story down, so that you can read it back to each other at another time.

➤ **Picture your love.** Make a collage of your love for each other. Collect items that are significant both for yourself and for your partner and then create your collage together.

➤ **Bring out the animal in you and your partner.** Animals are uninhibited when it comes to following their desires. Play a game in which the two of you are animals. Get down on your knees, close your eyes, and use smell and sound to find each other. See what you do with one another. See which animals you chose to be! Are those animals compatible?

➤ **Play a tune on your partner's body.** Professional musician Paul Ramana Das not only plays piano like a virtuoso, he plays music on the body of his beloved. This can be wonderful play for you and your partner. Pretend you are the musician and play a rhythm on any part of your beloved's body. You don't have to be a musician or know music to do this, as long as you let yourself feel what you want to express through your motions.

Tantra Tales

Mae collected CD covers and Greek recipes because her beloved is a musician who likes to cook; he brought used airline receipts and seashells because she likes to travel and walk on the beach. They told each other how they felt about their respective hobbies and interests, and how warm they felt about being ac-knowledged for their interests.

Tantra Tales

Ted surprised his beloved—and himself—by penning a love poem. "The words just came out of me," he explained. "I just sat quietly, thought of Caryn, and started writing." Like Ted, let yourself be inspired by the feeling without any second-guessing or judging. Don't worry about style, rhyming, or even making sense! Ted's poem expressed how relieved he was to allow himself to love again without being hurt. A verse reads:

"My whole body radiates with the warmth and joy of my love and our love,

It streams from my smile for all to see and glistens in the glow of my eyes ...

My body is relaxed and my mind is peaceful, calm and free;

Never again will I give up my love to protect from feeling hurt."

Creating Sex Magic Through Tantric Sex

Sex magic is an advanced art of tantric lovemaking. Of course, any part of your union can be magical; however, the phrase technically refers to creating what you want through tantric union and practices. Sex magic involves several steps:

➤ Create a vision of what you want to have in your life (more love/abundance/ happiness). Lie relaxed with soft music playing. Hold your partner's hand if you like. Let your mind wander until an image of what you would like to manifest comes to you (more love, happiness, even world peace!).

➤ Imagine sexual energy fueling your idea. Draw that energy up through your body using this book (concentrating, imagining, feeling, and directing your energy to move).

➤ "Feel" your goal silently, or state it aloud to yourself or to your partner. Have your partner repeat it to you, to strengthen the energy of your desire. Think about that vision when you are in the highest states of pleasure, such as at the moment of orgasm.

➤ Cry out "yes, yes" together to heighten permission for the dream to come true.

Creating sex magic.

Sex magic is possible through tantric practices because you can visualize what you want while in a heightened state of bliss, making it more likely that this will happen. This is based on a valid scientific theory that the brain does not know the difference between what is imagined and what is real; therefore, the more you imagine something desirable as happening, the more you condition your mind and body to move toward that reality.

You can do sex magic by yourself through the steps previously described. If you have a partner, you can take turns doing sex magic individually, or do it together (having a joint image of what you want).

Ecstasy Essentials

The Art of Sexual Magic (Tarcher/Putnam, 1996) by recognized tantra teacher Margot Anand includes lots of ways you can create sex magic in your relationship.

Toys for Tantric Play

In tantric sex, the best toy is your imagination, and every part of your body and soul and that of your beloved. However, because tantric sex is about fun, you also can use many real toys. Tantric sex toys have special requirements different from just any sex toys or love aids:

➤ They should facilitate the process of cycling your energy through your chakra centers.

➤ They should encourage sensuality more than sexuality.

➤ They should never distract you from the real focus of your attention—your energy exchange with your beloved.

➤ They should help you have greater pleasure and joy and hopefully contribute to your physical health.

➤ They should bring you increased calmness or excitement as desired.

Blocks to Bliss

Sex toys can carry bacteria unless you keep them clean. Tantrika Taylor Lamborne recommends disinfecting sex toys after use by wiping them with a solution of nutribiotic grapefruit seed extract (available at health food stores) and water (use 10 drops of extract to one cup of water).

Some suggestions of sex toys include the following:

➤ **Crystal onyx massage egg**   Stronger, healthier vaginal muscles add more erotic sensation and sexual energy. The egg is meant to help develop these muscles, like doing isotonic exercises. The woman inserts the egg inside her vagina and pulses against it. "Such skills help a woman master the ancient eastern art of *pompoir* (also called *playing the flute*), in which she stimulates the lingam just by her vaginal muscle movements," says Taylor Lamborne, creator of a Web site that sells such tantric items at www.LoveNectar.com.

➤ **Crystal Wand**   This 10-inch curved crystal, clear Lucite wand can be inserted in any sexual opening. It has different sizes at each end to stimulate either the woman's G spot or man's G spot (prostate). The S shape makes it easier to reach these areas than with your own fingers.

The Crystal Wand.

➤ **Natural rabbit fur massage mitt**   This soft mitt fits over your hand and feels soft as you glide it over a beloved's or your own skin.

➤ **Lubricants**   These applications make sexual activities—from touching to intercourse—flow more easily, and can be crucial for women with problems lubricating (from lack of stimulation or hormonal troubles). Also, gliding motions prevent damage to delicate tissues during prolonged sexual contact. Perhaps even more important, they feel good and are just plain fun!

Lubricants should glide easily, without feeling gummy or sticky. They should also be made out of natural ingredients. For example, some preparations of glycerin are made from 100 percent pure vegetables, are water-soluble and edible. Choose a lubricant that tastes good, too. Never use anything that disrupts the chemical balance of the vagina (such as baby oil or cooking oil, which some people reach for in a rush or when unprepared). Always use a natural substance.

➤ **Videos**   As tantric sex becomes more popular, there are more videos on its practices. These are chockfull of helpful tips (more about these in Chapter 18, "Sex, Song, and Videotape").

➤ **Vibrators**   Vibrators come in all colors, sizes, and shapes, just like real genitalia. Rather than be threatened that you are not providing enough stimulation for your partner if he or she wants to use a vibrator, see it as a help to spark for pleasure for both of you. The constant motion can be stimulating for men as well as women, on all areas of the body.

Blocks to Bliss

Be careful when applying a vibrator to tender areas. Ask your partner what pressure he or she likes. Never insert vibrators powered by electricity inside the body.

Gifts from the Heart

A tantric sex gift is anything that comes from your heart that you give to your partner. All the toys in the previous section could also be gifts. The following are other suggestions. Check Appendix C for ordering information for such items.

➤ **God or goddess wear**   Choose clothing that is loose-fitting and comfortable. It should be made of natural fibers, such as cotton or silk, but velvets and beaded scarves also are popular. Pareos or sarongs are also pop2ular, especially for men; these are large rectangles of material that can be wrapped around the body in various ways.

➤ **Mandalas, thangkas, mantra designs, and paintings**   These are artwork of symbols and designs depicting sacred scenes of divinities, nature, or geometric forms meant for meditation, as described in Chapter 3.

➤ **God and goddess figurines and statues**   Many gift shops that specialize in Nepalese and Eastern artifacts offer these.

➤ **Books or videos on tantric sex**   These can be instructional as well as stimulating. I particularly like the ones that add imagery of historical erotic art, like the book *Forbidden Art* by Miss Naomi, or the video *Hot Sex in Erotic Art* from Access Instructional Media.

➤ **Adornments such as earrings, necklaces, or bracelets that evoke tantric sex or that have the yin yang symbol**   In tantric sex men also wear jewelry as adornments and symbols of power, just as they did in ancient times. These include rings, bracelets, necklaces, and even earrings. Tantric adornments also include *bindis* (beaded designs that are affixed to the third eye), toe rings, and beaded straps that fit around the second toe and around the heel.

➤ **A can of Kama Sutra body dust** Smell is a powerful sense in attraction, and this powder smells wonderful!

➤ **Pleasure promise coupons** These are pieces of paper printed with statements of what you will do for your partner; for example, I will give you a massage, do a chore for you, take you to a romantic dinner, please you in any way you want for an hour. You can make any pledge that strikes your fancy. These coupons are available in stores, or in my book *The Complete Idiot's Guide to a Healthy Relationship* (Alpha, 2001), or you can make up your own.

Where to Find Tantric Love Toys and Gifts

Of course, there are sex shops that might carry some of the toys that fit the criteria for tantric sex practice; however, there are also vendors who specialize in such aids. You can find them at…

➤ Web sites for tantra teachers

➤ Resources listed in Appendixes B and C; for example, Eve's Garden, a pleasure shop geared toward women, which maintains a respectful attitude toward women and sex in general

➤ Recommendations from friends who practice tantra or tantra teachers

➤ Tantra workshops, where there are usually tables of tantra-oriented items

---

The Least You Need to Know

➤ Tantric sex practices are meant for your pleasure and joy; you deserve it.

➤ Be creative about what you do. Let your imagination go, sense your energy, and let yourself follow your feelings.

➤ The best sex toy is your own body and that of your partner, but if you purchase a sex toy make sure it's safe and respectful.

➤ Give gifts to each other to increase your fun and pleasure.

Chapter 16

Advanced Tantric Lovemaking Techniques

In This Chapter

➤ What makes a tantric technique advanced?

➤ Examples of advanced tantric lovemaking rituals

➤ Magical love rituals

➤ Advanced white tantra poses

➤ Aids for advanced tantric use

Now that you've mastered the basics, had a wonderful time on his and her "best nights ever," and discovered some new ways to play together, I am sure you are curious about what could come next. There are endless levels of training and practices in this tradition, as in many other paths.

In this chapter I will give you a taste of some advanced practices—to take you deeper into sacred love and the wonders of expanded consciousness.

What Makes a Practice "Advanced"?

It takes time and practice to become proficient at any skill, and tantra is no exception. Because moving energy in tantra is a powerful force, you need to respect the process and not rush. But once you've mastered the practices as I have described them in these chapters, you'll be ready for the more advanced exercises. These are characterized by the fact that they …

➤ Use breathing patterns in more complicated ways.

➤ Generate more intense energy.

➤ Coordinate more steps.

➤ Clear deeper emotions.

➤ Direct energy in more diverse ways.

Be prepared for powerful rushes of energy that will catapult you to higher states of consciousness.

A Slow Ride into Timeless Love

Some advanced practices might seem simple on the surface, but truly are more advanced because more skills are required to move energy in a new way. *Relaxing into ecstasy* is an advanced practice that California tantra teachers Steve and Lokita Carter discovered to be so effective in their lovemaking, they adapted it for students in their various classes at the Institute for Ecstatic Living. It is advanced in that it requires extreme sensitivity to very subtle movements of energy that elicit intense sensations. "We call it a 'slow ride into timeless love,'" explains Steve, "because it includes *micro movements,* where the partners connect with tiny motions that are no more than half an inch, yet the results are exceptionally intense."

Here are the five steps:

1. **Ritual**   Start your lovemaking session by telling each other what you love most about each other at this moment. This creates a feeling of safety and trust.

2. **Communication**   Agree to try something different. Tell each other how you feel about it and what you are afraid of.

3. **The experience**   Do whatever you enjoy to get aroused. Once you are inside each other and have made love for some time, slow down. Resist the temptation to have an orgasm. Melt into each other and move your pelvis ever so slightly toward your partner's pelvis (in micro movements) while looking into each other's eyes.

   When you both feel ready to do something different, contract your pelvic floor muscles a few times. Do this at the same time or alternately. Focus on these small movements, allowing the awareness to increase sensitivity in your genitals. Play with the speed and frequency. Tell each other what it feels like.

   After a while, come to stillness. With open eyes let your breathing and the contractions of your pelvic floor muscles carry you into timelessness.

   Include the micro movements, stillness, and contractions in your lovemaking. Move faster, and then return to the stillness. This creates a slow wave of ecstasy.

4. **Sharing**   After you have made love like this, share your feelings:

   ➤ Did you feel relaxed?

   ➤ Were you able to feel your ecstasy in the relaxation?

   ➤ Did you feel connected to each other?

   ➤ Is this something you would like to try again?

5. **Closing**   End your lovemaking by thanking each other and bowing to each other.

The Magical Maithuna Love Ritual

In Parts 2 and 3 of this book, I introduced you to various rituals in tantric lovemaking. The *maithuna* is the most elaborate of these rituals and includes many steps. At one of Bodhi Avinasha's teacher-training courses for Tantrika International, we observed Seattle tantra teachers Kirby Jacobson and his co-teacher Radhika demonstrate this ritual. "It is to be done with reverence," instructs Jacobson. "The power of the Maithuna is revealed when the couple believes that each movement is a dedication to themselves, each other, and the universe."

The sequence of the ceremony includes these steps:

1. Prepare the lovemaking space in the shape of a yantra (magical geometric design).

2. Purify and seal off the space with blessings in each direction (including the corners of the room, ceiling, and floor).

3. Prepare special powders, light lamps with special igniting substances (called "ghee butter"), make offerings to chosen deities, and massage each other's chakras (energy centers).

4. Use hand movements and mantra chants to invoke and connect energy between the partners.

This ritual could go on for days!

> **Tantra Tutorial**
>
> **Maithuna** refers to the coming together of god and goddess with the acknowledgement that everything is sacred, from food to acts of orgiastic proportions. The ritual is an elaborate performance using specific items as part of the sacred ceremony.

The Snake Dance

When you really follow your intense energy, it can feel like a snake coming up your spine. *Kundalini* is the name of the famous serpent power that lies coiled up at the base of the spine. Once awakened (through your practices), this energy travels up the spine. Its journey can take you into new intense sensations, if you go with its flow!

Intense power surges of this hot kundalini energy rushing up the spine can literally make you shake—with fear, fury, enthusiasm, or ecstasy. Lack of preparation can lead to a panic called a *spiritual emergency,* but with responsible practice you can follow the inner snake to where it takes you, ending up dancing primitively, seeing visions, feeling outside your body, or experiencing inner knowing.

Following the kundalini rising for an ecstatic experience.

If you feel uncomfortable, read the book *Spiritual Emergency: When Personal Transformation Becomes a Crisis* by Stanislav Grof and Kristina Grof (Tarcher/Putnam, 1989), or call the Spiritual Emergence Network for a referral.

Advanced White Tantra Twosome

Physical practices (yogic poses to move energy) complement your sexual practices, as I discussed in Chapters 5, "Prep Your Body Temple of Love," and 14, "Getting Fit Together for Tantric Sex." As you progress, these poses can become more advanced.

Here are two exceptional advanced poses, developed by New York City tantrika Carla Tarantola:

➤ **Earth to sky salute** Stand facing your partner with enough space between you so you can bend down without bumping into one another. Take a few breaths to center and connect, reach behind you and clasp your own hands behind your back with index fingers pointed out. Bend over slowly (one vertebrae at a time), dropping your head down as far as you can go comfortably and touching the back of your head. Lift your arms behind you as straight as possible with index finger pointing up to the sky. Breathe and feel the energy of the two of you creating a channel connecting earth with sky (Shakti with Shiva). Lower your arms and come up slowly taking care with your spine, and do a backward bend to balance. Repeat three times, then do the following pose.

Dr. Judy's TantrAdvice

Remember that every pose has a purpose in how you move your energy. Also, always do preliminary poses in a routine, to prepare your body for more physically demanding ones.

➤ **Tantric twosome trestle**   Sit in front of each other with your legs outstretched and slightly bent, with the soles of your feet pressed together. Reach forward to clasp your partner's hands and interlock your fingers. Keeping your body straight, raise your legs at the same time, keeping them between your straightened arms (or outside your arms if that's easier). Do five full synchronized breaths together while looking in each other's eyes. Notice how you maintain your balance in this position and how that is reflected in your relationship.

Earth to sky salute.

Tantric twosome trestle.

Advanced Passion Positions and Acts

The *Kama Sutra* contains many positions and acts, many of which are shown on various videotapes that I'll tell you about in Chapter 18, "Sex, Song, and Videotape." But tantra teachers and students often come up with new possibilities from their own practice; you can do this, too. The only prerequisites to be sure these fit the tantric tradition is that they …

➤ Connect chakras (energy centers) to move energy.

➤ Include breathing patterns.

➤ Are part of a practice rather than an isolated act.

➤ Honor one another.

➤ Use the intense energy for a higher purpose.

Dr. Judy's TantrAdvice

To come down to earth and re-enter the real world after such intense energetic experiences you must do closing ceremonies, such as releasing spirits, acknowledging your partner, or saying a closing prayer.

A sexual position is not just an acrobatic achievement. In tantra, it is the passageway to divinity, allowing you to be and see the god/goddess. Once you can arouse a forceful pool of kundalini energy at the base of your spine, intensifying it in your sex center and then circulating it through your body, you can then send it rising out through the top of your head in a unified spiral together, reaching higher states of consciousness, to the point where you sense an expansion of this unified mass merging with the universe in outer space. There are no boundaries. You have become divine and merged with the divine to know true and intense god/goddess consciousness.

Enflaming of the Dragon Goddess

I love this position because it invokes the dragon, the Chinese symbol of heavenly power conferred on man. The two steps allow the fulfillment of the ultimate purpose of positions: to connect with divine energy in yourself, your partnership, and all that is. "This position and practice just came through me, and I knew my advanced students would love it," explained New York tantra teacher Carla Tarantola, who discovered this technique while making love with her soul mate and beloved John.

Lie on the bed or floor on your back (head on a pillow for comfort and eye contact) with your feet to each other's head, base chakra pressed against each other, and thighs interlocking. Carla explains, "In this position, John kisses my feet, an act that opens up my appreciation and energy so much that I want to do anything to please him. I hold his lingam in my hands, and guide it to make circles at the entrance of my yoni. Then we make small circles with our groins pressed together, to move the energy."

Enflaming the dragon, first position, connects sex centers.

Carla continues, "We help each other up into the classical yab yum sitting position, with his lingam still in my yoni, so the penetration is deeper. We undulate while we do the fire breath and then draw the energy up into our hearts and the back of the brain. Then we hold the breath, press our heart centers together, and visualize spirals of energy and fire connecting us and lifting us higher, while our hearts expand and merge together. Exhaling, we make the sound 'ahhh' and allow the energy to come back into the genitals, visualizing a golden energy coming down from the universe, flushing and enlivening all the cells of our physical body. In this way, we experience a nonejaculatory body orgasm. Then we go into a meditative state and repeat the building-up process three times before John decides to go into an ejaculation."

Enflaming the dragon, second position, connects heart centers and visualizes divine connection.

The Kabazzah

It's no wonder that the sexual skills of the Japanese geishas gained such mystique with American GIs during World War II. The women practiced an ancient sexual art that allowed the man to lie blissfully passive. The secret: the *kabazzah,* in which the woman mounted the man and only moved her internal muscles to bring him to climax.

The Full Stop

In the *full stop* technique, you freeze in a position in the middle of lovemaking (take turns giving the signal) for one minute—becoming aware of thoughts and sensations instead of ongoing compulsive activity. The Easterners believe that only with such valleys can the peaks be higher.

The Two New Erogenous Zones

The advanced tantra man knows the full art of polishing the pearl (pleasuring the woman's clitoris). One new and effective way to do this is the *Kivin method*, in which the man stimulates the woman orally on two erogenous points on her genitals to bring her to orgasm within three to eight minutes. The method requires pressing one point (between the vaginal and anal openings) while applying pressure with the tongue on other points located on each side of the clitoral shaft. A videotape (www.kivinprod. com) demonstrates exactly how it's done, with an introduction by California sexologist Patti Britton.

Tongue Fu

In a Taoist practice, a woman strengthens her tongue by first pushing against an orange or a grapefruit. She also strengthens her vaginal muscles by attaching weights to hold. These practices are described by Mantak Chia in his book, *Tao for Women: Cultivating Female Sexual Energy*. Similar routines are described in Chia's corollary book for men, *Taoist Secrets of Love: Cultivating Male Sexual Energy*.

Ecstasy Essentials

The middle finger has more direct, intense energy than the fourth finger or pinky. Be conscious of which you use with yourself or your partner. Touch each other with different fingers, in different combinations, on different body parts. Feel the sensations of each.

Mudras

Mudras are positions of the arms, hands, and fingers that connect the energy centers. There are many combinations of these; they can be placed externally on many areas of the body, on outside points correlating with inner points, and even reached internally. Every finger that is used communicates a different energy, which you must learn to become skilled in sending energy patterns to your partner.

Advanced Visualization in Tantric Sex

Imagery sets pictures in the mind that the brain cannot distinguish from reality, so you are likely to act on these. Taking advantage of this, sexual visions can inspire physical actions that lead to blissful union when practiced in a meditative, disciplined way. Here are two examples:

➤ **The tantric triangle** Visualize yourself as a male god-like being with a triangle of white light at your third eye that points downward (the symbol of the female yoni), with the lower angle pointing toward the back of the tongue. The angles become the three doors of liberation, opening to the wisdom of great bliss.

➤ **The Shakti shine** Visualize the goddess Shakti with blue lights radiating from her body that enter your body through your genitals and melt a blue radiance throughout your body.

Advanced Tuning In: You, Too, Can Be Psychic!

People in love who are having great sex seem to really know what each other wants and needs. Everybody dreams of being so tuned in to a lover that you can read each other's minds—so you don't have to say what you want because your partner just does or says the perfect thing. Like Nicole, who was ecstatic when her new lover was walking in the street with her and blurted out, "I'm so proud to be with you." It was exactly what she always dreamed of hearing. Or like Pam, whose beloved Jim whispered huskily in her ear during intercourse, "You're the most beautiful woman I've ever known. I'll never leave you." That was heaven to her ears.

The desire to be known so well is one of the reasons people go to psychics, but the truth is, you can tap into your own intuitive powers. If you get calm and focus, you will be surprised at what you can accurately sense about your partner. Doing this deliberately is called a *psychic* (or *energy*) *reading*. I have been to many tantric weekends and massage workshops in which we did a psychic reading of each other. Everyone is always so surprised at how it is possible (after several preliminary exercises) to read another person's energy (without really knowing him or her before) just by putting our hands close to the other person's body. Once when I did this exercise with another tantrika, I felt sparks jumping out at my hands at even two feet away, telling me how much energy (and power) she has!

Do a simple energy reading with your partner. Sit in yab yum and breathe together for a few minutes to get attuned. With eyes closed, let your hands go to a certain place on your partner's body and say aloud whatever comes to your mind. Don't censor your words! You'll be surprised how accurate you can be. Some couples feel so in tune after this, they feel like being closer and making love. If possible, give your partner what you read that he or she needs. For example, Fred was reading his partner June and heard her (energy) saying, "I need you to hold me tightly like I've always wanted."

Eight Steps in Deity Yoga

In Chapter 4, "Awaken and Worship the God and Goddess in You," I introduced you to many gods and goddesses, and promised to tell you about techniques to bring their energies into you. *Deity yoga* does this. In this exercise, you can use your favorite gods and goddesses from that chapter—the ones you most identify with—or experiment with others. Follow these eight steps to actualize a particular deity to achieve a certain state of being within you:

1. Set intention. Meditating on any deity should always be toward the goals of wisdom, compassion, and service to others.

2. Sit comfortably in front of a picture or statue and focus. Relax, close your eyes, and let the image appear in your mind's eye. After a while, the image will become a radiant being of light. You will feel inspired and blessed; realizations will come to you.

3. Request the deity bestow blessings on you.

4. Picture the deity as light energy entering your head, allowing it to descend and then rise through your spine, dissolving into your heart. Feel the essence of the deity becoming one with you.

5. Focus on yantras, geometric forms that are associated with the deity and trigger desired energies.

6. Look at the geometrically shaped mandalas with the deity's image that triggers certain imagery or emotions.

7. Listen to music invoking such energies. (See listings in Appendix C, "Tantric Tools," for some ideas.) Choose CDs whose titles imply the energy, such as *Ecstatica* or *Trance*.

8. Perform mantras, prayers, and ceremonies associated with the deity and characteristics you desire. These can be simple or very elaborate.

The practice of "deity yoga," meditating on the divine to realize a desired goal.

Base Chakra Pleasuring

I will talk more about base chakra stimulation in the next chapter with regard to male sexual healing, but such exploration can also be a source of pleasure. Be aware that many partners will cringe at the thought, which can arouse shame, embarrassment,

Tantra Tutorial

While you can learn about tantra and deities on your own, such study is best under the guidance of an experienced teacher.

and fears (especially for heterosexual men, who may associate the act with being gay). Yet the presence of many nerve endings around the anal opening can lead to arousal. Always respect your partner's boundaries, go slowly, and follow your partner's cues about when, where and how to touch.

As I described in Chapter 3, "Spinning Your Wheels and Breathing to Ecstasy," the base chakra is associated with issues of safety and security; therefore moving energy from the base center to the heart, throat, or sex centers brings more solidity to expression in that area. Bring the energy there by sweeping your hand in that direction, and then holding a hand on each of two areas to connect them.

Base chakra stimulation.

Advanced Aids in Tantric Play

Just like toys are rated for use with age groups, sex aids are appropriate for different levels of lovers in their practices. Although there is no rating system, trust your intuition about which ones could be above your head (restraints, anal beads) for the time being. By all means surprise your partner with new sexual pleasures, but when it comes to some activities you know might be a stretch, discuss readiness together.

One such aid is the *Pearls of Delight,* a long strand of washable pearls (costing about $12.95), that can be worn around the neck but also inserted inside the vaginal or anal canal and pulled out slowly. "Surprise your partner," says Taylor Lamborne, a California tantrika who sells them. "Wear them when you go out for dinner as a signal of what's in store for your love play when you come home that evening."

Pearls of Delight.

Entering the Time and Space Machine

When you are really adept at tantric practice—specifically meditation—you can enter deep states of consciousness that take you across time and space. Some people can do this naturally, but most need a teacher as a guide. Attend a workshop on past lives or astral projection.

Past Lives Connected to God/Goddess

The idea of past lives might be alien to you, in which case some of these principles may be hard to accept. Put aside your skepticism for a moment and entertain possibilities of potential value for your personal transformation and exploration of sacred loving.

The principle of past lives is intrinsic, although not essential, to tantric loving because the gods and goddesses come from a tradition that is traced back to the beginnings of time. Becoming one with the lineage of all these deities helps you to unite with all that is, all that has come before, and all that will be. This merging of time helps you reach the state of bliss within yourself and the realization that you are complete without any partner.

Astral Projection

Advanced tantric sex partners can send their love and sensual connections through the airwaves, across space as well as time. This transmission is obviously useful for long-distance lovers, forced to be in different locations because of jobs, schooling, or other reasons. People who don't think they have psychic powers can find themselves able to do such projected communication—by deep concentration and "sensing" the other person.

Ecstasy Essentials

Some advanced practices require supervision or guidance of a teacher; seek that out freely.

The Least You Need to Know

➤ As you master the preliminaries as presented in this book, there are ever-increasing levels of information and practices to study.

➤ Practices become more advanced when they add more elements simultaneously, and intensify the energy cycled and the emotions that could be triggered.

➤ Advanced practices include rituals; white tantra poses, positions, and visualization; and connecting across time and space through exploring past lives.

➤ Allow yourself to come up with new practices and variations. Trust yourself to experience new dimensions.

Chapter 17

Sexual Healing to Set You Free

In This Chapter

➤ The power of sexual healing

➤ Who can be a healer?

➤ What happens during a healing?

➤ Guidelines for the healer and the receiver

➤ Healing the pain of abuse

➤ The effects for the healer and the healed

Until this point I have concentrated on telling you about practices that bring pleasure. Yes, bliss and ecstasy are the goals and rewards of your tantric path. However, along the way, emotions will arise. Sexual energy is powerful and any such power will trigger strong emotions. This could be the very reason people resist the practices—the emotions become too much to handle. The emotional release exercises discussed in Chapter 9, "Breaking Through Blocks to Bliss," can help you handle these—but you might want to set aside some time specifically to handle these feelings.

Specific sessions to free your expression from past pain are called *sexual healings*. In this chapter I will tell you about sexual healings, how they happen, and what you need to know to participate in this most powerful experience.

What Is a Sexual Healing?

Everyone has been hurt emotionally in some way by a relationship. These hurts unintentionally get stored in the first chakra (where feelings of insecurity and lack of safety are lodged) and in the second chakra (where feelings of shame and inhibitions are stored) in men as well as women, blocking the free flow of energy, emotions, and joy. The blockages can come from past painful relationships; abusive sex; physical conditions (such as a hysterectomy); emotionally charged experiences (abortion, miscarriages); shame and embarrassment; body hate; intimacy and commitment fears; religious prohibitions; or parental punishments.

A sexual healing involves specific rituals to assist someone through an experience to clear these pains or blocks locked in the body. It is important to distinguish these healing sessions from the nights of pleasure we discussed in Chapter 10, "Giving Her the Best Nights Ever," and Chapter 11, "Giving Him the Best Nights Ever." The healing sessions entail more ritualized interaction in which the healer and receiver have very distinct roles, with the focus on uncovering and releasing any blocks in the receiver's sexual responses.

Ecstasy Essentials

Love has healing power. At a recent conference of scientists, visionaries and healers (called the Prophets Conference), scholar Gregg Braden reported on research that showed that the human expression of love actually changed the molecules of water. This proves that emotions can change surrounding matter. Find out more at www. greatmystery.org.

When you heal your own past wounds in this way, your newfound wholeness extends beyond just you. In fact, you are healing all beings on this planet. And when you are the healer, you represent many divine beings who have healing powers. Your actions help heal everyone suffering from similar pain and heighten joy for everyone.

Both men and women can benefit from various techniques used for sexual healing. Hawaii-based tantra and yoga master Charles Muir is a pioneer in developing these healing techniques for men and women and has taught them to many trainees and thousands of couples.

Who Can Be a Healer?

There are two types of healers. Your loving partner is a healer every day, soothing a beloved from the stresses of the day. However, taking on the serious role of healer in this sense requires some training. Muir has proven that couples can learn to do this for each other in a one-weekend course. "Men can learn in one weekend how to free their goddess to be expressive and enjoy sex, after years of fears that have been locked in her vagina from past mistreatment by men," says Muir. "And women can learn how to heal their god from any past pains he may have suffered from her or other experiences in his past."

Other healers are highly trained dakas and tantrikas, some of whom have completed Muir's extensive training course. (The course in his methods requires a three-year commitment of two ten-day retreats, assisting at various introductory weekends, and producing case reports.) Some women and men who decide to be sexual healers and offer services to the public advertise on the Internet. Some do hands-on healing; using phrases such as "goddess spot massage" or "male sacred spot massage."

Blocks to Bliss

Just as there are good or bad therapists, and licensed or untrained health practitioners of all kinds, there are responsible or untrained sexual healers. Be careful when choosing someone to whom you are entrusting the most vulnerable places in your body and soul. Use the same criteria as in selecting a good therapist. Do research on the Internet at tantra sites, and network with people interested in tantra). Ask respected tantra teachers for referrals. Interview healers intensely about their experience and check references.

What Happens in a Healing

To set the stage for a healing, the healer should create a comfortable space. Spread out a pretty sheet or soft blanket. Light candles. Ensure privacy and confidentiality (for example, say, "I give my word that I honor your sharing with complete confidentiality. Whatever happens stays between us.")

Start with a ceremony that sets both the healer's and the receiver's intentions. Hold hands and speak a dedication. The healer might include words such as, "I devote myself to you and am here for you with the best of love and intention for you to have the most healing experience you choose." The receiver might say, "I thank you for being here for my healing and intend to be fully present for myself in whatever comes up so that I can be healed. In doing so I will heal others who are similarly suffering."

Healing the Goddess

Invite your goddess to lie down and relax. Ask permission to give her a massage. A healing massage has a different intention from the relaxing and pleasuring massage. Massage her thighs and entire pelvic and stomach area. When she is ready, put your hand over her pubic area and stay still. Put your other hand over her heart (if you feel

Ecstasy Essentials

As tantra teacher and master body worker Marci Javril describes, "Tantric touch in sexual healing massage is a special way to approach intimacy and genital contact. Complete compassion and attention gives the receiver a chance to really feel into the emotions held in the physical body and to release tension, frustrations, and anger that could have been stored for years."

she needs to feel your love) or over her power center (if you feel she needs to feel stronger). Make small movements around her pubic area.

Releasing painful emotions opens the potential to receive more pleasure, in more places, for longer periods of time. As a result, even though the sexual healing ceremony is deliberately not meant to arouse, it can actually cause heightened arousal from relaxation, trust, and release. Be aware of the receiver's potential escapes from intense emotions, such as ending the session, switching attention to the healer, or changing the energy to lovemaking. Gently invite the receiver to return to the moment and emotion that was happening before the withdrawal.

Encourage her to focus on the sensations and not to worry if there is burning or numbness (typical signs of emotional pain that is being brought to awareness), and encourage her to stay with any feelings that may arise. If strong feelings emerge (yells, screams, thrashing), tell her you are there for her and let her express them. Reassure her she is safe and loved.

When the goddess says that she is ready to go further, ask permission to enter her sacred space. Go slowly and move your fingers gently as a particular spot might trigger a reaction. Keep reminding her to breathe, as the breath is crucial to the expression of the motions, and ultimately of pleasure at the other end of the pain.

The yoni massage.

Each healing session can be different. One time the receiver might be calm and even joyous; another time deep pain and anguish can be triggered. Never consider any reaction bad or dysfunctional.

When the Goddess Love Liquid Flows

If the woman is feeling pleasure during her healing session, you can accelerate the stimulation of her internal vaginal canal and stimulate the G (goddess) area, as discussed in Chapter 10. (This stimulation might result in a female ejaculation.)

> **Tantra Tutorial**
>
> For more information, watch the videos listed in Appendix C, "Tantric Tools," about G spot massage and female ejaculation. Listen to Muir's tape about "Freeing the Female Orgasm."

Healing the God

Men can achieve the same sexual and emotional healing as women. Although we expect that men more often than women are the cause of hurt in relationships, men, too, suffer the pain of sexual rejection or emotional upset that needs healing. Sexual healing also helps the man learn to appreciate intimacy rather than just genital sex, and to become more open. Female partners are very appreciative, and touched, by a man opening up, exposing emotion, and demonstrating trust in her by doing so.

The man's healing can center around his base chakra as well as his sex chakra. Muir's healing techniques for the Shiva involve stimulation of the prostate gland (called one of the male G spots, a hot spot for arousal that is similar to the woman's G spot). Some men may be uncomfortable with this, and some critics challenge the process, but Muir has many examples of men who found it not only helpful to heal hurts, but also to release pleasure and increase their capacity to love.

Overcoming the Two Major Hurdles in His Healing

During the session, the woman prepares the setting and herself as healer in the same way described earlier for healing the goddess. There are two major hurdles to overcome in men's healing:

➤ The man has to surrender. Lying on his back in the more traditional female position makes him feel additionally vulnerable. This is more difficult for men than it is for women, as men generally much prefer to be in control. Continually encourage him: Say, "Allow yourself to surrender" or "I know this is difficult for you."

➤ As I mentioned in Chapter 11, most men have a great deal of fear and discomfort about being touched or entered in their anal area. This is because being touched there might arouse homosexual anxieties (although there are some heterosexual men who have discovered great pleasure in stimulation in the base center). To overcome this resistance, the healer must go very slowly, rest a finger gently at that area, and wait for him to invite her inside.

Instructions for His Healer

His healing, like hers, should always start with a body massage to relax him. After the general massage, pleasure his lingam using the techniques described in Chapter 11. Reassure him that he need not have an erection, but should just lay back and enjoy it. Vary the strokes, using those I've suggested or making up your own. Include pleasuring the testicles. Use all your body parts (fingers, side of the arm, breasts).

As Charles Muir instructs, move the energy from his lingam to his base chakra by stroking the lingam and gliding your hand to his base. Rest an oiled finger at his opening waiting for him to push against it to show his readiness. Ask, "May I enter you?" Remind him to breathe and allow whatever feelings come up, and invite him to heal. Enter slowly, inviting him to tense and release his anal sphincter muscles against your finger.

Doing a male sexual healing.

STIMULATE THE PROSTATE
THROUGH THE ANUS

Ecstasy Essentials

There are four male G spots. The two external ones are the frenulum (knob-like protrusion on the underside of the penis where the tip meets the shaft) and perineum (space between the testicles and anal opening). The two internal ones are inside his anal canal in a slight indentation (reached by curling a finger toward the front wall in a come-hither action) and higher inside the anal canal (rubbing around or on the prostate gland). Just as with the woman, this sacred space can house past pains, memories of either real or imagined hurts, rejections, intrusions, or abuse.

Expect him to deny feeling anything. Or he may have strong emotional outbursts (as with the woman when she receives) that could include anger at you. Don't take these personally. Keep encouraging him to express whatever comes up. Keep reassuring him: "You're doing great," "I'm here for you." Go only as far and as long as he wants. You can reassure him of safety by breathing with him and reminding him to breathe; this is reassuring when he is deep in the process.

Blocks to Bliss

Don't interrupt a receiver's process by saying, "Don't worry about that," or "Don't cry," because that stops the process. Also be careful to not interrupt because you are frightened or threatened; only do so if you feel the person is in too much emotional distress to continue.

Healing the Pain of Abuse

Sexual healings can have dramatic effects in cases of abuse. Sadly, so many women have suffered from sexual abuse of one sort or another, causing them to feel violated or taken advantage of. For example, many women I have counseled have been extremely traumatized by past abusive experiences with men in which they feel they were pressured into having sex or performing a certain sex act—even without force—and afterward felt "used" and angry. These feelings build over time—even years—creating low self-esteem and distrust of men.

It is important to note, however, that men also have been sexually, physically, or emotionally abused. As a society we are just becoming sensitive to this; it can and does happen. One man I know, Carlton J. Buller, had the courage to write a book about his experiences of suffering from sexual abuse and the steps he has taken to recover, in *Stolen Innocence: The Autobiography of a Lost Soul* (Fair Weather Publications, 2001).

Tantra Tales

A sexual healing can be a powerful release that is like a miracle for a woman who has been abused. I have witnessed many such healings; for example, in one teacher training course, we observed Muir work with one woman who had been abused. He continually offered encouraging instructions, such as "breathe" and "stay with the feeling"; and used expert hand movements. She resisted at first, but then screamed as if she were re-experiencing the earlier trauma. As the feelings intensified, she appeared to be reliving a prior attack, but this time told her attacker off. This empowerment was essential to her healing. Afterward, her facial expression and body relaxed, and she began to express signs of pleasure—later reporting that she felt as if a huge block had been removed from her insides and from her soul.

Handling Emotions in a Healing

Of course emotions can come up naturally when you have sex! I have certainly heard enough stories from women or from their partners, in which the woman has cried hysterically during or after sex, much to both her and her partner's panic. Or she might break out in laughter, causing him to think, "Am I doing something funny? I didn't think so!" I always offer reassurance that these are natural reactions, from powerful pools of energy that are stimulated and being released in a big burst. Crying, I always explain, does not always mean present pain; as I mentioned in Chapter 10, it can be the result of release from pain, or the contrast between present loving and past hurt.

Blocks to Bliss

When sexual abuse is uncovered in a healing, further help should be arranged, by support groups (of others with similar experiences) and professional therapy to work through the trauma.

Rules for the Healer

Effective healing requires careful attunement to the person's energy. For this reason you need great skill to do a healing and should only perform one after you have been to a workshop with a qualified tantra teacher. There are certain conditions for the healing session to be effective for the receiver as well as the healer:

➤ Create a safe space physically. The receiver must be able to relax and feel safe. This starts from the simple provision of privacy and quiet (phones off the hook, locked doors) and extends to an energetic feeling that he or she can trust the receiver and let go in this setting.

➤ Beautify the space. A person feels more at ease when the setting is clean, peaceful, and lovely. Dim the lights or light some candles. Put flowers and other items that invoke natural elements around such as a bowl of water and some rocks (for earth energy).

➤ Take care of whatever you have to so you can be fully present at the moment. This means get clean yourself, make whatever phone calls you need to, or go to the bathroom, so that these things are not on your mind during the session. Ground yourself beforehand, so you are not in your own head, and can be aware of the receiver's needs. Be aware of whatever problems, conflicts, or needs you have (anger at your partner, frustration, being turned on) as these could influence your reactions to the receiver's process. Set these aside, so you don't bring them into the session and project onto your receiver.

Blocks to Bliss

A healer, like any therapist, must not use someone for his or her own sexual or emotional gratification or needs. This is both unethical and criminal.

➤ Set intentions. Verbalize to yourself what you want to have happen. Speaking your intentions makes them more likely to happen. Say, "I intend this session for (the receiver's) highest good, keeping my own needs out of it."

➤ Be respectful, especially of personal boundaries. Remember that you are always equal even if the receiver seems in pain now. Pay attention to how the receiver feels and what his or her needs and limits are, what is okay or not okay for you to say, do, or touch.

➤ Be empathic. This doesn't mean feeling pity; rather it means putting yourself in the receiver's place, as if you are inside his or her skin.

Dr. Judy's TantrAdvice

Be kind to yourself as the healer. If something is too much for you (the emotions are too high, for example), it is better to let the receiver know than to proceed and muddy the experience.

223

➤ Don't take anything that happens personally. The receiver might get upset about something between you that happened in real life, but usually these emotions can be traced to earlier traumas and feelings. Never defend, judge, correct, or criticize.

➤ Follow the receiver's energy. Of course you might have some techniques in mind, such as those I have introduced you to in this book, but follow what the receiver wants and needs. This means he or she is in control of what happens and when, not you.

Rules for the Receiver

There are equivalent requirements for the receiver as for the healer, as shown in the following list. This follows the tantric principle that both people are creating a circle of energy and are equal. The receiver is also healer and vice versa.

➤ **Commit to being present in the moment**   Avoid distractions and keep your mind focused on the here and now.

➤ **Respect yourself**   You're not a victim with a sexual dysfunction but a beautiful being who wants to be fully released of anything that holds you back from experiencing the full potential of your love.

➤ **Prepare your body**   Take a bath, brush your teeth. Dress up in something that makes you feel wonderful. Ground yourself to be in your body, not in your head with worries, anger, and disappointments.

➤ **Set your intention**   Verbalize to yourself what you want to have happen. Speaking your intentions makes them more likely to happen. Say, "I intend to relax during this time and allow myself to experience whatever happens for the highest good of myself, my healer, and all involved."

➤ **Set your boundaries**   Let the healer know what your limits are. Are there any parts of your body that you do not want touched? Any actions you do not want him or her to take?

➤ **Make requests**   Say what you want from the healer, accepting the healer's boundaries, too.

➤ **Appreciate the healer**   It is a big responsibility for someone to undertake a sexual healing for you; that deserves your gratitude.

At the End of a Session

After a powerful experience a person needs to be nurtured and held. Cover the receiver with a blanket, or better yet, ask if you can hold him or her, and how he or she would like to be held. A good position is a nurturing one, either spooning the person by laying against his or her body outline from the back, or lying over the receiver's chest area (because the heart is very open and vulnerable now).

A sexual healing is a powerful experience, whether you laugh, cry, or think nothing much happened. Much *did* happen—because a strong intention was set, and because you both directed intense energy in some way. Sometimes the effects might not be felt for days, weeks, or months later. Share what you experienced and ask for feedback if you want to, or be silent and allow the experience to be integrated into your being.

Comforting and caring after a healing.

Be kind to yourself after a healing, recognizing that you have been through a powerful time. Don't just jump up and go about your business. Instead,

➤ Take time to allow the experience to sink in and be absorbed into your being. Stay still, lying in bed quietly. Breathe naturally. Let your mind and body rest.

➤ Drink water. Even if your body didn't move much to the outside world, it moved a great deal internally. As after any intense physical exercise, drink water to replenish your hydration.

➤ Take a shower or bath, as water soothes the soul and washes away some of the intensity of the emotions at that moment and helps you transition into your daily life.

Are Healings Effective?

There are no research studies that have been done to show the effects of healings (I did the first research on the effects of tantric sex trainings, which I'll talk about in Chapter 24, "Which Path Is Right for You?"). But many reports from men and women who have either been trained by Charles Muir, or couples who have taken his weekend workshops, attest to welcome and positive changes. Some even feel profoundly transformed.

Ecstasy Essentials

The process of facilitating someone else's healing can also heal the healer. Being energetically and empathetically connected to the other person, the healer may go through equally intense experiences. As a result, the healer might want or need to process whatever comes up for him or her. Decide on the best time to do this.

People often want to know whether there is ever a point at which they can say, "I am healed." It's the same question I have gotten from men and women who go through any other kind of therapy who want to know when it is over and they have been cured. Here are some ways to measure progress in sexual healings:

➤ The decreased intensity of emotional pain

➤ Increased feeling of trust

➤ Increased ability to experience joy

➤ More feelings of giving and receiving love

➤ Less physical pain upon touching various parts of the genitals

➤ More freedom in sexual expression with a partner

The experienced healer will also be able to tell whether there is reduced trauma in the genitals and more joy in the person in general. Muir has said that the healed goddess feels more moist inside, her body moves more freely, her vaginal tissue is softer, her vagina is more open and welcoming. The vaginal muscles become more elastic and responsive to the lingam, able to pulse and massage the lingam, expanding to receive him and contracting to embrace him. She will look younger, make more joyful noises, and even smile more!

Some people might require many sexual healing sessions, especially in cases in which there has been abuse of any kind, and particularly sexual abuse. Others might feel the need for only a few such sessions.

Some tantric partners request a sexual healing when they are feeling stressed and want to concentrate on releasing some inner blocks, even if they are not feeling a serious problem. You can request such a session at any time; remember it does not have to start with or lead to pain. Joy can motivate healing, too!

The Least You Need to Know

➤ A sexual healing is a powerful session that should be taken seriously; it can lead to intense results whereby stored-up or even fleeting pains can be released.

➤ If you do a sexual healing on your partner, it is best to have training from an experienced tantra teacher at a special workshop or private coaching.

➤ Appropriate conditions should be set for the healing session including creating safety and setting boundaries.

➤ The receiver of a healing has a responsibility to tell the healer what he or she wants and needs.

➤ People who advertise themselves as sexual healers should have extensive training by a professional; you should inquire about their background and experience.

Chapter 18

Sex, Song, and Videotape

In This Chapter

➤ The importance of music to set the mood

➤ CDs to spark your tantric thrills

➤ The new specialty of tantric videos that tantalize and teach

➤ Picking videos that are right for you

➤ Tantra on the silver screen, over the air, and on the Internet

Tantric lovemaking is about arousing the senses and includes even more exquisite attention to detail than other sex traditions. That means stimulating your aural as well as visual senses. These senses are important in your tantric practice, so in this chapter I give you some suggestions about which CDs and videos can help your love life (flip to Appendix C, "Tantric Tools," for details on how to order these materials). Some of the videos have great tips that even I enjoyed—and I thought I'd seen and heard it all!

Tantric Music

Music is key to setting the mood of your tantric sessions. In this chapter you'll learn how to use sound to spark your mood and some music that is the best for your practices. List your favorite music for lovemaking in the exercise in this section. Ask your partner to list his or her choices, too, and see if your choices overlap. Put your choices in order, as if you put them in a five-CD changer. Make sure to identify the mood the music evokes, as that will determine the tone of the lovemaking experience, and give you some clues about whether you and your partner will be on the same wavelength.

Music for Our Tantra Love Date

	Artist	CD Title	Specific Cut	Mood
My choices:				
1.				
2.				
3.				
4.				
5.				
Others:				
My partner's choices:				
1.				
2.				
3.				
4.				
5.				
Others:				

I have my favorite tantric music handy to load into my CD changer or to take with me when I lead tantric seminars or teach tantra at workshops or conferences. The mood that the music evokes varies, and so applies to different tantric practices; for example, meditation, massage, yoga, or dancing up a storm (as in the Shakti Shake or Dynamic Meditation described in this book). I have favorite artists in the hard rock, grunge, and even heavy metal style, and others like the classic Barry White that are undeniably meant for seduction. There's an increasing library of music that is specifically designed to be compatible with and facilitate tantric practices and moods. These are designed to open the heart and stir progress from sensuality and tenderness to tantalization and erotica to a crescendo of ecstasy and bliss.

My favorites include:

➤ *Spirit of Love* by Awakening Heart; it has a great song "Give Yourself to Love," which I play over and over at classes.

➤ *Journey Into Love* by Sophia, with another terrific song I play all the time in classes, "Heal Me With Your Love."

➤ *Sex 'n' Violets* by my good friend and brilliant Maui musician Jaiia Earthschild, whose song "Learning How to Love" is beautiful for intimate settings. Other songs speak of honoring the goddess or the environment.

➤ Raphael and Kutira's *Music to Disappear In,* which sweeps you into an ecstatic, quietly peaceful state. All their music invokes beautiful prayers and rituals, such as "The Calling" and "Prayer."

➤ Gabrielle Roth's *Waves* (although others of hers are equally exciting, such as *Bones, Trance, Totem,* or *Ritual*). Some of these have one of my favorite music styles, what I called "techno tribal trance." Roth's music takes you through various stages of activity and sensuality.

➤ Robert Frey's *Opening to Love,* a classic in the tantra world for heart-opening and inspiring healing, and personal growth (also used by midwives, churches, and hospice groups). Tracks 6 and 7 are especially valuable at the end of a tantric meditation or lovemaking session.

➤ *River of Romance* and *Worlds of Love* by Paul Ramana Das Silbey, with piano melodies that inspire a romantic mood. Silbey describes how he "channeled" the music, meaning that he tuned in to ecstatic states and let his fingers just flow over the keyboard.

What Makes Tantric Music Special?

Certain themes are emphasized in tantric music to facilitate your practices. These include choruses that create harmony between lovers, rhythms that are consistent with breathing patterns, hypnotic repetitions to still the mind, and tribal sounds to activate the body.

Tantric songs imply blessing the beloved, as in "Blessed One" written by Frey and Ashana Lobody:

> Love so divine, love so compelling
> Love with a radiance that outshines the sun
> In your divinity I see my reflection
> In your tender glance I find my heart
>
> Chorus: Woman and man there is no separation
> Goddess and God are one and the same
> Children and elder united together
> All rejoice at the sound of your name
>
> Breath of my life you shall always be with me
> Sweetest Beloved and joy of my heart
> Let me return to you all you have given
> This treasure unfathomed
> This gift of your love

231

Tantric songs also invoke honoring, as in this wonderful message from Jaiia Earthschild:

> I have to feel honored by you, That's what it comes down to.
> You speak to me with words of love but I feel incomplete.
> Words are fine—should be enough but I listen with my feet.
> To my feet love is a verb. It's what you do that will be heard.
> I have to feel honored by you, And when I feel honored by you
> Then I will unleash my passion for you.

Some tantra teachers have made tapes that talk you through a transformative tantric experience. Excellent ones in this genre include Raphael and Kutira's *Tantric Wave, Oceanic Tantra,* which guides you through the steps of ecstatic lovemaking from breathing, to sensuous touch, to heart opening and sex magic. Another is Robert Frey's *Inner Male/Inner Female,* a guided meditation that evokes male and female energies and brings them together in a sacred inner marriage in which integration, cooperation, and harmony are possible.

Tantra Tutorial

Not surprisingly, many magical tantric musicians come from the island of Maui on Hawaii, the land of gods and goddesses; and San Francisco, known for being experimental in all realms of exploring consciousness.

Dr. Judy's TantrAdvice

Make a special CD for your lovemaking. Take turns being the disc jockey during a lovemaking date. See what moods each of you likes to create.

Let the Music Flow Through You

Tantra is flow of energy. Performing tantric music, like tantric breathing techniques, is always attuned to the energy of the moment. The most gifted musicians know that they are in the flow, feeling the music from the inside. I knew that magical feeling when I played in a band; I loved playing the same sets over and over, and really getting into the flow of the music. Musicians "feel" the music. Keyboards virtuoso and daka Paul Ramana Das calls his music and performance "vibrational engorgement" and "tantromatic." "This means I attune myself to the piano as a feminine divine entity," says Paul. "I approach the keys as 'her' senses, and respond to the inner flow with appropriate melody, rhythm, flow, and passion." This is the energy with which he also "plays" on his beloved's body.

Sounding Chakras

In Chapter 2, "The Basics: Yes, Yin Yang, Yoni, and Yab Yum," I described the sounds associated with certain energy centers. Chanting these sounds evokes their energies: lam, vam, ram, ham, yam, ooo, oomm. Voice and sound healer Karin Schelde suggests using your voice on your partner's body to evoke energy. Put your mouth close to your partner's chest and make any sound at first to express yourself; then the "ahhh" sound of the heart chakra. It is fascinating in Karin's workshops to see how some people cry when this is done, feeling touched in their hearts. Her audiotape *Classic Sound Healing* takes you through the chakra sounds to achieve releases.

Ecstasy Essentials

Tantric music might sound "new age" but it's not always slow and melodic. In fact, some tantric exercises described in this book have chaotic rhythms and fast beats, intended to create faster breathing and activation of the body. The Osho dynamic meditation is a good example of a chaotic action, meant to energize, progressing to quiet meditation states. Gabrielle Roth's *Bones* CD is a good example of music cuts that progressively move through the stages of relaxation, arousal, and resolution in a typical lovemaking sequence.

Chants That Charge Your Connection

Have you ever heard a song that you can't get out of your head? When that happens you are no longer the singer; the song is singing itself. That is how chants work. As a form of mantra, a chant puts you in a meditative state by simple, repetitive, and memorable rhythms. Often about love but never sad like the blues, chanting assists you in the journey to joy and peace. Lyrics can sound almost like a tantra lesson, invoking god/goddess, grace and beauty, and choruses that hypnotically still the mind and move the body. Often they inspire tribal movements and are done at tantric gatherings, either in circle or free form.

Henry Marshall, master of chants in CDs such as *Mantras, Magical Songs of Power,* offers mantras for different purposes. The mantra to attract a partner evolved from Marshall's own problems finding a mate. Here's how it worked for him. First, he found himself chanting. "As I continued chanting, I began to feel that the mantra was sending a signal from all levels of my being to my soul mate, and I knew I'd find her." After considerable practice chanting and imagining sending the signal, he began to hear from friends about some woman who seemed to meet his expectations. With more chanting, their paths crossed repeatedly and they eventually got together for a date. "Success takes at least 40 days of this practice," Marshall explains, "but you must sing from the heart 108 times every day or else start from scratch." Marshall

Ecstasy Essentials

Tantric songwriter Michael Stillwater, who holds ChantWave Celebrations in San Francisco, describes using song and singing as "movement that carries awareness into the field of the ecstatic open heart, using song and chant as the vehicle."

also tells the story of a man who was estranged from his wife and began chanting. After a while, he had a vision of his wife as a beautiful goddess, and they got back together.

Mantras can also be sung to a beloved, to heighten the love energy. Tantra teacher Robert Frey writes songs that are sung at many tantra gatherings because the lyrics stimulate loving feelings and are meant to be sung to others (not to mention they're repeated over and over, making the words and tune easy to remember!):

> I behold the beauty in you, I know you are divine
> I am inspired by your Light, Shiva Shakti am I

Another beautiful chorus to sing to a beloved is this one from tantric musician Sophia:

> I open my heart to you
> and let your love flow through me.

Tantric Videos That Tantalize as Well as Teach

What you see is as important as what you hear in tantra. Instructional sex videos are becoming more and more popular in the market of sex-oriented videos. Tantric sex videos usually cost between $19.99 and $39.95, but they're worth it. You can watch them more than once, and even use them as background inspiration to your lovemaking without paying specific attention to it.

Tantra Tutorial

Reportedly more than 10,000 new titles in the adult video category were released last year, with rentals totaling more than $3 billion. Obviously there's an interest in seeing the subject of sex on celluloid.

Of all the hundreds of instructional sex videos I have seen over the years, most of those geared toward tantra are appealing and interesting. Some have captivating tantric soundtracks; gorgeous tantric imagery; and visual depictions of goddesses, colors, and special effects that evoke the visions of blending energies dissolving into bliss.

Research by recognized professional sex therapists has shown the value of *Video Assisted Therapy* (*VAT*) in helping couples get over inhibitions about sex, learn specific techniques to solve sexual issues (premature ejaculation, anorgasmia), and learn healthy sexual functioning. Toronto-based psychiatrist and sex therapist Frank Sommers has couples watch his videos at home or in another room, and then discuss what they saw.

Many tantric videos contain valuable lovemaking tips; for example, lessons on techniques for the man to delay ejaculation by contracting his PC muscles firmly and frequently.

Don't believe the myth that men are visual and women are not. Women can be just as sexually stimulated by what they see as men. That's why the tantric man dresses up for his goddess on her night and dances for her—to give her a visual delight. Research even shows that women are renting erotic films in increasing numbers.

Watch videos on your own or with a partner. Use the videos for enjoyment, or as a way to learn about yourself and your relationships. Here are some key questions to ask yourself:

➤ What scenes made me excited or anxious? What is going on in those scenes that relates to my life and relationships?

➤ What can I learn from the video? Would I feel comfortable acting out a scene I liked?

➤ How comfortable am I letting my spouse know that I am watching these videos? Can I talk to my partner about what we see?

The Kama Sutra *Series: Videos with a Tantric Twist*

Some companies specialize in sex videos and have a long history of such involvement. Several are even run by trained sex therapists who have spent years in the field, studying and teaching about sexuality. One of these is Dr. Michael Perry, the sexologist who did the original research on the G spot. Perry's company, Access Instructional Media, has a number of videos perfectly suited to show you what other people do sexually. These couples-friendly films have just the right mix of instruction and stimulating erotica. The *New Lovers Massage* video presents clear instruction on giving and receiving sensual pleasure. There's nudity but no explicit sexual activity. *Sexual Massage* is much more explicit, showing actual massage strokes for the erogenous zones including the G spot.

The *Kama Sutra* series, hosted by Perry and California sexologist Patti Britton, lives up to its name. It combines ancient secrets and modern techniques you're learning about in this book. The set includes *Kama Sutra, Tantra and Tao: The Ancient and Erotic Techniques for Incredible Sexual Pleasure, The Ecstasy of Exotic Sex: The Joys of Total Sexual Ecstasy*, and *Hot Sex in Erotic Art*. The latter is like taking a trip around the world reviewing sex

Ecstasy Essentials

Access Media's video *The Amazing G Spot and Female Ejaculation* shows an inside view, as never before seen on video, of the inside of the vagina during stimulation of the G spot and female ejaculation. Seeing the moist lining and coloring of the internal female organ provides a positive image that can help raise self-esteem.

235

in ancient and modern times, and bringing museums of erotic art to life. Perry quotes the Kama Sutra, saying, "You can have health, wealth, and spiritual well-being but without good sex you have nothing."

Honoring the Goddess on Video

You can read about how to honor the goddess, but seeing it happen with beautiful imagery can give you extra inspiration. Charles and Caroline Muir have made a beautiful film about tantra and female ejaculation. *The Secrets of Female Sexual Ecstasy* contains detailed instructions and is erotic and visually exquisite, with gorgeous Hawaiian scenery, original tantric soundtracks (including by Jaiia Earthschild), and original tantric artwork that is a sight to behold in itself. The Muirs narrate and demonstrate the processes of their workshops. The film is explicit but not X-rated, and shows sexual loving infused with intimacy and caring. The video includes secrets of erotic kissing and touch, techniques to achieve male ejaculatory control, and instructions about how to do the female sacred spot (G spot), massage, and achieve female ejaculation (a topic on which the Muirs are truly experts).

Other Videos

Initiate Secrets of Sex and Spirit: How to Worship Each Other in Bed shows lovemaking tips and demonstrations by mature couple Paul Ramana Das and Marilena. There is lots of useful information here, too; with the most powerful lessons being the use of music in lovemaking and humming on the yoni, as music is Ramana Das's expertise.

Ancient Secrets of Sexual Ecstasy for Modern Lovers includes comments from many of the top teachers, book authors, and workshop leaders in tantra, including the Muirs, the Ramsdales, Nik Douglas, and Margot Anand. Informational sound bites from these experts are interspersed with staged but sensuous scenes of five couples demonstrating tantric techniques such as breath control, ejaculatory control, goddess spot stimulation, lovemaking rituals, full-body orgasms, and simultaneous orgasm. Lori Star's expert demonstration of breathing techniques is very helpful (in case you can't get to a workshop and learn it in person).

Sluts and Goddesses is by Annie Sprinkle, who has worked as a porn star, sex counselor, and workshop leader. Her very risqué video is presented like a "transformational workshop" that is visually fun, very entertaining, and full of exercises for women to bring out their inner goddesses and allow wild expression. Her suggestions include penciling your eyebrows to look like an Egyptian; playing with wigs; decorating your body with jewelry; changing clothes to change your consciousness (high heels, biker boots, or Victorian bustier); posing for sexy shots; and experimenting with crystals, vibrators, feathers, and rattles. Sprinkle mentions every possible trick of the trade, some of which are very racy.

Kama Sutra II: The Art of Making Love from *Penthouse* magazine's video collection is 60 minutes of an extensive and excellent lesson on sexual positions. The scenes are sensuous and the words used have a tone that's consistent with tantra. There are scenes in which the woman controls the activity tantrically so the man can last longer. The narration starts with foreplay, learning about each other, taking time to touch and caress, letting partners know what to do to give pleasure, and progresses to oral sex and intercourse.

Positions include those Kama Sutra–like titles, such as *Twining of the Creeper,* in which the woman rests her head on the man's stomach while looking up and he gazes lovingly into her eyes; *Mixture and Season and Rice,* which entails encircling each other completely with arms and legs; and *Milk and Water Embrace*, in which she sits on his lap and he embraces her from behind.

Let your touch travel all over your beloved's body. Include light, gentle touches and "pressing of nails" (an essential tantra technique that sends shivers up the lover's body). Start at the neck and run down the body to the hips. Go up the chest and down and up the arms, around the shoulders, down the chest to the hips, making circles. Travel down to the pelvis area, and massage and pull at the thighs between the legs. Keep coming back to the chest (breasts) to heighten feelings of love.

Blocks to Bliss

Some of the positions in these videos are complicated and require agility, as in the Kama Sutra itself. Kneeling for a long time can also be a strain for most people. Only do what's comfortable for you. Work your way up to these positions. While many videos do use "real" people, don't feel like you have to look like any beautiful couples in other videos.

Tantra-Related Workouts to Watch

An increasing number of fitness experts who practice tantra have developed workout programs that are compatible with tantric sex principles and practices. *Stephanie's Tantric Toning* combines the physical practices of yoga, T'ai Chi, chi gung, and light aerobics with guided imagery that invokes tantric meditative states. At the end is a *color light meditation* that reinforces self-esteem. *Chakra Yoga* with Toronto-based yoga teacher Gurutej Kaur shows an interesting exercise program of very gentle poses (mostly sitting) that balance each of the energy centers (chakras). The 16 poses come from the kundalini yoga tradition.

Related Videos on Sex

Educational videos about treating sexual dysfunction were first produced in the 1970s, and the numbers keep increasing. My cabinets are already full! Some classics in the field present a variety of proven therapy techniques for sexual dysfunction, hosted by top educators and therapists and used by many professionals over the years. They include the *Better Sex* series (with titles like *Sharing Sexual Fantasies, Sex Games and Toys,*

237

and *Advanced Sexual Techniques*); and the *Great Sex* series from psychiatrist Sommers, who has done extensive research to prove the effectiveness of using videos to help couples' sexual and marital life.

The latest trend is that women are producing sexy videos, meant to present sexuality from a woman's point of view. Candida Royalle is a pioneer in this effort. Through her company, Femme Productions, she has produced many videos that depict women's fantasies and realistic scenes where women are sexually respected and pleasured by men the way women like. "Many of my films are highly erotic and show very exciting fantasy sequences," says Candida, "but there's always some relationship, not just rushing to some sex act." Titles bespeaking the female spirit include *Christine's Secret*, *Sensual Escape*, and *Rites of Passion* (the most tantric-oriented selection, in which a woman discovers ancient lovemaking secrets from a "mysterious Adonis-like master").

Tantra on Radio, TV, the Silver Screen, and the Internet

Tantra is becoming an increasingly popular word, in large part because of shows and story lines being aired about the topic on radio, TV, and in the movies. For example, tantra was heavily featured in the film *American Pie 2,* a coming-of-age movie in which teens dealing with adolescent angst end up in a perfect world where all the women are gorgeous and available, and every guy gets his dream come true. As expected, tantra is portrayed as a mystical Eastern trip to perpetual orgasm.

A Hollywood feature film has been produced about Charles Muir's tantra work, which follows couples who have been through his workshop. Years ago, the film *Bliss*, starring Terence Stamp as a daka, was based on Muir's work. Other tantra teachers have been approached by producers to make movies about their work; some of these projects are being pursued.

The popular TV show on HBO called *Real Sex* often airs segments about workshops run by tantric teachers. And HBO's popular series *Sex in the City* included a subplot in which one of the girlfriends attended a tantra workshop, fearing something was wrong with her sexually because her boyfriend had fallen asleep during sex!

Now that you know more about tantra and tantric sex, it will be amusing for you to notice when scenes about it pop up in different TV shows or films. Be a watchdog, and notice how accurate the portrayals are (the topic can be sensationalized!). When you notice, let me know!

Tantra Tutorial

Celebrities also make household words of whatever they practice when they reveal it publicly. Likewise with tantric sex, in which several celebrity names often are mentioned whenever people talk about men being able to last for hours in sex.

Over the many years I've studied tantra and hosted call-in advice shows on the radio, I have talked extensively about tantra. My co-host Chris Jagger and I even did one show in which two friends who were tantra experts demonstrated a pleasuring of the goddess experience, in which the tantrika had a female ejaculation, thanks to the daka's expertise (a classic Lovephones show that many people still ask me for a copy of!). Of course we had to do a running commentary to describe what was happening, since it was radio after all, but it was vivid enough that listeners could hear the yelps of joy and celebration.

Like everything else, tantra is spreading to the Internet, a topic I discuss more at length in Chapter 25, "A Healing Force for Now and the Future." Host Bob Berkowitz's eyada.com Love Bytes show was a pioneer program that used the Internet to talk about sexual issues. I've done many advice shows on the Internet; on my site at www.cameraplanet.com you can send in your questions by e-mail or by video and I will answer them!

The Least You Need to Know

➤ Your tantric evening of pleasure must have music to reflect and set your mood. Pick anything that appeals to you, but try CDs especially made for tantric lovemaking.

➤ Music tones vibrate similarly to the chakras, so you can control energies you want to stimulate with the music.

➤ The value of videos that show couples in loving interactions has been proven by research; it can be healthy to watch educational videos about sex with your partner.

➤ There are an increasing number of erotic films being produced that are specifically made to demonstrate tantric practices and sexual positions.

➤ One measure of how much a topic is becoming part of the popular culture is how often it shows up in the media. This is happening with tantra, as more shows include the theme in their broadcasts and projects. The Internet also offers a wide opportunity for sexual topics to be discussed.

Part 5

Dating and Mating Tantra Style

Hopefully you're convinced by now of how good love and sex can be—or have had an experience of "the best ever." Now what about the impact on your relationship of doing these practices? What if you're excited about this new path but your partner is not? Or if one of you finds someone else to share with? Or perhaps you're enticed about what you've been learning in these pages, but don't have a partner to practice with?

All is not lost! Yes, on any powerful new path such as this one, things can get rocky. But there is always a solution to any problem. In this part, I'll help you find those solutions. If you're looking for a tantric partner to practice such delicious loving with, I'll give you suggestions about how to find one and manifest the love you want! Deep, passionate, exhilarating love IS possible—you'll see that in some amazing stories about couples who are sharing the tantric path, tying the knot, and doing it in grand tantra style! The beauty of their love, and what is possible for you, will be inspiring!

Chapter 19

Singles, Sex, and Tantra

In This Chapter

➤ You are the beloved: loving yourself first

➤ The search for Mr. or Ms. Right

➤ Attracting a tantric mate

➤ The two love lessons you should know

➤ Safe sex when practicing tantra

Now that you've been reading all these undoubtedly compelling things about tantric sex, you must be excited about the experiences. Hopefully you've had a chance to practice them—with or without a partner. Of course, practicing tantric exercises is more fun if you do them with someone. I have said, after all, that tantric sex is about union to reach bliss.

But if you don't have a partner now, don't be discouraged; you can reach this bliss on your own—by being your own beloved. You can benefit a great deal from your solitary tantric practice and continue when another beloved comes along. No excuses! Your path of channeling your sexual energy to higher states of consciousness and bliss is possible no matter what else is going on in your life. In this chapter you'll learn just how to do that. I'll tell you how singles can enjoy tantric sex alone—but also, how to approach that search for your beloved, and where to go to find like-minded singles interested in pursuing the tantric path.

You Are the Beloved

Whether or not you are with someone, always remember that you are the beloved; this is a basic principle in tantra. Whether you have a new boyfriend or girlfriend, a mate that you have been with for a short time, or a lifetime partner, you are still whole within yourself. The first step in tantric sex is to create that wholeness within yourself—the union of male and female energies and all the qualities that implies, as outlined in Chapter 2, "The Basics: Yes, Yin Yang, Yoni, and Yab Yum." Tantric sex gives deeper meaning to a statement you are likely familiar with: You have to love yourself before you can love anyone else. So look in the mirror and fall in love— with *you*!

Fall in love with yourself as the beloved.

One of my favorite exercises to help people develop self-esteem is to take yourself out on a date. That means you treat yourself as well as you imagine you would be treated by someone else. In Chapter 7, "Setting the Stage for Your Tantric Nights of Pleasure," I described how to prepare for a tantric date with a beloved. Refer to that chapter and do all the steps described there, but for yourself! In summary that means …

➤ Clean up your house as if that special someone was coming to call.

➤ Take a bath or shower, and shave or put on make-up as you would if you were about to see someone special.

➤ Pick out a special outfit that you've been saving for that special someone to appreciate. Choose something particularly sexy or alluring. Remember that tantric clothes are flowing, comfortable, enticing.

> ➤ Choose a place to go that you would take a special someone. You can go out to dinner on your own! What movie did you always think would be great to see with someone you could cuddle up to? Treat yourself to that movie.

> ➤ Take that special walk, gaze at the moon, or whatever romantic, fun, or exciting thing you would do with that special someone.

Remember that *you* are that special someone. The more you practice loving yourself and treating yourself well, the more you will create that loving aura around you. People will notice and be drawn to you. You may even have noticed that as soon as you stop looking for that special someone (and appearing desperate), that's when he or she appears in your life. Check out some great ways to build your self-esteem in *The Complete Idiot's Guide to Dating.*

Meeting Your Match

Looking for that perfect mate has traditionally been referred to as the search for Mr. or Ms. Right. In recent years, the slang term for this has been *hooking up*, which actually means anything from meeting someone you really enjoy being with, to sexual interactions with that person (and even then, the term includes anything from kissing to a one-night stand to seeing someone regularly).

In tantra, the phrases for meeting your match are different. To me they sound more spiritual, more flowery, more respectful, more honoring. The most common word used is *connecting.* A phrase would be that you "feel the energy between you." These words are meant to express the energy between two people, which is intrinsic to the tantric way of life and implies not only a sexual interest, but a deeper spiritual attraction.

Conscious Flirting

In tantra, everything is done consciously. That means you are aware of your actions and have only positive intentions, which results in the best outcome for all. Francesca Gentille and her partner Brian Bourke, a tantra teaching team, lead workshops in what they call *conscious flirting* (see Appendix B, "Workshops, Web Sites, Teachers, and Tantra Communities"). Participants are asked to identify their intentions when meeting someone new. Knowing this intention also helps if you are "striking out." "If you flirt to make yourself feel good you won't be as successful as if you do it for the others person's good," says s. Being conscious of your behavior and intention allows you to look at what you might want to shift, making you more effective.

Other exercises include role playing how you flirt, to see more objectively how you come across and decide whether you like what you see in yourself and how you make the other person feel (some are shocked at what they see!). Bourke notes two exercises that particularly empower men to choose whether to follow up an interest. In the *steel ball,* they imagine themselves as a steel ball rolling down a slope. The steel ball is

Tantra Tutorial

Tantra demands respect for other's boundaries. Being careful about approaches is important in today's society. Be aware of differences in what is acceptable according to different cultures and alert to approaches that are unwelcome and therefore subject to being considered sexual harassment.

Ecstasy Essentials

Because men can go too slow or too fast in dating, tantra teacher Brian Bourke advises them about the *pacing window,* meaning they should ask a woman outright what she wants ("Do you want me to call you tomorrow or next week?").

symbolic of moving with determination toward that goal but slow enough to stop at will. In the *pass up the pass,* the men practice exchanging smiles with an attractive woman but walking by and just enjoying a warm feeling inside without having to follow through.

Who Is Mr. or Ms. Right?

In tantric sex your whole idea of the perfect mate can change, as you look beyond the superficial values at who the person really is. This means seeing the god/goddess divinity as opposed to thinning hair or size 14 dress. Be open to the possibilities. You could be surprised who shows up in your life—that someone special could be someone you never imagined!

Remember that the basic—and beautiful—spirit of tantra is to look beyond the physical being to see and connect inner souls. Remember one of the basic exercises is to look into the eyes of another to see the god/goddess within that person. Look into his or her eyes and see beyond age, race, height, and any of your preconceived notions of whom you should be with. It is striking, isn't it, how different this concept is from our culture, which is so bound to the physical and so rooted in our stereotypical images. Eight out of ten men today still rate a woman's looks as the first thing that attracts them.

Yet in tantra, when you truly look beyond the physical, you find new love matches. In my book *How To Love A Nice Guy,* I wrote about how women can find the true love they seek if they look beyond their usual love criteria—beyond a dashing Armani suit, flashy Mercedes, or shiny Platinum card—to assess instead whether he's a nice guy who will really treat her well.

Of course, there are factors that make a couple more compatible. There are lots of tests you can take of your compatibility in my book *The Complete Idiot's Guide to a Healthy Relationship.* Couples are more likely to get along when they agree on several important dimensions of a relationship: how to raise children and spend money, what kind of sex they like, what kind of lifestyle (quiet country dwelling or bustling city life) they want, and basic values to follow. But here's my general rule: You can make any relationship work, if you really want it to work—if you both are really committed to getting along, and you deeply love and respect each other enough to work out any differences. Yes, you might have to work at the relationship to get past your own or one another's prejudices, but you can make it work if you want to.

The Beloved Shows Up in Surprise Form, If Only for Now

If you walked into a room of couples doing tantric sex workshops, you might be very surprised. You might see married couples, or singles who connected for the first time who don't fit a classical mold of the perfectly matched couple. Why is that? Because people following the tantra path are drawn energetically to each other and fall in love based on deep emotional connections that have nothing to do with mere physical attraction.

Tantra Tales

Frances is 54 years old, 5'2" with gray hair, and admittedly twenty pounds overweight. In one tantra workshop she sat next to Octavio, a 21-year-old, 6'4" Brazilian man whose stunning looks turn women's heads. When asked to energetically find someone to pair up with for the next exercises, they turned to each other and ended up doing an emotional release process together. From that time on, Frances curled up into Octavio's arms during the rest of the workshop. "She's beautiful," Octavio told me. "She's certainly not my typical type—I date tall, stunning, Spanish-looking models. But I need to be with a real woman here who is kind and who can help me grow."

Over-50 Pauline, a fiery, outgoing Italian woman, met 26-year-old Lee, a quiet guy of few words. Pauline was well into her career and owned a house; Lee was still in school and lived at home. But Pauline fell for him; as she explained, "He was kind and faithful and I could count on him for everything. He would always come when I needed him. He set up my computer. He listened to all my worries. Best of all, he learned all the tantric sex practices with me." They were inseparable for several years, but even Pauline herself knew that it was not forever. "I had been hurt so often by so many men and Lee was safe. Being with him taught me how to trust again." Pauline's new boyfriend is her own age. "Lee was my training for love," she explains. "Often there are relationships that prepare us for the next true love."

*Energetic connections go
beyond age.*

Quiz: Are You Ready for Your True Tantric Sex Partner?

Answer the following questions about what qualities your tantric partner might possess. Add more questions, if you like.

Can Your Tantra True Love ...

1. Be much younger than you?
2. Be much older than you?
3. Be of a different race?
4. Have less money than you?
5. Have dark hair instead of blonde hair?
6. Be balding?
7. Come from another country?
8. Be a different religion from yours?
9. Have children from a previous relationship?
10. Be a night owl when you're an early bird, or vice versa?
11. Dress differently from the way you do?
12. Other:

If you answered "yes" to six or more questions, you are open to love without being tied to convention or preconceptions about whom you should be with. If you answered "yes" to fewer than four questions, your concept of who is right for you could be preventing you from making a wonderful connection. Go back over your answers and see what it would feel like if you answered differently.

Sensing, Not Scoring

Whether you consider being a sex object politically incorrect or even enjoy it for a momentary thrill, tantric sex will shift your mind from that to a whole new attraction. Even women who have been more aggressive in scoping out men for reasons of sexual desire find themselves using new attraction criteria. As one woman, Marcy, put it, "I used to walk into a room and decide who I was going to hit on, which hot guy I would take home for the night, but now that I've been practicing tantric sex, I realize that's empty. My body is my temple now, so I don't want just any man."

Now that she doesn't just zone in on hot guys for sex romps, "the pickings are a little slimmer." Indeed, for Marcy and other men and women practicing tantric sex, the choices for partners might seem slimmer because she is more discriminating. In fact, there are more possibilities of partners when you look beyond the obvious and into someone's inner being. As another woman said, "I don't care how old or rich he is, I just care if he's big enough to hold my energy, to accept my anger, and to invite my love." Quoting singer Sheryl Crow's song lyric, "Are you strong enough to be my man?", another woman said, "I want a man who gets who I am, instead of having some Barbie doll fantasy."

Similarly, men want a woman who sees beyond their income potential or the kind of car they drive. As Andrew said, "I'm sick of women who just want a rich guy." And Joe wanted to know, "Where are all the women who want nice guys instead of all those guys who treat them badly but they think are cool?" Fortunately, as a woman matures, she more often goes for the nice guy. Any woman can learn to pick these more loving men; I've laid out a 10-step plan to do this in my book *How to Love a Nice Guy.*

Dr. Judy's TantrAdvice

Because the lingam and yoni are energy transmitters, it is wise to be discriminating about having sex with someone, since doing so invites their energy into your body and soul.

Finding Your Soul Mate on the Tantric Path

Of course, once you've committed to a tantric way of being it can be wonderful to find a like-minded person on a similar journey. This makes life easier because you understand what each of you is striving for, in yourselves and in a partnership. You're on the same wavelength because …

➤ You already have a common language. You know what she means by "chakra" or what he means by his appreciating your "Shakti" energy.

➤ You can encourage each other in your practices and remind each other to do the breathing exercises or yoga practices.

➤ You can support each other in your affirmations.

➤ You can accept all parts of each other, even at difficult moments.

➤ You can trust that you will strive to treat each other with respect and honesty.

➤ You can create sex magic together, knowing the steps to do this.

➤ You can give each other space to grow.

➤ You know the feeling of being "one" together and with all that exists.

Blocks to Bliss

Don't assume that a student of spiritual sex is automatically emotionally mature, sexually liberated, and psychologically healthy. He or she can have the same problems in relationships as others. Problems with intimacy and commitment can be even more intense at times, since practices and emotional release processes might trigger previously unnoticed conflicts.

A soul mate is someone you feel is a perfect match for you. Usually a soul mate is recognized in these ways:

➤ You feel you've known each other forever.

➤ You can sense what your mate feels before even talking.

➤ You feel you were destined to be together.

➤ You know and appreciate each other on a deeper level than you feel with almost anyone else.

➤ You might feel you shared past lives.

Most people are searching for that perfect soul mate. Some experts on the topic say there are only a few perfect soul mates, *twin souls* or *twin flames*. More optimistically, it is possible to develop a relationship that feels deeply intimate and touches your soul with a partner who might not fit the previous characteristics.

Practicing tantric sex offers even more hope, because tantric sex means connecting; not on the superficial level, but at your soul level. Also, according to tantric sex, every person is considered a divine soul. As a result, you can connect with his or her divinity if you open yourself to it. According to this point of view, you might find more soul mates out there than you thought.

Astrological readings to connect spiritual singles are consistent with tantric respect for the heavens and balanced matches. There are dating services based on what's called "Indian vedic astrology," a particular system of interpreting the effect of the planets on your life that promises profiles specifically geared toward earthly gods and goddesses on the tantric path. (One such site is www.tantric-soulmate-connection.org.)

Getting Ready for the Beloved

Of course you have to be prepared for that special beloved to enter your life. That means you have to clear your conflicts about being in a relationship and any problems you might have stored up from past relationships. I have encountered many men and women who say they want commitment but who are unsuccessful at meeting people. If you are not attracting a partner, look inside yourself to make sure you really want a commitment and are not unconsciously sabotaging your efforts to meet someone. Also, confront the limiting beliefs you might have about finding your tantric match, such as:

Tantra Tutorial

Research shows that certain chemicals flow in our body when we encounter some people. There is also conditioning involved with attraction in that if we have positive experiences with a certain type of person we tend to want to repeat those experiences; negative past experiences tend to make us avoid people who remind us of those times.

➤ There are no good ones left; they're all taken.

➤ Even if I find someone, it'll turn sour anyway.

➤ I can never be happy in love.

➤ Whenever you have sex with someone, it always ruins the relationship.

➤ I always get hurt in the end.

➤ I'm destined to be alone.

➤ I'm better off being alone.

➤ Tantric lovers are always prone to affairs anyway, so I'd never have someone to myself.

➤ It didn't work out last time, so what can I expect now?

Catch yourself in these beliefs. Read each one and turn it into a positive affirmation that states how possible this type of love is for you. For example, change the phrase "I can never be happy in love" to "I *will* be happy in love." Feel how much happier you already feel when you say it the new, more positive way!

Bringing in the Beloved

Tantra practices are all designed to open you to love; therefore it is not surprising that some singles have found true love after starting their studies. As Celia told me, "I realized after my third weekend that even though I was complaining I didn't have a man, I was closed off emotionally and angry at men for using me in the past. Once I got over that anger and learned to love myself and my yoni, I was open to Bill when I met him and I could let a man touch me deeply inside and out again."

Because tantric sex involves rituals, some people do rituals to draw in the energy of a partner. You might think of these as witchcraft or black magic; if anything it is white magic, as we are talking about bringing in love—not doing harm to anyone.

A ritual to bring in a beloved might involve this process: Look at the moon, especially when it is full. Invoke spirits (of Mother Earth and Father Sky, god/goddess, grandparents, those who love you) to be your aides. State a desire clearly, such as "I declare that my beloved will come to me by next week." State what qualities you would like. End with assurance, "It is done" and an affirmation that "It is for the good of all."

Bringing in the beloved.

Where to Go

So many people ask me, "Where do I go to meet someone?" My book *The Complete Idiot's Guide to Dating* is chock full of advice about where to go (and what to say and tests about who is right for you). From all of that, my favorite advice is: Go to places where you will enjoy yourself. This works for several reasons:

➤ You will be happy; therefore you will glow and people will be attracted to you.

➤ People with similar interests will be in the same place.

➤ You'll be so involved in what you're doing that you won't seem like you're looking for someone (which can be a turnoff).

➤ Even if you don't meet anyone, you will have had fun!

Here are some concrete suggestions about where to find tantric soul mates:

➤ Tantra seminars, parties, and introductory events.

➤ Classes in yoga, T'ai Chi, and related Eastern fitness programs.

➤ Spirituality conferences and retreat centers.

➤ Flyers posted in bulletin boards at spirituality bookstores, health food stores, and meeting places.

➤ Stores that sell Eastern items or gifts.

➤ Bookstores in the section that sell books on tantra and related spiritual practices.

➤ Workshops on related topics (relationships, personal growth, spirituality) through organizations such as the Open Center, Learning Annex, Seminar Center, and Omega Institute.

➤ Events and retreats related to spiritual leaders (Osho and others).

➤ Personal ads posted in magazines, newspapers, or on the Web.

➤ Through friends and people you meet about tantra. (You never know whether the person sitting next to you on a plane could be your next tantric beloved. It has happened to at least two women I know who almost gave up on finding their beloveds.)

➤ On the Web. Surf for sites related to tantric sex (just type the word "tantra" in your search engine or start from www.tantra.com); join tantra newsgroups; join in on chat rooms. Set up your own Web site and include your interest in tantra.

➤ Refer to the listings in Appendix B.

Once you go to one of these events, you will become networked into the tantra community and more resources will naturally come your way.

Two Love Lessons You Wish You'd Learned When You Were Young

Dr. Judy's TantrAdvice

Instead of waiting for the perfect tantric mate, you can develop loving friendships with tantra buddies. These are platonic friends with whom you share some practices but who understand that you are not romantically committed partners.

Wouldn't it be nice if you didn't have pain in relationships, and if you didn't feel you wasted your time trying to make something work that was wrong all along? Colorado tantra teacher and psychologist Shavana Fineberg suggests the following two lessons to keep in mind to prevent those problems. "These can save you a lot of aggravation," she says.

➤ Just because you're incredibly attracted to someone doesn't mean it's a good match. Lust and looks can be deceiving, whereas real energy between people is more lasting and genuine.

➤ If the amount of energy you're putting into a relationship isn't the same as what you're getting back, don't pursue it. Fineberg recounts a female friend who handles dating wisely. If someone is not really interested in her, says Fineberg, she doesn't have to force herself to resist calling him like so many other women— she is genuinely not interested. She says, "I have enough problems, so if the other person doesn't want to be with me, I don't want him with me either!"

Safe Sex When Practicing Tantra

Some experts estimate that there is a risk of sexually transmitted diseases (STDs) in the tantra community because of the accessibility of intimate contact between men and women, men and men, women and women, and even groups. Partners might be misled into unsafe sexual contacts because of the expectation of "trust" surrounding the practices. This expectation could lead to unwise assumptions and prevent someone from quizzing others about their sexual past and present health status.

I have been invited to lecture about the importance of safe sex at some tantra seminars, and have noticed there is not enough attention paid to this subject. One fact that should be emphasized to prevent the spread of disease is this: Even if you don't notice any symptoms, you can still have an STD and pass it on to someone else (as is the case with herpes and early stages of hepatitis C). I implore all tantra initiates and experts to pay attention to this issue!

Be aware, too, that some people with an STD that stays in the body (such as herpes), do not admit this, rationalizing that they are not contagious because their energy has no intention to do so. When Lara found out that Don had herpes but insisted he would not spread it because he had no such intention, she was understandably furious about not being informed.

Be vigilant about asking, and telling, your partner about your sexual health history and risks before you engage in any intimacy. Always practice safe, protected sex to protect against STDs and unplanned pregnancy.

Blocks to Bliss

Tara had unprotected intercourse with a new tantric lover who proclaimed that he did not have any diseases, but she contracted a yeast infection from him. Find out what a person means by "disease." Also be aware that men as well as women can transmit infections. And of course, always use protection!

Keeping Confidence

My advice to singles throughout *The Complete Idiot's Guide to Dating* is to enjoy life and keep confident that love is possible—and everywhere. Tantra teacher Joan Heartfield, co-founder of Conversations That Matter for singles agrees and says, "Your love relationship is waiting for you at each unique moment."

The Least You Need to Know

➤ You can enjoy a tantric sex lifestyle even if you are single. There's no need to wait for the beloved; *you* are the beloved!

➤ When you see the divinity in all beings, you can expand the possibilities to find someone to love.

➤ To find other singles who are interested in tantra, go to events for tantra, search the Web, and talk to other people about your interest.

➤ Two love lessons are best learned early: Real energy between two people is more important than a mere physical attraction, and the amount of energy you and your partner contribute to the relationship should be about equal.

➤ Like any sexual activity, always practice safe, protected tantric sex to protect yourself against STDs and unplanned pregnancy.

Chapter 20

Tying the Knot Tantra Style

In This Chapter

➤ How tantric marriages are different from traditional ceremonies

➤ Examples of beautiful tantric wedding ceremonies

➤ Dedications that couples make to each other

➤ Personal stories from tantric brides and grooms

➤ How couples continue to dedicate their love

Practicing tantra with a partner can lead to such intense and beautiful love between a couple that they want to celebrate that love in a marriage ceremony that integrates some of the rituals they have learned and cherish. Although not a legal process according to state laws, these ceremonies are meant to mark a couple's commitment and honor their union—for themselves and for their friends and family.

These ceremonies are often exquisitely original and elaborate, with eloquent dedications of love. In this chapter, you'll meet several couples who have created such joyous festivities. Of course, the love and joy of any wedding is precious, but I know you'll find these stories interesting, and maybe even inspiring!

The Unique Aspects of a Tantric Marriage Ceremony

Every culture has its beautiful—and idiosyncratic—rituals for important events such as weddings. Greeks dance with handkerchiefs; Jews lift the couple into the air on chairs; I've even witnessed two Christian weddings where the couple was wrapped in a braided rope to symbolize their union. Tantra, too, has its special rituals.

Bridal magazines and books today are filled with wonderful ideas on making the ceremony special. There's even a trend for couples to be quite original—such as marrying while scuba diving, sky-diving, or hot air ballooning! Tantric ceremonies are equally creative, although they vary from tradition in some ways:

Dr. Judy's TantrAdvice

A tantric wedding ceremony needn't be elaborate or expensive to be profound. The rituals, dedications, and guest participation can be just as (or more!) moving than my $30,000 wedding with eggs made to look like penguins, and a Viennese dessert table that could fill a bakery.

➤ The wedding does not have to be traditionally legal. The couple might never get a state license or they might get one at another time. Declarations of devotion often will do.

➤ The only people who need to be present for the marriage are the tantra bride and groom! Vows can be said that feel binding without anyone actually presiding over or witnessing the ceremony.

➤ Priests and priestesses who preside over the ceremony do not have to be traditionally licensed either; they could be friends given the honor to perform the role. Often the couple's tantra teacher officiates.

➤ The couple might have many marriage ceremonies and events, to commemorate and celebrate their love.

Many tantric wedding ceremonies have similar elements that mark the occasion. These include:

➤ **Symbolic places to make vows**   The choice of locale is influenced by the elements the couple would like to call in. It might be a forest for its earth connection, as a symbol for being grounded with each other; a mountaintop at dawn for more visionary, sky energy; or a secluded cave, dusty desert, or other holy place where spirits abide. Ceremonies near water are always magical and consistent with tantra's emphasis on cleansing.

➤ **Creative dedications** More couples today are adding their own statements to traditional wedding ceremonies even if they are strictly religious. Tantric weddings have no boilerplate, so partners let themselves be totally free with what they say to each other.

➤ **Being in the moment** Tantra teaches you to be present in the moment, so it's no surprise that some couples unite on an impulse. You've heard of quickie Las Vegas weddings; well, in tantra, couples can be as spontaneous, deciding to marry at a beautiful moment, walking on the beach at a particularly beautiful sunset, during a party where friends are already present, or sitting together in their bathtub!

➤ **Picking an auspicious time** Some tantric couples wait for a particular day, consistent with the tradition of correct timing (as with Chinese philosophy where certain times are more auspicious than others and predict a happier future for the couple). The determination often rests on the moon's shape or the particular alignment of the planets.

➤ **Specific references to uniting male and female energies** Because tantra is based on the balance of opposites, tantra marriage ceremonies often include references to the coming together of male and female energy.

➤ **Acknowledging that we are the world** Tantric consciousness reaches out to the world, so the activities and spoken words in the ceremonies reflect this universal consciousness.

➤ **Including more than two** This is an advanced idea in tantra. Because love can extend to several people, more than two people might want to create a ceremony to testify to their love for one another.

Feast for the Tantric Wedding

The food served at tantric marriages is purposefully chosen to be consistent with the tantric principle of sensuality. The choices include foods that stimulate all of the senses with scent, taste, and color, such as strawberries, chocolate, and avocados. Celebrants may offer food to each other as a symbol of offering love.

Music for the Tantra Marriage

The music for tantric weddings is often original, performed by musicians who practice tantra themselves or make original music consistent with tantric practices. Some of these musicians and their work are listed in Appendix C, "Tantric Tools." It is common to have drummers who drum passionately for hours on end. Guests are often welcomed to play drums, shake rattles, or participate in any imaginative way.

259

Guest Participation

Often friends are given roles in tantric marriages. Like priests and priestesses in a temple, they might say dedications or perform dances for the delight of the couple and the other guests. Guests are encouraged to bring original songs to sing or poems to recite.

Special Ceremonies for Tantric Lovers

I'm honored to share with you the wedding ceremonies of several friends in the tantra community (who are also tantra teacher teams). They really know how to celebrate their love! Blessings to them!

Christina and William's Tantric Marriage Ceremony

I introduced you to Christina Sophia and William Florian in Chapter 15, "Make It Juicy with Magic and Play," when you read about their advice on the joys and benefits of belly dancing and other dance. Christina and William's wedding was exquisitely tantric in its elaborate attention to ritual. Both Californians, they decided not to get a state license because, as William said, "we do not recognize the importance of involving the state in our commitment to each other." Many friends were invited to play a role and also to serve as witnesses.

Tantra Tutorial

A **sweat** is a Native American ritual gathering in which groups of men or women (or both) gather in a teepee–like structure where stones are set on a fire and participants incant prayers.

Tantric wedding rituals often begin the night (or even days) before the actual vows, either in rituals the couple does alone, or that the guests do together. The night before their ceremony, Christina and William's friends met for a *sweat*.

The wedding took place at a friend's home in California. Everyone was in festive costume, with the couple in sensual and colorful Gypsy-like costumes. The groom, William, wore no shirt.

Many elements of the event reflected typical tantric rituals, such as dancing, inviting spirits, chanting, a sensual feast, and doing the yab yum position. (The couple was also serenaded and surrounded by the sounds of the didgeridoo, an Australian flute-like instrument.)

The festivities started at 6 P.M. Men congregated at the pool and women gathered in the living room, holding flowers and chanting a Sanskrit mantra ("Om ManiPadme Hum"). In keeping with the tantric theme as the union of male and female divine energies, the men and women met in a circle, dancing and chanting, with the men singing, "I am the god, I am the father, all acts of love and pleasure are my ritual," as the women chanted, "I am the goddess, I am the mother, all acts of love and pleasure are my ritual." Every so often they all chanted, "Pleasure sacred, sacred pleasure." They also reversed the chants of the opposite sex with the women singing, "I am the god ... " and men singing, "I am the goddess ... "

Christina and William celebrate their tantric union.

In another demonstration of the embrace of opposites, the group gathered in a circle chant, with the men starting on the outside and the women forming an inside circle. The men danced counter-clockwise as the women circled clockwise. But then the women passed through the raised arms of the men, moving to the outer circle and allowing the men to enter and create an inner circle. After a few minutes they paused and bowed to one another and then came into one big circle, completing the union.

Ecstasy Essentials

Following ancient tradition, both a priest and priestess are often chosen as masters of ceremony (to facilitate the activities), further maintaining the balance of male and female energies.

William and Christina entered the room carrying flowers and crystals as a friend recited a poem. They placed gifts for each other on the altar as guests hummed in chorus.

To synchronize the group energy, everyone was invited to face his or her beloved or someone near them, to eye gaze and breathe together, recite a blessing, and affirm being a "circle of family." The couple introduced the guests with a few words about who each is to them and their appreciation to them for being family. There was much drumming and chanting; everyone proceeded into the couple's ceremony area, chanting, "I am god/goddess, the mother/father, all acts of love and pleasure are my ritual."

In true tantric style, the couple took time just being there, present in the moment, moving slowly, taking time to breathe deeply. They even did exercises I have described in this book, moving energy into each other's heart.

Christina sending love energy into William's heart at the wedding.

Dancing is an integral part of the ceremony—many tantric couples are well versed in this art (Christina and William teach it together). Dances include blessings of the different energy centers (chakras).

The couple made dedications and vows, ringing a crystal bowl after each one. William's dedication was, "Part of our relationship is that we each have our individual goals, intentions, and aspirations, which we work toward and put energy into. We want to share these with you." His other statements to everyone included:

Ecstasy Essentials

Spirits are invited to the ceremony (including family members not present), as is everyone from the couple's past, all of their previous lives (for those who believe in previous lives!), and spirits of the elements (fire, water, earth, air) and of love and sacred marriage. Everyone bows in *Namaste* (the Hindu greeting acknowledging that "god/goddess in me greets and celebrates god/goddess in you").

➤ We believe in service and extending our love and relationship into the world through our work together. We recognize that we are on a journey of growth and healing as individuals and together, and it is our desire to become increasingly conscious and aware of ourselves on every level.

➤ We have chosen Tantra as part of our spiritual practice because we believe the path to god/goddess realization, and conscious evolution must include the body and all that we are.

➤ We also recognize that we have shadow sides and we are committed to have, be with, and love all parts of ourselves. We believe in the spiritual path of relationship and see all our experiences as opportunities for growth and healing.

➤ It is okay to be imperfect, to not know, to be open to possibility. We believe in learning through joy, fun, and pleasure.

➤ We revel in our many dimensions and saying yes to being partners with god/goddess in creating heaven here on earth.

➤ We experience profoundly in our bodies the love that we feel and generate together, and when we fall into a fixation that is not of this loving space the affinity that is in every cell of our bodies and permeating our beings always brings us back to this simple truth.

➤ Support our love.

William's vows to Christina were:

➤ I love you and I love myself without conditions or reservations.

➤ I vow to continue with you on our path of growth and service to myself, each other, our family and community.

➤ I know that I shall love you forever and beyond forever, and that my highest good is served by acting in alignment with this great love.

After the vows the couple sat in yab yum, kissing and breathing together, as the Didgeridoo sounds blessed them.

Christina and William connecting at their wedding.

As I have mentioned many times throughout this book, setting intention is a fundamental part of tantric lovemaking. Christina and William's intentions included the following:

➤ I am devoted to my spiritual path, bringing forth all the talent, artistry, knowledge, wisdom, and love that is my birthright for the evolution of my being and all others. I ask for your support of this intention.

➤ Most of all I wish to grow and deepen the love for myself and you in this sacred union, and our capacity to work together, cooperatively and tantrically. I ask for your support of this intention.

➤ I intend to be of service to both men and women and to help bring about a more loving, peaceful world. I ask for your support of this intention.

Christina added, I am a mother and will always love my children. I intend to be there for them as much as I am able. I ask for your support of this intention. William's similar intention was, "I am a brother, son, friend, and family member to many. I intend to be there for them as well as your children and the new family I am entering into as much as I am able." And he added, "It is my intention to allow for the free flow of abundance, travel, creativity, music, enjoyable work, health, playfulness, and bodily pleasures. I ask for your support of this intention."

Acknowledging truths and each other is another intrinsic part of tantric love tradition. Christina and Williams's acknowledgments included these:

➤ We acknowledge that we are multidimensional beings, different yet equal. We acknowledge that there are infinite possibilities and we seek to know exactly what we want so we can delight in the joy of creating it.

➤ We follow no one religion, rather we seek to understand the spiritual truths contained in all. We embrace Tantra as a way of life which gives us the key to healing, knowing, and opening our hearts and bodies to truth, and celebrating all of life and the divine essence within all things and all beings.

➤ We honor, celebrate, and care for our physical bodies as the temple and we say yes to full embodiment here, bringing together in harmonic vibration and expression the sacred union of our inner male and female energies and our consciousness.

➤ We are committed to nourishing ourselves body, mind, and spirit; and keeping our bodies healthy and vibrant. Let any division between body and soul be healed completely in this loving relationship.

➤ Our love does not forsake others; it embraces all others.

Rundy and Lisa's Four-Day Wedding Ritual

The pretty and fit mother of an adolescent daughter, Lisa writes greetings cards for a living but performs her own exquisite poetry. Rundy is a tall, dark, and handsome actor, yoga teacher and professional athlete, who also is a tantra teacher. They met at a yoga class and she knew he was her prince. Lisa joined the training classes that Rundy was teaching, giving them added time to be together, as she was still living in Cleveland while he was in California.

These meetings gave them an opportunity to have many magical settings for their vows to each other. One night, particularly auspicious because of the placement of the moon in the sky, they traveled to the top of a mountain, despite the cold, to be closer to the sky and slept outdoors to be connected to the elements.

Consistent with the tantric tradition of taking turns, as described in Chapters 10 and 11, "Giving Her the Best Nights Ever" and "Giving Him the Best Nights Ever," Rundy and Lisa each had their turn to be giver and also to receive the other's nurturing, service, honoring, and loving. Their marriage ceremony lasted four days, and included many ritualistic and beautiful choreographed steps:

➤ **Day 1: Honoring the goddess** Lisa's day started with Rundy nurturing her with massages and baths scented with candles, oils, and hibiscus and rose petals, following an eastern wedding tradition. All day long he fed his beloved exotic fruits, surprised her with love letters and small presents, sang to her, read poetry, brushed her hair, and kissed every part of her to make her feel honored and cherished.

➤ **Day 2: Honoring the god** The following day was Rundy's turn to receive. During those 24 hours they made love without coming to climax, breathing in each other's desire, allowing the energy to build inside their bodies.

Tantra Tutorial

Rebirthing, summarized in Chapter 16, "Advanced Tantric Lovemaking Techniques," is a sacred process in which a person's birth is re-enacted, but ensuring that it is a positive experience. The process is attended and assisted by those who greatly honor and respect it, and treat it with great reverence.

➤ **Day 3: Rebirthing** This day was dedicated to the advanced tantric ritual of rebirthing, followed by a feast. The foods represent colors of the energy centers (for example red tomatoes or green artichokes) to symbolize total connection. Lovemaking continued without coming to orgasm, to continue to build energy and desire.

➤ **Day 4: Taking the vows** At sunrise the couple went naked to the top of a cliff overlooking the ocean, near their home, with a *shamaness* minister (enlightened being) as a witness. As the sun came up, they exchanged their vows in a Maithuna-style ceremony (described in Chapter 16). They sat in yab yum with lingam inside yoni to create a total connection, looking into each other's eyes, honoring the 108 gods and goddesses in each other. They spoke their heartfelt promises for their life together, written by them especially for the occasion.

Other rituals in Rundy and Lisa's ceremony:

➤ The shamaness brought in the energies of the four directions, earth and sky, and all the ancients so that their bodies would become one with each other's and all of the cosmos.

➤ Rundy and Lisa did extended breathing together, connecting all their chakras (sex, heart, third eyes kissing), their bodies vibrating (not having orgasm), melting deeper and deeper into each other.

➤ The couple lay back to back with their sacrums touching, to allow their powerful kundalini energy to rise, as the sun rose.

Rundy and Lisa celebrate their love.

Mark and Patricia's Hindu Fire Ceremony

Mark Michaels and Patricia Johnson are a tantra teacher team. They got married in a tantric ceremony, at which their dear friend and teacher Bhagavan Das performed a *Hindu fire ceremony,* assisted by his wife Mira. Guests included their parents, who participated in the ritual. Later, a small group of tantrikas gathered to invoke ancient traditions and bless their union.

"It was a beautiful and profound experience," says Mark. "We feel it is only one of many marriage ceremonies we will have." This is consistent with the tradition of the Hindu wedding ceremony, in which you make a commitment for seven lifetimes.

"Perhaps more important," Mark adds, "we view marriage not as a state of being or something brought into being by a ceremony. Rather it is a process, an ongoing unfolding. Thus, we are constantly in the process of marrying each other. "Conjugal" comes from the same Sanskrit root as the word "yoga." The root, *yug*, means yoking or union. Dr. John Mumford (their teacher) tells us that it is the most difficult yoga of all. As in other forms of yoga, the process of marriage is not about achieving a goal, it is all about what happens along the way."

Tantra teachers Mark and Patricia at their wedding.

Tantra Tales

Tantra teachers Sasha Lessin and Janet were at a conference at a California retreat center, attended by many tantric friends, when they decided one evening to get married, and created a ceremony on the spot. The bride and groom were lifted in the air in chairs as friends (and anyone else at the conference!) danced around them in celebration.

Keeping the Fires Burning

Antoinette and Dick Asimus, teachers at Tantrika International, have maintained their monogamous commitment to each other in a marriage that has lasted more than 30 years. "Our love is stronger because of our tantric practice," says Antoinette. How do they do it? Antoinette shares two of their secrets. "We honor our commitment to each other every day by making love and including some yogic and spiritual practices in our lovemaking. And every two or three months, we make a date for a tantra day where we experience the timelessness of tantric lovemaking for a whole day, celebrating at the end of the day with dinner at a five-star restaurant." "Yummy!" she adds.

Tantra teachers Paul Ramana Das and Marilena Silbey have been married in a tantric union for more than a decade and call their partnership an *alignment and aloinment,* meaning they are lined up spiritually and sexually no matter what their individual paths. On a trip to Hawaii to celebrate Marilena's 55th birthday, they made a promise to have "a honeymoon every day." They also wrote a partnership constitution, in which they pledged to continually practice the following:

➤ Love in their hearts for each other.

➤ Good intentions.

➤ Clear communication.

➤ Positive language.

➤ Celebration of their male and female aspects in the healthy dance of sacred sexuality.

➤ A deep commitment to an ongoing intimate relationship.

"We encourage everyone to come up with their own list of decrees for their love," says Ramana Das. "This gives you a sense of joint willingness to weave a strong relationship and build love forever."

The Least You Need to Know

➤ Tantric marriage ceremonies include many rituals of song, dance, and dedications to honor spirits, gods and goddesses, all guests, and each other.

➤ Couples who marry in tantric ceremonies do not always go through legal civil ceremonies or get state licenses, yet still consider their union sacred and definitive.

➤ Tantric marriage ceremonies always include personal statements from the couple and sometimes from guests, to set intentions, make acknowledgments, and state lifetime pledges.

➤ Tantric marriage ceremonies are usually one of many, to signify ongoing commitment.

➤ Ongoing and shared tantric practice can help solidify a couple's long-term commitment.

Chapter 21

When He Resists or She Strays

In This Chapter

➤ When you're sure about tantric sex but your partner isn't

➤ How to change a skeptical partner's mind

➤ Making it work despite different points of view

➤ Can tantric love survive an affair?

➤ Energy boosters: what you can do to re-ignite the spark

Surely you are excited about your tantric journey. You've shifted your perspective about sex and love, and are becoming intrigued with the possibilities for the deepest connection you have ever known. But wait—there's a rock in the road. What if your partner is not as intrigued as you, even after you've shown him or her this book? What can you do? Can you ever convince someone to share your new vision? This chapter will help you with that dilemma.

Worse yet, what if you've already convinced your partner to enjoy tantalizing tantra, but then he or she took it further than the boundaries of your relationship, and let the sexual energy lead him or her into bed with someone else? Or perhaps it's you who is tempted to taste the treasures of another tantric lover and fears the havoc it will wreak on your present relationship. What to do now? This chapter addresses those issues, too.

When One of You Is Convinced But the Other Isn't Sure

If you're in a relationship and you both agree to find out what tantric sex is all about, it's easy to begin practicing immediately. You've started already, by getting this far in this book. You can start right now to put into practice what you're reading. Check Appendix B, "Workshops, Web Sites, Teachers, and Tantra Communities," for workshops and recommended teachers, and sign up right now for a seminar to learn more.

But what if you've discovered tantric sex and really want to pursue the exciting things you're reading about in this book, but your current paramour is unsure? It is not uncommon that one person in a relationship is intrigued and ready for a new path whereas the other has reservations. Don't despair; all is not lost. I can offer you some hope. I've seen it happen: A partner can come around. Here are some suggestions to approach a resistant beloved with your desire to travel this path together:

➤ Be prepared for the excuses. Your partner might say there's not enough time for practice or money for courses. Instead of protesting, listen and accept his point of view. Resistance only gets stronger if you argue or make your partner wrong.

➤ Understand and accept the fears. The practices in tantric sex can make you feel vulnerable, as feelings come up that might have been suppressed for years. It's not easy to be present in the moment. Instead of getting angry, empathize that your partner might not have the strength at this time to be so open and vulnerable.

➤ Explain your point of view and your interest in the practices clearly and without defensiveness.

Talking through your differences about tantra.

➤ Point out the benefits that she can relate to. If your partner values physical fitness, emphasize the health benefits. If she is more psychologically oriented, describe possible growth from an emotional point of view.

➤ Supply your lover with videos, Web sites, books, and audiotapes (check those listed in Appendixes B and C) to illustrate that this is a sacred practice. Explain the mood, energy, spirit, and philosophy of tantra to your partner. Sometimes a picture is worth a thousand words, so videos can offer clear pictures of what tantra is about, especially helpful for beginners on any spiritual path. Audio tapes can help too, as they offer a more personal touch than an advertising flyer, with a voice talking to you. Tantra master Charles Muir sends a free audiotape on request that describes the practices in a clear and engaging way (you'll find his contact information in Appendix B).

➤ Be honest about what you think and feel. Offer to show your partner what you have discovered and why you feel tantric sex is a wonderful lifestyle choice. Speak to your partner up front about your desire to study tantra. Give him a chance to be supportive.

➤ Don't nag. Attitudes can change, so bring the subject up every now and then, but not with persistence and annoyance.

➤ Avoid climbing on a pulpit. It's difficult to convert someone to what you think and believe. Honor your partner's path. Allow your partner to be herself—and you to be you. Like philosophy or religion, deep thoughts regarding spirituality and sexuality are unique to each individual and are very personal choices.

➤ Ultimately support your partner's position, as that is the spirit of tantra. Continue your lovingness, as that is the goal of the path.

Hell No, I Won't Go!

The dread, of course, is that you are really gung ho about taking this high road to bliss, but your partner is dead set against it. It can happen. But don't be so quick to throw in the towel on the relationship. Partnerships have survived when one person studies tantra but the other doesn't. Of course it would be better if you both spoke the same language. Of course, it's more serious than if one of you likes sushi and the other cringes at the thought of raw fish; or if one of you likes romance movies and the other prefers classic comedies; or if one of you wants to climb the Himalayas and the other can think of nothing better than vegging out on a beach. It's more serious than that, because tantra is a commitment to a lifestyle. But when your love is working on other levels, you can still be a team, raising kids, sharing your dreams, and even making love.

Know What's Best for You

Stay on your personal path. Recognize your own fears of being alone or disagreeing with a partner whose opinion or approval you value. When you maintain your integrity you might suffer some consequences, but you'll never lose yourself; in the last analysis, you have to decide what's best for you. If your partner just won't share this path with you, you might have to go on the journey alone. But you can still stay together—if you bring home the love you learn to generate and make it benefit this relationship.

A partner's reaction is a test of his or her character. Karin's husband told her, "If you feel you'll be happy finding out what this is all about, go for it. I'm not interested but I support you doing what you need to do." That shows true love! On the other hand, Donna was so dismayed at Frank's desire to go to a tantra introductory class that she threatened to date other men and hid mail that he received from the tantra organization. Her intolerance revealed her true character, that had not been as evident before. Eventually Frank knew it had to be over.

Dr. Judy's TantrAdvice

It is possible that pursuing tantric sex can draw you toward like-minded people with whom you share more time and intimacy, which can lead you to decide that your primary relationship is not so satisfying. That's the time to talk seriously with your partner about your future together and to consider seeking professional counseling.

Honor Your Agreements

Tantra teaches honor. Respect your agreements with a partner, especially regarding the most sensitive issue of commitment and exclusivity about sexuality. Be honest about what your intentions are. Offer reassurance—if you can do so honestly—that you will not engage in any activities that are not in alignment with your relationship agreement. Your partner deserves your love and respect. Make sure you are studying tantra with a practitioner who will honor, respect, and support your relationship agreement; ask the teacher any questions that you have about your situation, to get some advice and support.

Don't Sneak Off to a Tantra Talk

Be honest if you decide to attend an evening event or class, or see a practitioner or healer without your partner. Explain that your intention in gaining this knowledge, experience, or healing is to grow and transform your ability to deepen your love, in this relationship and in all of your life.

Share Your Growth

After your tantra class, private healing session, or tantra seminar, share what you experienced with your partner, even if he or she doesn't have a deep appreciation or understanding of what you are going through. As you learn, show your partner the immediate effects of your training and your newfound sensitivity, loving ways, caring attitudes, and spiritual depth. Keep making a low-key invitation to join you at some entry-level event that would be especially safe and nonthreatening. Be patient. Remember to allow your partner to keep sharing his or her concerns over time and give you feedback.

When the Going Gets Tough

Be prepared that a partner's differing experience, feelings, or judgments about tantra can precipitate a confrontation in your relationship. I know this could be traumatic, but welcome it! Don't blame it directly on tantra. A blowup just means that you were headed toward some pivotal moment anyway; this just happened to be the catalyst—it could have been something else!

The topic of tantra presses people's hot buttons, because it's associated with sex (already a threatening subject) and promises transformation (worrisome if you fear the unknown). Reread and share with your partner the sections about the corrections of myths about sex and tantra in Chapter 1, "What Is Tantric Sex?"

When a Relationship Has to End

Blocks to Bliss

If you attend tantra functions, don't keep it a secret from your beloved. This kind of deception is contrary to tantric practice and erodes the energy that you are trying to purify. In fact, your practices may make you more vulnerable to being caught in any deceit, because they make you more transparent in the course of being open and loving.

Blocks to Bliss

A partner's resistance to tantra might be based on past abuse that has been repressed. Unconscious conflicts and fears might be triggered at the thought of being open to feelings and love.

Sometimes you can thank your lucky stars that things came to a head, and that you and your partner broke up because of your separate paths. Be grateful you found out now that you were incompatible. Don't second-guess what could have happened. Face the sadness and use the experience as a real-life experience of tantric principles: that the love you have never leaves you even though particular people might.

Tantra Tales

Cassie dragged Steve to three tantra weekend workshops around the country, desperate to break through his controlling nature and get him to be more intimate. "I love making love with him," she said, "but when he's deep inside me he gets to thrusting fast and I try to get him to feel the love we have, but it's too late." Steve enjoyed some of the exercises during the workshops, but back home he complained that he had no time or interest to do them; eventually he told her "I can't do this anymore," and asked her to move out. Cassie came to see the value of being set free from this unfulfilling relationship and honor her own desire for a more intimate connection instead of being obsessed with changing Steve.

Tantric Tolerance

In these modern times, there are many relationship paradigms that are acceptable. More and more people are choosing to define their own rules. Couplings that were once seen as alternative are now more mainstream, and people are becoming more open about their choices and living what's real for them instead of leading a double life in fear of what others and society think of them.

This new era is seeing a re-emergence of the open relationships that bloomed but bombed in the 1970s. Couples choosing more love for all, called *polyamorous,* accept and invite third, fourth, or fifth parties to join their intimate circle, including sexual activity. Polyamorous men and women face challenges with commitment and jealousy like traditional monogamous pairs, but feel this new way of relating is more satisfying for them. There are communities and conventions for couples sharing this lifestyle (see Appendix B for references).

What to Do About Tantric Sex Affairs

Most affairs are painful, and can be even more so when tantric sex practices are involved, because of the association to higher levels of eroticism and therefore deeper connections. One partner's sexual relations or liaisons that the other does not sanction are inevitably hurtful. Before betrayal sends you off the deep end, evaluate the situation, including the reasons it happened, your choices about what to do, and what new level you can reach in your relationship as a result.

An Affair as Energy Booster

The reasons people cheat are diverse, including intimacy and commitment fears, situations that separate partners or put two people together under intense circumstances anger toward the partner, or even a different philosophy of life. Some people don't want to be monogamous and their cheating doesn't necessarily point to any underlying problem in the relationship. In many relationships, however, an affair is a wakeup call to a situation that desperately needs to be addressed.

In tantric terms, seeing relationships as energy, there is another reason for affairs. It's called a search for an *energy booster*. Because everything in tantra can be seen as energy, an affair is not necessary; all that is necessary is a new and equally exciting way to boost energy.

A related theory postulates that people seek what is called *New Relationship Energy* (NRE). As described in *Loving More*, a magazine about the polyamorous lifestyle, this defines the high-energy spark and rush of chemicals felt when you meet someone new and get a surge of excitement from the attraction. *Extra Relationship Energy* or *External Relationship Energy* has the same effect, but comes about between people who have known each other a while and had infrequent contact.

Affairs arise from an illusion that someone outside of the relationship has more attractive energy— they appear more sexy, exciting, and desirable because they're not the one handling bills, taking the cat to the vet, or messing up the bathroom. A good way to affair-proof your relationship: When you're tempted to stray, always imagine what it would be like in daily life with a new lover.

The most common area that breaks down in long-term relationships is sexuality. Either the sex itself isn't good, or other problems arise and lovemaking goes from infrequent to never. Anger or guilt shows up in impotence or withdrawal from sex. Couples build up resentments and disappointments that, if left unresolved, could erode a couple's ability to open up in sex. If the problem is never addressed, the entire relationship erodes and

Ecstasy Essentials

We often are attracted to, and attract, lovers who reflect unresolved issues we had with our primary caregivers while growing up, and then want to hurt, cheat, or leave them. Identify how present partners resemble past important people in your life in some physical, emotional, psychological, or energetic way, so you don't keep repeating the same patterns.

Dr. Judy's TantrAdvice

As a therapist, I am constantly struck by how much couples take each other for granted so soon in a relationship. Instead of looking for sparks with someone else, create that desirable energy by tapping into new parts of yourself with your partner.

can lead to a breakup over something that seems unrelated. You have to have courage to talk about what your sexual needs and problems are and get help.

Tantric partners are tuned in to energies within themselves and the people around them, so they are more likely to sense when something is awry. If you sense a problem brewing in your relationship, address it now with your partner before it gets bigger and more difficult to solve. Trust your tantric intuition!

Considerations About Tantric Affairs

If one of you has an affair, it's time to ask some hard questions of yourself and your partner. Use these questions as a guide to clarify some issues and start a confronting conversation:

➤ Are you or your partner involved romantically in a relationship with someone else but not having sex with that person?

➤ If sex is involved, what type of sexual activity is it?

➤ Is protection being used?

➤ What types of diseases are you being exposed to?

➤ What are your agreements about fidelity and has either of you violated those agreements?

➤ What is the nature of the "other" relationship? Is the "third person" an ongoing lover or a fleeting relationship?

➤ Are you both being honest now, or telling lies?

➤ Do you both really want to know what's going on?

➤ What are the motivations behind the affair?

➤ How have you each contributed to this situation and to any behavior you find upsetting?

➤ What steps can you do to improve or change the situation?

➤ Do you want the relationship to end?

➤ Is the relationship already dead and you just haven't buried the corpse?

➤ Do you want to continue and try to fix the relationship?

Tantra Tutorial

An affair always involves some breakdown in communication in a relationship. Learn to effectively communicate your wants and desires to each other. When you open up, you might be surprised at what you each have longed to share. From that place of openness, all things are possible.

It's not easy to have a confrontation, but when it's necessary, have the courage to do it. In the course of a lifetime, everyone experiences disappointments in love, rejecting and being rejected; abandoning or being abandoned. Neither position feels good. Always keep in mind that denial only postpones pain; discussing difficult issues leads to some relief—and resolve.

The Energy Booster Checklist

Ultimately an affair is an opportunity for healing—either yourself or your relationship. Look at everything that happens as a winning situation for you in the long run. As a relationship therapist for many years, I know that any relationship can work if both people want it to. You can heal from tantric love affairs if you work at staying together.

Reflect on what you and your partner can do to give your relationship an energy booster so you continue to be fascinated with each other. Can you learn not to interrupt while he is talking? Take a class or find other interests to become more well-rounded? Lose weight to feel more attractive about yourself? Make your list here. Ask your partner to make a list, too.

Your Relationship Energy Boosters

What I Can Do to Infuse More Energy in My Relationship: **What My Partner Can Do:**

1. _____   _____
2. _____   _____
3. _____   _____
4. _____   _____
5. _____   _____

Look over your lists and talk about which energy boosters you can both put into practice. How do you feel about each other's suggestions? Decide to implement at least one of these each week.

The Least You Need to Know

➤ It is possible to pursue tantric sex to enlightenment and ecstasy whether you are single or in a couple, and whether or not your partner is committed to the same path.

➤ When one partner wants to pursue tantric sexuality but the other doesn't, the relationship is put to a test. Some survive if communication and love keeps growing.

➤ Studying tantra makes you more intuitive and sensitive to the energy between you; therefore, more attuned to potential problems. Trust your intuition.

➤ Temptation for liaisons with others on the same path is possible and can lead to affairs that could cause a breakup. However, staying together despite sexual dalliances is possible if the couple really wants to.

➤ The tantric lifestyle demands honesty, so eventually if one of you has an affair the truth has to be faced and new agreements made about your future together.

➤ Be clear about your agreements concerning exclusivity, and be sensitive to each other's needs sexually and otherwise.

Part 6

Tantra for Everybody in the New Millennium

Now that you've learned how powerfully these practices can manifest sexual energy, empowering you to have more joy, passion, and love, you'll wonder whether they can apply to you and people you know. The answer is yes: No matter what relationship you are in, no matter what your age, tantric principles can make your life a thousand times richer.

Tantra is about honor, respect, and healing. So in this part you'll learn how to extend that respect and healing to yourself, to be ready to adjust to life changes with new life force. And you'll see how you can apply tantric principles to every aspect of your relationships—and every living thing—around you. This will take you beyond sex to a more intense force that can actually reach out and help heal the planet.

Chapter 22

A Lifetime of Tantra: Learning to Love at All Ages

> ### In This Chapter
>
> ➤ How tantric sex keeps you young
>
> ➤ Easing mid-life transitions
>
> ➤ Adapting tantric sex practices for teens
>
> ➤ Preparing kids for a healthier life
>
> ➤ Teaching tantra in schools

So far we've been concentrating on tantra for adults. But the principles and practices of tantra are good for all ages. Everyone can learn to love at any age—and see the benefits in all of life.

In this chapter you'll learn how tantra is a genuine fountain of youth—and can even help the young. I don't mean to imply by any means that kids should engage in sex, but I do mean that practicing tantra yourself and teaching certain principles associated with tantra can help raise healthier kids and create better relationships for all.

Want to Feel and Look Young Again?

In our youth-oriented society, everyone is in search of the fountain of youth; in tantric sex you can actually find it! After tantric lovemaking, you can look at least 10 years younger—and other people notice. I've heard men say to 40-year-old women after tantric sex, "You look like a kid again!" Their faces dramatically change, skin glistens and lines disappear! Eyes sparkle and open wide, and smiles spread from ear to ear.

Tantra Tales

The benefits of tantra happened for Nancy. After her husband died, Nancy panicked, fearing, "There will never be another man who knew me as a young lover, who saw my face at 20. No one will remember how pretty I was as a young woman." However, practicing tantric sex provided a solution: Much to her delight, new lovers remarked to her anyway, "You look 20."

Tantra Tales

Tantrika Carla Tarantola is 59 but looks much younger, something she has been told by lovers. "I'm convinced it is my tantric sex practices," says Carla. "I know that bringing my sexual energy into my heart and living from love every moment of my life is what makes me look so much younger."

Rejuvenation happens on several levels. Psychologically, you feel young! And physiologically, there are real changes. The physical activities in tantric sex practices—cycling energy, breathing deeply, exercising muscles through white tantra (yoga) practices—keep organs vital by being fed with blood and nutrients, and keep the body supple and toned. The neurons in the brain are activated, and the immune system is stimulated, contributing to all-around health and maintenance of youthfulness.

The Real Fountain of Youth in Amrita Flow

Some very experienced tantra teachers and tantrikas, such as Caroline Muir in Maui, credit the flow of amrita (the liquid emitted during female ejaculation) for rejuvenation. (The techniques for bringing about the flow have been described in earlier chapters on how to arouse the woman and stimulate her goddess space or G spot.) "Amrita is considered the "nectar of the goddess," the key to her immortality and youthfulness. "It is a woman's gift to herself and her lover," says Caroline, "and definitely keeps me young." Another expert disagrees, claiming that the amrita flow ages women. Although this dismissal can be consistent with Taoist beliefs that a man's ejaculations drain his energy, most women I know who have this experience (myself included) agree with Caroline and treasure the experience and its positive effects. As one woman said, "When my love liquid flows, my whole face and being is so full of joy and so relaxed that of course I look young again!"

Tantra in Older Years

As the percentage of the population over 65 has tripled during the past century, understanding sexuality throughout the entire life span has become essential for everyone. Contrary to popular beliefs, sexuality can and does play an important part in the lives of older adults. Those people who were most sexually active in their younger years are most likely to remain sexually active as they age. Such sexual expression among the elderly has been identified as a predicator of general health.

Forget any notions you might have about cutting back on sex as you age. Studies show that although sexual activity does decline with age, this is partly due to illness and unavailability of partners. Sexuality is normal and natural in older years! Studies show that sexual activity is possible and takes place through the 70s and beyond. In any case, remember that tantric sex as the transmission of energy goes way beyond any specific sexual activity or intercourse; therefore, pleasure and bliss are possible for your entire life.

Facing the Changes

Our sexual desire is bombarded with challenges from emotional, psychological and physiological onslaughts. As we age, hormones can wreak havoc on our physical, emotional, and sexual life. Emotional challenges escalate at critical ages, such as the classic mid-life crisis. Some experts claim that mid-life crises are even starting now as early as age 35, especially in our youth-dominated society. Even younger men and women in their mid-20s are going through what I call the "quarter-life crisis," stressing out that they are no longer "young" and now have to bear huge responsibilities as adults in a fast-paced, competitive, and money-obsessed society. Baby boomers bemoan passing years, as their parents become ill, children grow up and leave the nest, friends suffer heart attacks at younger ages, and they face the ever-dreaded life review with regrets or broken dreams. But if you keep your energy surging, as through tantric practices, biological slowdowns and emotional lows don't have to ruin your life.

Easing Her Time Through Menopause

Given physical and psychological benefits of tantric sex as described throughout this book, moving your energy this way can ease the symptoms of menopause. These include body aches and pains, night sweats, headaches, and even depression. The flexibility and shape of the vagina can change, and thinning and shortening of the vaginal canal and less lubrication can lead to pain and avoidance of sex. However, tantric sex practices limber the body, help the mind focus on other pleasures, and can even create more lubrication

Tantra Tutorial

Several research studies show that continued sexual activity keeps you healthy and that general satisfaction with life, love, and sex helps you live longer. Both men and women who continued satisfying relationships had fewer physical ailments and lower mortality rates.

naturally. Instead of "drying up," the mid-life menopausal woman can experience an increase in her sex drive and a sense of sexual freedom that she's never felt before.

As tantric lover Pam says, "I sailed through menopause without even noticing except that I stopped having my period." Menopausal women like Pam who practice tantric sex also accept their change of life, seeing it as a blessing—a "reunion with the ancient mother." Even though fertility is revered in the tantra tradition, the goddess appears equally in older age in the form of the wise woman.

Spiritual counselor Barbara Bizou runs workshops for people in life transition. An expert on ritual and author of the book *The Joys of Everyday Rituals*, Barbara recommends this ritual that a menopausal woman can do to celebrate her life stage and acknowledge her transition into a new—and rich—stage of life. Invite your friends over, including those who are also going through menopause, and ask each to write down a memory about some painful time at another stage of life, to release the energy of that old memory and make room for the new stage that they are entering. Then burn the pieces of paper in a big pot in the middle of the room, and as they burn, each woman should light a candle and say a prayer for healing the past and opening up to the start of a new life.

Tantra Tales

During the change of life one of the major problems is lack of lubrication. However, tantra practices can make you moist again. Says Nancy, "Now at 49, I don't get as excited instantly as I did before but the tantric practices have taught me how to move my pelvis and loosen up the energy flow in my body. When I add the movements to my breathing, within 10 minutes I get very lubricated. Sometimes I don't even need to reach orgasm because the practices and pleasure is enough."

When He Has a Mid-Life Crisis

Similarly, tantric sex practices can ease the symptoms of what has become known as male menopause (or *andropause*), when men gradually have less testosterone as they age and go through slumps and depressions similar to women. Lowered hormone levels can lead to a man's reduced sex drive, along with less interest in relationships and career. As with mid-life women, the mid-life man can get tired, anxious, irritable, sweaty, and achy. He could feel helpless and hopeless. Sexually, he worries about being less potent, having less ejaculate, and even whether his penis is shrinking.

Tantric sex helps these men by reviving a great storehouse of their energy and teaching them to shoot it through their bodies (instead of just out the penis!). They learn to generate more energy in their sex center; more blood there leads to stronger erections and a seemingly bigger penis. And they learn to enjoy new levels of love and creativity, energizing them in every aspect of their family, relationships, and business life.

By learning techniques to prolong sexual stimulation before they come, as I outlined in great detail in Chapter 12, "Make Lovemaking Last … and Last … and Last," men gain more control over their ejaculation. The result is more pleasure in their sexual relationship, which becomes an escalating positive cycle of better sex, more love, more happiness, and feeling more potent. What a good deal!

Seven Keys to Happier Life Transitions Through Tantric Love

Practicing tantric sex offers many ways to keep you fit through all of life's changes in many ways:

➤ Tantra unleashes feelings, emotions, and attitudes that you've always wanted to express in a relationship. It focuses you on intimacy, closeness, affection, and tenderness toward a partner, which sustains sexuality, and provides self-esteem and inspiration—all essential with passing years.

➤ Tantric sex takes you way beyond sex as just intercourse to realms of intimate expression so that just looking in each other's eyes or breathing together can set off orgasmic waves. Romance, kissing, hand holding and oral sex are all honored to create closeness even when intercourse is not possible. Exploring these options deepens sexual expression, love, and intimacy.

➤ In tantric sex, limp lingams are just as loveable as erect ones. In fact, energy can be generated from the lingam no matter what its state.

➤ Tantric sex creates more lubrication for the yoni and relaxes, heals, and revitalizes the woman at any age.

Ecstasy Essentials

There are many benefits of tantric orgasm to the body and brain. Cycling sexual and orgasmic energy throughout the body vitalizes major organs and body systems (including the circulatory, cardiovascular, nervous, immune, and endocrine systems). Stimulating the pituitary and pineal glands is especially positive, because they are central to the pathway to bliss in the brain.

➤ Because synchronizing the partners' energies is fundamental in tantric sex, some physiological changes (such as a man taking longer to achieve an erection or ejaculation) can benefit the couple's lovemaking.

➤ Tantric sex emphasizes loving touch, which triggers chemicals from the body that are proven to strengthen the immune system, and therefore ensure longer life—besides making you feel loved and good all over.

➤ Tantra encourages expression and leads to higher states of sexual and emotional satisfaction, which result in higher self-esteem, further intensifying an overall sense of well-being.

Filling the Empty Nest

Parents often suffer distress from what's called "the empty nest syndrome," when kids leave home for school or marriage. Depression can result from being separated from children as well as from being faced with a spouse whom they hardly know anymore because the marriage took a back seat to child-rearing or careers. Yet, this can be a terrific time for starting tantric practice, when the couple needs to get to know each other again and when they now have more time to spend together.

When a Partner Dies

The largest obstacle for older couples is illness or the death of a partner. When this tragedy happens, you don't have to end your tantric love life. Go back to being your own beloved and pleasure yourself. After you've mourned, seek a new love and relive days of happiness—believe that you won't be betraying your partner and that you deserve pleasure.

Tantra for College Students

Meghan Lambert and Ryan Deluz are a California-based teacher team trained in Kriya tantra yoga (through Tantrika International) who specialize in teaching college students. As college students themselves, they consider their age group "indigo children" or "children of the golden age." According to Ryan, this means that their spiritual consciousness has naturally evolved into an awareness of heart connections and subtle energies. "This allows us as teachers to do a lot more with the group," says Meghan, "since they bring with them a creative passion for this material, which amplifies the group energy."

"Young people are ready to discover who they are as a creative and sexual being and to channel it in a way that will bring them to a deeper place of intimacy within themselves and within all forms of relationship," explains Meghan, who once referred to herself as "Morning Star" and is author of a self-published book on dolphins, called

Free Like a Dolphin. "Because they are so open to experience themselves and because they feel so comfortable with us—since we are college students, too—our groups get very juicy," she explains, "which means everyone is excited and having fun."

"Having knowledge of tantra at this age when you're having a lot of insecurity in yourself and your relationships, can eliminate a lot of stumbling and experiences that end up being unfulfilling," says Ryan. "If you receive the teachings as a young adult, imagine what kind of marriage you can create, and imagine how rich and powerful your relationships will be at 30, 40, or older. You are learning right from the start how to use your relationships and life experiences as opportunities to evolve spiritually and to heal yourself."

Tantra for Teens

Teens even younger than college students can also relate to tantra, although formal workshops for this age group are still in their infancy. "It's ideal to get young people thinking about entering their lives of loving from a tantra perspective," says Boulder-based psychologist and teen tantra teacher Shavana Fineberg. "In my work, teens get wonderful lessons about how to connect from their heart and redirect their sexual energy both within their own bodies and toward their actions in the outside world, so they don't feel that the only thing they can do with this powerful energy is to have sex."

"People get scared when they think of teen tantra," says Fineberg, "but this work is not about teens being sexual. In fact, the exercises give teens more power to choose abstinence. The workshops are equally appropriate for teens choosing abstinence, those thinking of being sexual, and those already sexually active." In group discussions, girls particularly enjoy hearing what the boys have to say about "What do boys really want?" and boys really like the meditation exercises, says Fineberg.

Being honest and learning to say no (to what you don't want or to going out) is another favorite lesson. Boys can feel a new sense of freedom and confidence when they learn that they can be the one, besides girls, to say "no" to sex. One 17-year-old boy told Fineberg, "Learning how to say no to a girl when she was coming on to me was a new experience."

Tantra Tutorial

Most teens in tantra groups are referred by their parents who have taken tantra workshops and realize the value of teaching their teens about self-esteem, responsibility, communication, friendship, and love as contexts for sexual sharing.

Healthier Kids When You're a Tantra Parent

Following a tantric lifestyle can help you raise healthy children. Here are several ways to do that:

➤ Be a model of a loving relationship. Kids learn from what they see at home; if you are loving, they are more likely to be loving, too.

➤ Work out any of your own problems. The happier you are as a person, the better mood you will be in when you relate to them. If you harbor anger toward men or women, they will pick up on it.

➤ Show affection. When I'm asked, as I so often am, "When should I teach my kids about sex?" I always respond, "You teach them about sex from the moment they are born by how you hold them." Hold them often, to give them comfort and security.

➤ Give them a positive attitude about sex and love. Too many men and women I have counseled suffer from fears, embarrassment, and shame about their bodies or about sex; you can prevent this by not instilling these attitudes.

➤ Teach youngsters stress-reducing techniques such as meditation.

➤ Play with kids in ways that heighten their sensitivity to relationships and to their bodies, and let them have fun! One mother told me that on rainy days she used to do veil dancing with her children. "This was a wonderful game that taught my kids to feel comfortable with their bodies. Even though people think of veils as sissy, it was a great activity for my son, to help him get past the macho ways his father was always teaching him."

Dr. Judy's TantrAdvice

I've seen so many women and men suffer from negative attitudes in their childhood about masturbation that ruined their sex lives and self-esteem in adulthood. Parents can prevent this by not telling children they are "bad" or punishing them for such behavior.

Tantra Tales

The adolescent daughter of one of my best friends was getting depressed about all the normal problems of her age group (school, friends, body changes). Then she decided to redecorate her room as a meditation sanctuary, asking her mom to paint stars on the ceiling, draping gold cloth over a dresser as an altar on which to set a statue of Buddha, and collecting other objects that felt spiritual to her (crystals, painted boxes). Doing this helped her relax and feel more empowered, making her feel connected to strong spirits.

How the School System Can Be Tantric

Certain schooling practices may actually be tantric in nature, even though they are not identified as such. Certainly they are not meant to be sexual, but they *are* meant to increase a child's sensory perception. That skill prepares children for more self awareness and greater capability to be totally present in each experience and each moment.

One certified pre-primary teacher, who is also a tantra teacher and my good friend, recognizes the astounding similarities between adult tantra training and teaching young children. While doing her tantra training, she noticed how some of the exercises were similar to the exercises that she has used in her 14 years of teaching 3-, 4-, and 5-year-olds. "Of course the exercises for the children are not intended for sexual purposes," she told me, "But the value in terms of sensory perception, and encouraging spirit, self-awareness, and presence in the moment are equivalent—and wonderful."

Examples of these exercises include one that stimulates sensitivity to the environment by having kids truly smell the air when they go outside. Another encourages the capability to truly experience and distinguish different sensations. For example, in a fabric game, kids pick pieces of fabric from a box that match the texture of fabric rubbed on their palms. Or they hold cotton, jersey knit, or velvet and answer the question, "Are these the same or different?"

In a fruit play game, strawberries are put on the kids' tongues and they answer the question, "What does that feel like?" In another exercise, the kids are given 12 containers with substances inside that represent different scents (like peppermint, vanilla, or coffee) and are challenged to put the containers with similar scents side by side.

Sensory ("tantric") exercises also encourage kids to fully experience each moment—the same goal of adult tantra training. "The kids' eyes would sparkle the more they tuned in to their senses," the teacher said, "because they felt pride over mastering their environment."

Tantra Tutorial

Women enjoy soft, sensuous touch in lovemaking, yet fewer men than women have the natural knack for sensuous massage. For this reason, it is especially helpful to teach young boys how to develop keen sensory perception.

The Payoff of Sensory Training at All Ages

"Children more fully experienced in tactile sense tend to be more sensitive, tender, and loving toward their peers," the teacher also told me, calling the phenomenon, "gentle hands for gentle creatures." Such sensory training helps develop respect, honoring each other, and more expressiveness in communication. "They approach each other with hugs as opposed to the aggressiveness that is more common in children who are not trained in this way," she said.

Sensory awareness similarly improves adult communication and self-esteem. For example, the more that adults are sensitive to touch, the more nurtured the cells in their body feel, and the more softly they approach and touch others.

The Least You Need to Know

➤ Tantric sex practices are rejuvenating and help you look and feel younger.

➤ Tantra can help men and women deal with the emotional, psychological, physiological, and hormonal changes that come with menopause and mid-life transitions.

➤ The principles of tantra help teens and college-age kids develop healthier attitudes toward sex, have higher self-esteem, and make wiser choices about their relationships.

➤ Raising children with tantric sex principles in mind does not encourage irresponsible sexuality; rather it helps them grow up to be loving people.

➤ Teaching the principles of tantra to people of all ages makes them more sensitive toward the world around them and kinder to other people.

Chapter 23

Lifestyles and Situations: Tantra for All Relationships

In This Chapter

➤ Tantra in the world of cyberspace

➤ Seeing beyond the physical to the soul

➤ Tantric sex for gay men and women

➤ The value of tantra in disability

➤ Tantra in new models of relating

➤ How tantric loving energy benefits everything around you

In the last chapter I talked about how tantra teaches valuable lessons and love for people of all ages, but what about all persuasions? Yes, the practice can apply to every relationship or situation you're in, because tantra is based on the union of energies, not specific entities or even specific genitalia. This makes the practices applicable to everyone regardless of sexual orientation, physical form, or even presence in the flesh—since tantra, like every other topic—is taking on a cyberform!

Cybertantra

With the increasing presence of the Internet and advances in technology, some people are becoming technological tantric partners, including practicing *cybertantra*. That means that just as in other aspects of relationships, the practices of tantra are being exchanged over the Internet with tantra enthusiasts communicating with each other, or even clients seeking sessions over cyberspace.

In the latest edition of my book *The Complete Idiot's Guide to a Healthy Relationship*, I devote an entire chapter to the upsides and downsides of new technology on relationships and how to use it to your advantage. Get a copy and read that chapter to get a full picture of how this new world is changing and how you can keep your love alive in the midst of it all! All the valuable advice given there serves as a good foundation and addition to what I am sharing with you here about practicing tantra.

The Pros of Cybertantra

Tantra is about opening one's heart to love. For many people who are too shy or afraid to be open in personal relationships, the distance of the Internet allows them to be more open in an apparent shield of safety. Connecting through technology rather than in person can help those who are insecure about setting their boundaries learn to do so.

Cyber-connecters can also practice getting close to others and test their limits to intimacy. They can allow hidden aspects of their self to emerge, without as much fear as those who meet face to face, because they can pretend to be someone other than who they really are and escape easily. The Internet has allowed people to achieve "instant intimacy" by writing e-mails, pouring out their most intimate feelings and needs to strangers, or developing "deep" sharing with people whom they hardly know and have not met in person.

Blocks to Bliss

Be very cautious in pouring out your most intimate feelings to a stranger, keeping in mind potential predators on the Internet. Deal with known tantric groups on the Web; check them out first or get a reference. Don't give out personal information to a stranger, and if you must meet face to face, arrange to meet in a public place.

Technological advances beyond even cell phones and beepers allow ever-increasing connections between people, so that long-distance love is even more possible and physical separations less painful. Advances such as sound cards, video streaming, and camera attachments on top of your computer now allow both voice and visual contact between people, increasing the potential for closer connections. Computer technology is further making contact easily possible between peoples around the world, facilitating the world view that is consistent with tantra.

Tantra and sacred sexuality are best studied in person because they are about human connection. Yet energies can also be felt without being face to face—even electronically. Tantric lovers can stay in touch by typing out instant messages or sending e-mails describing exactly what they are doing; for example, writing messages such as "I am exhaling now, sending my love energy out my heart and into your heart."

The Cons of Cybertantra

There is a downside to cybertantra connections. Tantra is about honesty, authenticity, and being who you really are; in contrast, the Internet allows dishonesty in relating. People do pretend to be something they are not, and they do lie about their looks, age, or sex. Great disappointment and deception are possible.

The depersonalization of some technological mediums can facilitate emotional distance and offer escapes from true intimacy and commitment. This depersonalization is the bane of relationships today! The method of interaction through words and writing on the Internet itself can provide an easy escape for those who have deep fears of intimacy or commitment, letting them pretend to be close but actually keeping them away from person-to-person contact. People can withdraw from interactions easily, logging off and disappearing into the safety net and ether of cyberspace.

Dr. Judy's TantrAdvice

An increasing number of tantra coaching and courses are being offered on the Internet. Explore their value to you, but don't use them as replacements for face-to-face meetings. Attend gatherings or take courses in person whenever you can; these are available in cities across the country.

Seeing Beyond the Physical

Millions of people in this country are unhappy with their weight. Over the years of being a sex therapist, it has been painfully clear to me that such unhappiness has also wrecked millions of men and women's sex lives; considering extra pounds unattractive, they withdraw from sex. Tantra teaches love for your body that can help heal self-hatred about one's own weight. It also teaches us to see beyond the physical, which can prevent partners from judging others by the way they look.

Tantra Tutorial

The Web's depersonalization has created an even greater need for methods that facilitate people meeting and connecting in a face-to-face way. Tantra offers this through its workshops and coaching sessions.

Lasting Love for Seemingly Odd Couples

Tantra demands seeing beyond the physical, deep into the soul of the other being— seeing the god or goddess within. As I've mentioned, as soon as you do that, love is possible where it once might never have flourished. Seemingly odd couples become deeply committed, as the typical external perfect matches are vastly overshadowed by the meeting and melting of inner souls.

295

Couples who practice tantra might have larger age differences than even the average couple, as well as differences in race, background, economic status, and every other characteristic you can think of. Increasingly common are the pairings between older women and younger men and different races.

Joshua Smith is a 35-year-old Black man and Laurie Handlers is a 5'2" 50-year-old Jewish girl who readily admits her figure is not shaped like a supermodel's. But Handlers is a powerhouse, and Josh knew it the moment he laid eyes on her. "She's the most amazing woman I ever met," Josh says. "I know she is the female equivalent of me—she is the goddess to my god. I am in awe of her. She keeps me in line because she always tells the truth. I dated a lot of women who I lied to and cheated on, but I could never do that to Laurie because she calls me on everything I do and makes me own up to it. I like that. I grow from being with her every day."

Josh and Laurie share a special love despite differences in age and ethnicity.

Facing Society's Opinions

Seemingly odd couples often have to deal with the criticisms or discomfort of others who are not used to unusual pairings. Parents can have a particularly hard time accepting their children's choices. Don't be dissuaded by others when you know what's right for you. Discuss your differences with your parents, to help them understand and accept your choice of partner.

The New World of Sexuality

Having a space to express intimacy, as is created in tantra, gives people a chance to explore a broad range of feelings in whatever way fits their boundaries and is mutually agreeable. This allows for relationships between people that go beyond sexual roles or orientation. Even though I've explained how tantra emphasizes the union of male and female, you'll recall I keep emphasizing that these are meant as *energies*; not genitalia.

Tantra Tales

Josh knew his mother was unhappy with his choice of Laurie. "I knew she would prefer that I have someone younger and my same race. At first she was cold to Laurie, but I told my mother she had a choice: Either accept my choice of woman or not see me! Gradually she warmed up. At first, she came to accept Laurie as a "sister" because they were the same age. But after taking several of Josh and Laurie's workshops (they co-founded Butterfly Workshops), Josh's mother came to truly love Laurie, and now thay have a beautiful relationship.

Learning to integrate and be open to these two energies can lead to more openness in any type of relationship in which you see beyond the physical into the soul. Heterosexual people could surprise themselves by exploring a same-sex relationship or find themselves bi-curious (attracted to people of both sexes). Following this principle, tantra is equally applicable to any relationship regardless of the particular sex of the partners.

Tantric Sex for Men Who Love Men

Bruce Anderson is a pioneer in applying tantric principles for gay men. Trained by noted tantra teacher Sunyata, Anderson has led classes in California and a weekend workshop for gay male singles and couples (see Appendix B for content info). Anderson notes a difference between heterosexual tantric sex seminars and those for gay men: "Gay men are far more eager to interact with everyone in the group, compared to heterosexual groups, in which women put many more limits on intimate interactions."

Anderson's groups do not include emotional clearing exercises (as others do), concentrating instead on learning the cobra breath and yoga postures. Here's one of his favorite exercises (after reminding partners to always practice safe, protected sex). He instructs, "As part of your erotic play, move into a position in which you sit facing each other in a spider legs position [a modified yab yum in which one leg is crossed over and the other leg crossed under, instead of one partner's legs inside the other's]. Have your lingams touching. With one hand on your beloved's sacrum [at the base of his spine], use the other hand to create erotic delights for yourself and for him. As you feel the sparks rising, take deep breaths, concentrating on the inhalation, feeling a warm current rising up your spine. Stimulate with the intention of surfing on the edges of orgasm!"

Foreheads touch in the tantric kiss.

Keep gazing in each other's eyes. As you are moved to ejaculate, allow your love to rise up and ride the crests, pouring it through your eyes, your heart, and all of your being into your partner. Stay connected as you enjoy and follow the infinite blissful delight as the divine courses through you and your lover.

Anderson became motivated to teach tantra for gay men, because as a gay male himself, he discovered that intensifying his own erotic play led to his most profound experiences of the divine. "Tantra speaks to men who love men," says Anderson, "because it starts from the same premise and impulse upon which we know that we are gay: deep listening and understanding from the core of our bodies."

Anderson explains that the basic tantric sex concept, which is built on the union of polar opposites (male and female) has to be interpreted as an *alchemical marriage* of male and female within oneself, not between the partners. "According to physics, opposite poles ground each other in tantra," he explains, "but in gay tantra, like poles—of two men—create a tantric spark. It's just a different flavor."

Tantric Sex for Goddesses

There are not yet groups exclusively for women who love women similar to Anderson's groups for men. But some women who do not identify themselves as gay are drawn to working with other women in classes or women-only workshops especially devoted to healing the goddess. "I found myself really understanding the meaning of the word 'sisterhood,'" one student told me, "but even more, I found myself appreciating being with other women in ways I never did before."

"Women are ideal healers for each other," one tantra teacher told me. "They are naturally warm, loving, and sensitive." In one exercise in which women break into small groups and practice dancing sensuously for each other, some women end up really enjoying watching and holding each other. They can feel safer with other women than with men, even in doing *sacred sector* healing work. This is especially true if they've been hurt by men in the past.

Tantric Love for Those with Disabilities

Mitch Tepper had already had his accident—diving into a shallow lake when he was just 20 years old, that snapped his spinal cord and confined him to a wheelchair—when he met Cheryl. She says she never noticed the chair. When she met Mitch in college she fell in love with his charm, humor, and intelligence. Nineteen years later, Mitch can give a woman a good whirl around on his lap at a dance party, and the limited movement in his legs and hands hasn't stopped him from enjoying sex, or running a popular pioneer Web site all about the subject (www.Sexualhealth.com).

Tantra Tutorial

A woman's **sacred sector** is another term that refers to the most sensitive areas within her vagina. Other phrases are "goddess space" and "G spot."

"Tantric sex practices are a perfect fit if you're not the perfectly fit specimen," says Mitch, as he describes the unique perspective that tantric sex takes. Tantra shifts the attention away from intercourse or any particular sex act and onto slowing down, focusing on sensations, connecting with your partner, and exchanging energy.

Here are some exercises that Mitch recommends:

➤ Look at your right hand for a few moments and pay attention to what you feel, then focus your attention on your left hand. Pay close attention to the changes you feel from one hand to the other. If you are able, slowly move your hands closer together until you can feel the energy between them. Then you can practice moving that energy around by changing the distance between your hands or the positions of your hands.

➤ Control the pace of your breathing to a slow, relaxed pace with equal time on the inhale and exhale. If you can sense your heartbeat, you can use that as a clock to time the breaths.

➤ Learn to connect with a partner by matching the pace of your breathing while gazing into his or her eyes. You might want to place your hand near your partner's heart while doing this.

➤ Develop sensitivity to touch by paying attention to tiny sensation. Become aware of the feelings and sensations that you have, subtle as they might seem at first.

Tantric ecstasy and orgasm do not need a buildup of sexual tension, friction, ejaculation, or muscular contractions. In fact, there is no need for the traditional idea of sex at all once you have discovered that orgasm can be a deeply relaxing meditation.

Healing Relationships with Your Parents

Some people who experience a growth experience want to share it with everyone important in their life, to bring them closer or to heal the relationship. Tantra teacher Laurie Handlers finally convinced her father to come to a tantra weekend she was teaching. "I had stored up so much anger toward him over the years," she explained. "He never listened to me and always made promises he never kept, even as minor as saying he would call and then not calling for weeks." But after her father attended the weekend, their relationship took a major turn for the better. "I finally told him how I felt all those years and for the first time I felt he really heard me—and he apologized. That did wonders for me."

Her partner and co-teacher Joshua Smith had similar success getting his mother to come to a tantra weekend. "She was always angry with men because my father left her and she had such bad relationships, that I felt she took it out on me and expected too much of me," he told me. "But after she did the workshop, she felt so much better about herself. She knew for the first time that she could be happy, so she is much less angry and controlling of me."

Ecstasy Essentials

Research has shown that stroking your pet lowers people's blood pressure. Feeling love for your pets can inspire you to feel more prone to healthy sexual activity with your partner.

Tantra with Your Pets

Hold on, before you have any visions about what I mean here …! Being tantric with your pets means being loving, and every pet owner knows the value of that. Being loving and open in your heart space will transmit to all living beings around you—including your pets—and inspire them to respond with health and well-being.

There's no doubt that pets pick up on human emotions. The happier and more joyous you are (from better sex and more love), the better you will treat your pets and the better they will respond. Every dog owner knows how sensitive animals can be to their owner's moods; the calmer and more blissful your mood from practicing tantra, the more similar to that vibration will be your pet's disposition.

Research has shown that pet owners often feel closer to their pets than to other humans. Although the precepts of tantric sex would require that you open your heart to other people, single people or those without love partners can express loving energy to their pets and receive the benefits of a heart connection. Pet owners and animal lovers know the joy of talking to a pet, letting out deep emotions and feelings, trusting the animal—allow yourself this as a rehearsal for deep sharing with another human being.

Tantra with Your Plants

I hope I've convinced you about the value of sending love energy to your pets. So am I pushing it too far when I say you can extend the same loving energy to plants? Stay with me on this one! All plant lovers know that plants, like other living things, are sensitive to human emotion and caring. The happier you are, the more attuned you will be to the needs of your plants, from the amount of water to any extra nutrients you give. But research has suggested that plants also respond to people's emotions; growing healthier in a happier environment.

In summary, love and positivity become a cycle: The more you surround yourself with healthy living things, including people, pets, and plants, the more your own mood lifts, and the more motivated you will be, in keeping with tantric practices, to send that positive mood and love back into the world.

The Least You Need to Know

➤ Today's advances in technology can help tantric practitioners stay in touch, but should not take the place of in-person contact.

➤ The theories and practices of tantra as the exchange of energy and honoring of self and others are appropriate for every relationship, regardless of its nature, and allows people to explore all parts of themselves without fear.

➤ Even though tantra technically represents the union of male and female opposites, this refers to energies rather than gender; therefore tantric practices are equally applicable—and proving valuable—for homosexual partners.

➤ The road to higher consciousness and bliss is possible no matter what your particular circumstances or health status.

➤ Every relationship you're in, whether with people, pets, or plants, can be positively affected by your tantric sex pursuits by generating more loving energy.

Chapter 24

Which Path Is Right for You?

In This Chapter

➤ Why guidance is so important

➤ Making sense of the different traditions and schools of tantra

➤ Different opportunities to learn tantric sex

➤ Various types of workshops offered and what they cost

➤ Orientation of different teachers

➤ Choosing the path that's best for you

As in every spiritual practice, philosophy, journey, religion, and school of thought, tantric sex practices have been passed down through the ages and many different disciplines have evolved. As such, there are many practitioners of different styles of tantric sex, many schools of tantra, and different teachers to whom different lineages have been passed down. This chapter will help you sort out those differences so you can choose which path might be best for you.

The common denominator in all the tantric sex practices is harnessing sexual energy for the attainment of enlightenment. The highest goal is to use the energy generated by the spiritual union of two divine beings for the good of all humankind and the universe.

The Importance of Guidance

The use of the breath to move sexual energy through the body is a process that should not be taken lightly. It can be dangerous to engage in some advanced breathing practices, healings, and other rituals before one is fully prepared both psychologically and physically. Thrill seekers and over-enthusiastic students can be left in serious emotional trauma or even develop physical disorders by rushing too quickly down the path to expected bliss. For example, one expert in tantra says that when he was a novice at the practices, sending strong rushes of breath up and down his spine released powerful emotions that caused such violent shaking of his head that his spinal cord was injured, leaving him with serious disabilities.

Contrary to myth, great sex does not always happen intuitively. Even ancient wisdom maintained that sexual arts had to be taught. Teachers help by …

Tantra Tutorial

In his book *Introduction to Tantra: A Vision of Totality* (Wisdom Publications, 1987), Lama Yeshe has likened the need for proper guidance in a teacher/student relationship to the confusion that would arise if instead of getting a Rolls Royce you got a pile of unassembled parts and an instruction manual. Unless you already were a skilled mechanic, you would likely be completely lost.

➤ Giving you feedback on how practices should be done for maximum benefit and safety.

➤ Showing how all the practices fit together until you actually feel it for yourself.

➤ Supporting you in your pursuit and answering any questions you have.

➤ Helping you derive benefits from association with a lineage, as enlightened experience is often passed down to chosen students. In addition, some teachings might not be recorded anywhere and are meant only for oral communication from teacher to student.

➤ Giving you individual tutoring in complex individual practices (such as whether the breath in a practice goes up and down the spine, or central body). (I remember being so worried about whether certain experiences, such as flashes of light or colors, were "right.")

➤ Inspiring you, because they have achieved the goals you seek: of sacred love union or of specific practices such as prolonging orgasm or delaying ejaculation.

Blocks to Bliss

In the ideal world, all teachers and types of tantra would peaceably coexist, allowing you to freely sample from all types. However, as with so many other areas of specialty, competition and schisms have arisen between different schools of tantra. Fallouts happen over many issues such as violating the rules of certain practices, forcing some students to choose between teachers. One advanced student of tantra had a falling out with her teacher and felt excommunicated from the entire tantra community. Be careful not to fall into the approval trap, thinking that anyone holds the key to your enlightenment or acceptance.

Finding the Right Guide

It can be difficult to sort out the best direction for your tantric practice. Ideally a teacher would be a model of developing beyond selfishness, transcending petty concerns while still living in the world, and being dedicated to wisdom and the welfare of others. Some are better examples of this than others.

As the field grows, there are an increasing number of practitioners from all backgrounds. These can include men and women who call themselves "healers," "tantra teachers," "tantra educators," "tantrikas," "dakinis," or "dakas." They could be spiritual counselors and body workers, sex workers, or professionals licensed in a field of study such as massage or dance therapy. Others have training and might be certified by a tantra master who offers training courses; others are not. Only a few are medical doctors with MDs or psychologists with Ph.D.s. The maze can be as complicated as sorting out any counselor who is right for you, for any problem, from depression to anxiety, to a marital problem.

Here are some guidelines to help you choose a teacher who is right for you:

Blocks to Bliss

The spirit of tantra is to unleash your own individuality, your own specialness—to find your own special path. Don't blindly follow someone else's path because you are insecure about your own choices or fearful of trusting your own experiences. Also, be very wary of wounded healers themselves—or worse yet, sex addicts or energy vampires (people who suck energy out of others for their own selfish use).

➤ Check what is written in this book about what tantra involves, and about specific teachers and schools. Refer to Appendixes B, "Workshops, Web Sites, Teachers, and Tantra Communities," and C, "Tantric Tools."

➤ Surf the Web for sites about tantra and follow all links.

➤ Mention your interest to friends and other people you know. You never know who might have similar interests, experience, or contacts.

➤ Contact potential teachers for their materials and get references of other students.

➤ Check the teacher's background training. What is his specialty? What schools did she study at? Assess qualifications in yogic practices, spiritual journeys, and in other health professions.

➤ Follow your intuition. Let yourself be guided about whether this teacher is the right person for you to learn from.

Ecstasy Essentials

There is no uniform certification system or licensure to ensure a teacher's credentials, but some established teachers have offered certification in their methods.

It has been said that a true master does not want to be called "a guru" or a "master," because being enlightened involves a state of detachment to a title, ego needs, or having followers. (One teacher suggested the term *fellow journeyer*.) True gurus, it is said, want you to find the guru inside you. In truth, everyone and every experience is our teacher—but tantra teachers have much to share with us.

Charles and Caroline Muir teaching a class.

Bohdi Avinasha playing music at a tantra teacher training.

Tantra teachers can give sessions or run workshops individually or work in teams. Learning from a committed couple can present an example of a loving relationship, which can be inspiring to students. Another advantage is that you get both a male and female point of view. Some of these couples are listed in Appendix B.

A young couple, Meghan and Ryan, who teach tantra.

The Different Traditions of Sacred Sexuality

Adding to its complexity, tantra has filtered through and intertwined with many other spiritual paths. Indian tantra of Hindu heritage varies from Tibetan tantra of Buddhist heritage, which differs from tantra of Japanese Zen or Chinese Taoist heritage. Within each of these flavors of tantra are many splintered paths, each more liberal or conservative than the root path they sprang from. Yet they also have dramatic similarities, as between tantra as practiced in Eastern cultures and that of the American Indians. Let's look at some of the traditions or terms that describe these practices.

➤ **Hindu**   The Hindus can be credited with the origins of this sacred path since tantra studies flourished in the temples of India centuries ago. Its practices are most commonly known by the texts of the Kama Sutra, the ancient "Bible" of lovemaking that describes not just sexual positions but the value and practices of love.

➤ **Buddhist**   Tantric sex practices spread from India through Nepal and into China, where the Taoist traditions incorporated sacred rites and added their own specific movements, philosophy, and practices. There are many books you can read to explore these different traditions in detail; in this book I introduce you to techniques from various traditions (I always teach and treat clients in a holistic way) so you can design your own program that works for you.

➤ **Taoist**   The major principle of this tradition is unswerving adherence to ejaculatory control, consistent with the view that not to do so ruins a man's health. One of the best-known teachers is Mantak Chia, who has written extensively on the Tao of sex (see the next page).

➤ **Quodoushka**   Originally practices of sacred sexuality from ancient Mayan and Toltec schools of learning, this once-secret Native American Indian system is now being revived. Similar to some forms of tantric sex based on breathing techniques and chakras, Quodoushka teaches the "Fire Breath" as a means to full-body orgasm. The teachings are based on the medicine wheel, whereby a sexual encounter is meant to align the four directions, elements, and corresponding powers; for example: trust and innocence (south); introspection and intuition (west); wisdom and knowledge (north); and enlightenment and illumination (east).

Tantra Tutorial

Seattle tantra teacher Kirby Jacobson has deeply connected to the tantric teachings of many different lineages. He says his teachers have been very generous with him and he's happy to share the knowledge. You can contact him with any questions at earth2kirby@yahoo.com or 206-579-4421.

➤ Trained teachers introduce this knowledge to others, including information about five different levels and types of orgasm for men and women.

➤ In its original form, adolescent males and females would spend three days and nights with no food and water to purify themselves in preparation for initiation into sexual knowledge and behaviors by a Spiritual Fire Woman (also called the Phoenix Fire Woman). This instructress would take youngsters through rites of passage and teach adults more advanced practices (how to please different genital types, achieve five different types of orgasm, and do different breaths) to reach ecstatic states.

➤ Similar to other forms of tantric sex based on breathing techniques and chakras unique to this tradition is the concept of the *medicine wheel* (sacred hoop) that connects all peoples and elements. As such, a sexual encounter honors the four directions: south (representing water, heart, plants); west (representing earth, body, rocks); north (representing wind, mind, animals); and east (representing human beings). Sexuality is in the center, representing the soul, the life force that and connects the body and mind, all beings, and all that exists.

The Tao of sex.

Male
Heart

Female
Heart

Female
Sex

Male
Sex

Osho: The Spiritually Incorrect Mystic

Osho is a Hindu mystic who transcended all religions and traditions. Formerly known as Bhagwan Shree Rajneesh, and referred to as the "spiritually incorrect mystic" in a recent biography, he wrote extensively about tantric practices as a vehicle for transformation and achieving personal, interpersonal, and universal freedom; ecstasy; and enlightenment. Unlike other meditation gurus who demand celibacy, Osho celebrated

physical pleasures, becoming embroiled in scandals in the 1970s and 1980s that resulted in his deportation from the United States. Osho came to be called (to his displeasure!) the "Sex Guru." Although he died years ago, his spirit lives on at his popular ashram in Pune, India; devoted followers teach his techniques throughout the world. Many current tantric masters, like Margot Anand and Bodhi Avinasha, were early students of Osho and credit him for the origins of many of their teachings as well as for their personal transformation.

An example of Osho's teaching on love: "Become loving. When you are in the embrace, become the embrace. Become the kiss. Forget yourself so totally that you can say, 'I am no more. Only love exists.' Then the heart is not beating, but love is beating. Then the blood is not circulating, but love is circulating. Then eyes are not seeing, love is seeing."

Ecstasy Essentials

Perhaps the most popular of Osho's exercises is the dynamic meditation (described more fully in Chapter 6, "Amp Up or Damp Down Your Sexual Energy"). It is done in four steps: accelerated breathing, emotional release, quieting the mind, and celebration.

Blocks to Bliss

Just as you should in picking any doctor or health consultant, check credentials and background of any healer or tantra teacher. Use the tips throughout this book and recommendations in Appendix B to help your research. Interview the person thoroughly. Ask for—and talk with—references.

Different Trainings

Teachers of tantric sex usually offer a varied menu of services, including individual sessions, evening seminars, weekend or week-long workshops or teacher trainings. These are held around the country and in many places around the world. By contacting the central office (see Appendix B), you can find out about those in your area or request that teachers come to your area.

Some trainings are more geared toward sexual practices (such as learning ejaculation control or helping women free their expression), while others include practices like meditation and emotional clearing. You may find different trainings helpful at different points in your journey. I recommend that you get a balanced experience, so that you don't just experience sexual energy in sexual activities. The goal should be to achieve higher states of consciousness that unite body, mind, and soul for spiritual enlightenment.

Me teaching a tantra workshop.

Types of Healers and Other Practitioners

As with tantra teachers, there are various kinds of healers. Tantrikas, dakinis, and dakas are Sanskrit terms for the male and female teachers who have been trained in advanced experiences of tantric transformation, and are able to transmit these teachings to others. In ancient times they were considered holy beings. Today they are healers with expertise in diverse fields related to healing (you should ask about their backgrounds), such as philosophy, yoga, sacred sexuality, metaphysics, and intuitive counseling. Some are devoted to tantric healing as their job while others have a career in other fields.

Some of these healers might interact with their students to demonstrate how specific practices are done, supervise couples' practices, or engage in hands-on educational sessions or more intense healings as described in Chapter 17, "Sexual Healing to Set You Free." They might describe their "sultry voice" or "clear blue eyes" and advertise their services on the Internet as "sacred space healer" or "priestess of sexual arts"; and offer services such as temple dances, sacred spot work

Tantra Tales

The source of one tradition of tantra (called tantric Kriya Yoga) is an immortal called Babaji, supposedly born in 203 A.D. and living in his original form in a cave in the Himalayas. Babaji guides those who seek his help and transmits the practices to many students who have adapted the methods to their own particular branch. When I saw Babaji's image I couldn't tell whether it was a male or female—exactly the goal of tantra! Babaji is honored in the Tantrika International tradition.

(described in Chapter 17), various kinds of bodywork and massage, bathing and love-making rituals, and goddess celebrations. Tantric priests might offer similar services for women.

There are far fewer male healers than females (partly because women are more nurturing by nature). Male healers often use their given Western name, as opposed to female healers who often assume Indian or exotic names. Some men and women who train as sexual healers don't practice it as such, but do so for their own learning. As one said, "In real life I have a day job."

Starting and Keeping Up Your Practice

When you are considering a path, go to introductory tantric evenings to experience whether it's a good fit with you. After workshops and weekends, you can continue your study with booster sessions that some teachers offer to keep your individual practices growing and the community cohesive.

Continuing Your Tantra Education

Most established tantra teachers offer workshops on various themes as well as different levels of training. These usually start with an introductory weekend workshop and progress to a week-long course. Many students want to participate more because they enjoy it so much and it gives them support in their practices; you can repeat courses you like (usually for a reduced rate) or take a teacher training course even if you don't plan to teach.

Dr. Judy's TantrAdvice

Treat levels of tantra expertise with the same respect as you would getting a black belt in karate. It is unwise to dabble in tantric sex, read a book or take a course, and then proclaim, "I am a tantrika" and to announce this to potential partners, or use this to entice lovers.

Related training in other areas (such as meditation, dance, or making relationships work) can help your tantric practice, but be careful not to get distracted by too many other pursuits. For example, shaman training greatly deepened my appreciation for spirituality and even the role of spirits in healing. As a result, I spent considerable time at temples in Nepal and studied with a Tibetan shaman as part of a training program given by an American expert in shamanism, Larry Peters.

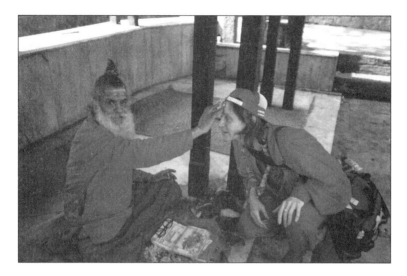

Being blessed at the shrine of Kali in Nepal.

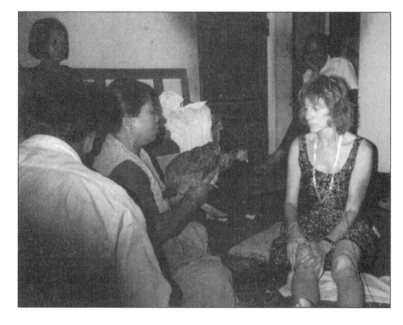

Training in Tamang Buddhism in Nepal.

A Few Things to Be Aware Of

If you go to a tantra gathering, be aware of certain aspects that might cause some discomfort for you. Ask ahead of time about the following concerns:

➤ **Can I stay with my partner?** If you come as a couple, ask whether you will be allowed to stay together for all the exercises, or if you will be asked to interact with the group and choose people you don't know as a partner for some exercises. Some participants are insecure about a partner's commitment, and get jealous seeing him or her working with—and perhaps deeply connecting with—another person, even if nothing comes of it.

➤ **How will I be paired up if I come alone?** If you come as a single, be prepared to be asked to pair up with someone of the opposite sex for some exercises, although your choices and boundaries should always be respected. Most tantric sex workshops are designed for singles as well as couples, and make serious efforts to achieve an equal number of males and females. Various games create these pairings (picking matching cards, wandering the room to whomever your energy draws you). Where numbers are not balanced, you might be asked to play the role of the opposite sex.

➤ **How much time is required?** Everyone is busy, but you do not want to be distracted by phone calls and other business when doing your practices at home or when participating in a workshop. It's best to devote full attention to the experience, and not be preoccupied with phone calls or checking e-mail.

➤ **Will there be nudity?** While exhibitionism (displays of nudity) is generally frowned upon, some workshops create a safe space for you to take off your clothes during exercises if you choose. In others, various states of disrobing occur, especially for certain massage experiences (although nudity is not intended to be sexual). Couples might do exercises together unclothed, but have no interaction with others in the group; in others, there might be massages or other exercises in groups of varying numbers. More advanced classes obviously are more relaxed about such things. Be aware of your own comfort level. Ask beforehand what's in store so you are not caught unaware or disturb others by unpredicted distress.

Dr. Judy's TantrAdvice

Check the level (beginner or advanced) of events. For example, one tantra event was advertised as "We strip down and are covered in oil by multiple attentive hands." Know whether you are prepared for this.

➤ **Is there sexual activity?** Actual sex is not what the workshops are about, but some places and teachers are more permissive and activities can go on after class if people so choose. There is some controversy within the tantra community over physical contact. Be clear about your boundaries and the teacher's or healer's orientation. If private coaching by specific types of healers includes some intimate activity at your request, this will usually be obvious from their Web site or an initial conversation. More conservative practitioners—certainly those who belong to professional's organization and are state licensed—will not engage in such interaction; giving couples exercises to do at home in private.

Don't look to tantric sex workshops to solve serious emotional or relationship problems. Seek professional advice. At one of her week-long workshops, Margot Anand offered a unique service: counseling sessions with qualified therapists. The therapists were myself, a licensed clinical psychologist, and a medical doctor, Harold Kornylack. This proved highly successful and useful for participants, because the exercises in the workshop, while pleasurable, also stimulated some deeper emotional issues. For example, one woman remembered for the first time after 20 years having been abused as a child. Another woman became intensely jealous about her husband appearing to flirt with someone. A man became distraught over rejection when he was not chosen to do an exercise by the woman he eyed. Ask about the availability of such assistance, or referrals.

Costs

Costs of individual evenings average about $20, or are based on contributions or ability to pay. Weekends can cost from $180 to $395. Discounts are available for couples, or if you sign up several people, work as an assistant, or repeat the course. Because many trainings like to have an equal number of men and women present, they might offer better discounts if they need an extra Shiva or Shakti. If you sponsor or organize the weekend and invite a qualified teacher, you can come free or even earn some money for your work.

Do Tantra Weekends Work?

The first research ever conducted on the effects of teaching sacred loving and healing the god/goddess was done on a group attending a weekend workshop led by master yoga and tantra teacher Sasha Lessin. He was assisted by me and his wife, Janet Kira Lessin. Before the workshop, many of the female participants described themselves as shy, embarrassed, and even shameful about sex—feelings that were often linked to dissatisfaction about their body (mostly feeling overweight), fears of intimacy and rejection, and past sexual abuses.

After the workshop, participants reported useful lessons in improved communication, honoring themselves and their relationships, and feeling more open and trusting. The results indicated an improvement in the quality of intimacy and communication, and in the amount of pleasure the women—and the men—felt in their sexual and everyday lives.

Ecstasy Essentials

Budget your money for your courses. Consider it an expense for continuing education. What could be more valuable for your growth?

New Trends in Tantric Experiences

Gatherings is a recent term referring to a playful social that provides some organized activities and ice breakers (games, pujas, massage round-robins, potluck meals) to facilitate connecting with like-minded people in a sacred, sensual, loving, and safe environment. These gatherings are consistent with tantric principles and lifestyle but are more free form than workshops. Although there is some structure, you never know

exactly what's going to happen, because each gathering is co-created by the group and its unique combination of people. The events often include dance, singing, drumming, feasts, and depending on the facilities, outdoor activities such as hiking or spending time on a beach. Often people bring favorite foods and musical instruments. Come dressed casually.

Some tantra teachers are now offering exotic escapes that are like vacations, but consistent with tantric lifestyle and practices. These are held at elaborate homes (sometimes their own) or other locations with sensual environments (complete with hot tubs, saunas, lakes, and indoor pools). These might be the same places where they hold workshops, seminars, and private coaching; however, the mini-vacations offer a less structured and more fun atmosphere.

Tantra Tutorial

In the tantric sex community, *playshops* refer to gatherings that focus on the pursuit of pleasure and give permission for people to play together as couples or in groups. Be aware of the kind of openness this could involve.

Harmony in Paradise in Boulder, Colorado, is the site of tantric getaways.

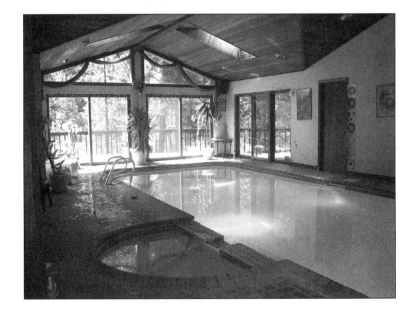

Dolphin and whale trips run by tantra teachers are also increasingly popular. Dolphin consciousness is part of the tantric wave (the undulation that is characteristic of ecstasy). Certainly, awareness and preservation of these amazing beings is consistent with tantric appreciation of preservation of the environment, nature, and all beings.

Various retreat centers are known as locales for seminars and workshops about tantric sex and workshops on related topics, often taught by noted teachers and experts. The surroundings and facilities are particularly conducive to heart-centered events and opening to loving energy. These include Harbin Hot Springs, two hours north of San Francisco; the Omega Center, which has headquarters in New York but a retreat center upstate; and the Zen Center, east of Los Angeles.

Integrating Tantric Sex with Other Techniques

Many of the techniques of tantric sex described in this book and used by noted tantric masters are adapted from emotional processes used in other therapeutic modalities or spiritual practices. For example, the emotional release processes are adapted from techniques used by other Western therapists, and some meditation and breathing practices are taken from various Eastern traditions.

The practices of tantric sex can often be smoothly integrated into spiritual growth routines with many other disciplines. Western practitioners of tantra are increasingly following this trend, as more collaborate on developing workshops, and as the techniques of tantric sex become more popular. Tantric practices are increasingly used by more traditional therapists who follow different Western disciplines. Therapists like myself, with extensive training in clinical psychology and backgrounds in psychoanalytic theory, use tantra in a mixture of many other therapeutic tools and techniques. This holistic approach can include disciplines like cognitive-behavioral therapy, neurolinguistic programming, and Gestalt therapy. I call it being an "eclectic" therapist—custom designing the approach for whatever the person needs.

The Least You Need to Know

➤ Tantra is a growing discipline, with an increasing number of options available for seminars, workshops, and evening events you can attend.

➤ Because there are no uniform guidelines for the certification of tantra teachers, it can be difficult to choose one; do considerable research and get recommendations from others before making your choice.

➤ Research tantric teachers and events, but also follow your heart about what's right for you. Attending an introductory evening is a good idea.

➤ Engaging in some advanced breathing practices, healings, and other rituals before one is fully prepared can be dangerous; find a qualified teacher to guide you.

➤ Budget your money and time to allow for your continued education to keep you focused on your practice and to advance your growth. Take ongoing courses at different levels, repeating courses or getting individual coaching.

Chapter 25

A Healing Force for Now and the Future

In This Chapter

➤ Tantra as a global community

➤ How tantra can interrupt the terrible cycle of abuse

➤ Turning away from artificial highs

➤ Tantra as a healing force in the face of illness

➤ More tolerance is possible the tantra way

➤ How tantra can help heal the world

You've learned throughout this book that the principles of tantra and tantric sex are to keep an open heart and to heal hurts. Tantra knows no prejudices for any humans, living things—or any things, for that matter—in the world. Therefore, you can express your loving heart energy in many directions and receive the benefits from that experience. This approach can fuel your connection to all beings and ultimately to the universe, protect you from the normal devastation of loss that people suffer, and open you to new dimensions of loving toward all beings.

I've also emphasized how tantra can be healthy for every aspect of your life. As we move forward in this new millennium, life becomes more complicated and challenging, and world conflicts more threatening. Tantric sex can help in adjusting to the fast-paced, stressful, and technologically digitized world we live in. In this chapter, you'll learn how the tantric lifestyle can help you survive—and thrive—in this new age and make a better future for you, your loved ones, and the world.

You Are Not Alone

People on certain paths or with similar interests tend to travel in similar circles and pursue similar interests. This is especially true when it comes to tantra. One of the most touching aspects of studying tantra is that you become connected to a group of people referred to as the "tantra community." Serious students even refer to the "tantra family." Of course this can lead to all the typical conflicts that might arise in any family (from petty complaints to big fallouts). However, in general the participants feel a sense of belonging and mutual caring that is especially valuable in these trying, isolating times.

The Internet has made it possible for everyone to communicate more freely all around the world. For tantra enthusiasts, this means an expansion of the tantra community globally. It's easy to join the Internet global tantra community to feel more connected to the world, ask questions, and share your experiences.

Sending Energy, Especially in the Face of Tragedy

With a growing spiritual community and more people committed to healing, there are an increasing number of global events intended to heal the planet. The annual World AIDS Day is a model for this paradigm, in which people all over the world are invited to focus their attention on a particular subject; in this case, AIDS. The tantra community has promoted such events, consistent with tantric principles of spreading love energy.

When the devastating tragedy of the terrorist attacks on the World Trade Towers took place in September 2001, e-mails of love and support instantly flooded the Internet. Members of the tantra community were particularly active in sending out messages of support and healing. I posted many such messages on my site at www.cameraplanet .com, including "mini" therapy sessions with people I met on the street who wanted advice about troubling issues. One man wanted to know if it was okay to want more sex; he was ashamed to feel this way in the face of others losing their lives and loved ones. I reassured him that was normal. Another woman asked me if she should divorce her husband, as she was consumed with anger that she needed to talk about the tragedy but he refused to discuss it.

Any threat to life can lead to depression and withdrawal from relationships and sex, or the opposite—a desire for deeper connection in love and even more sex, out of a desire to reaffirm life. For example, one San Francisco hospital reported more babies born nine months after a devastating earthquake. And think of the number of marriages and babies conceived before men went off to World War II. When life is threatened, people need love. It's the time for the spirit, energy, and practice of tantra, with its emphasis on love.

Tantra Tales

People need to be told how much they are loved, and fear that they won't get the love they need. Saying "I love you" is a basic teaching in tantra. After the World Trade Center attacks, one Arab college student asked me whether girls would not date him now out of distrust for people of his ethnicity. A young woman asked my help to get her boyfriend to commit to her. She had asked him what he would do if she were in danger, a question I told him really meant that she needed him to tell her how much he cares. He finally understood her needs and agreed to her requests to spend more time together.

At one session of our advanced teacher training with Tantrika International, Bodhi Avinasha invited students to spiritually join a similar advanced group in Germany, to put our energies together to send healing energy to the planet. The practice started with a process called *Yoga Nidra*, leading to deep relaxation. This was followed by guided imagery, in which Bodhi described exactly what the hill in Germany where the group lived looked like, and the route of light energy that we would ride to get there. Several of the participants in both countries successfully had the experience.

Tantra Tutorial

Yoga Nidra, known as "sleep of the yogi," is a technique to progressively relax body parts and still the mind, to reach that moment when you feel about to fall asleep but are still awake. This is a magical time to direct your consciousness and empower your intentions. Being in that state is also useful to help people stop smoking and beat other addictions.

The next time you are with your beloved, send love energy you have charged through your chakras and cycled together out to the world—for love and healing for all (as shown in the following illustration).

*Sending out healing love
energy to the world.*

Healing the Cycles of Abuse

The number of women and men of all ages who have been abused—emotionally, physically, or sexually—is shocking. I have heard so many of these sad tales from people calling my radio show to share their stories. Fortunately, people are paying more attention to these traumas, facilitating healing and preventing further victimization. But more needs to be done! Tantric practices can actually create a future with less prevalence of such violations in several ways:

➤ Tantric practices encourage men and women to set their boundaries, respect the rights of others, and communicate with more loving intention. In this way, there will be less possibility of misunderstanding or power struggles that lead to sexual harassment or more serious issues.

➤ By fostering self-esteem in youngsters and teaching them to expect respect, they will be more capable of resisting peer pressures that get them in trouble, and instead make wise decisions and develop healthy relationships.

➤ Tantric practices can actually reduce the possibility of becoming a victim of abuse. This is partly due to the fact that becoming sensitive to energies can help you detect potential dangers and deflect attacks.

➤ Such awareness about energy can help youngsters resist potentially predatory behaviors. By learning that their body is a sacred area, they can understand the lesson that no one has a right to see or touch their sacred areas without their permission, and if anything bad happens, they will be more likely to tell an adult immediately and express their feelings.

➤ Practicing tantra can help heal women and men who have been abused to regain self-respect and trust, because the philosophy puts such emphasis on respect, equality of partners, maintaining control over your own body, and self-expression. Having a partner who honors these principles and generating loving energy can also help these women and men trust new beloveds to allow healthy physical contact and healthy closeness.

➤ Tantric practices can help stop the victim/victimizer cycle by focusing on feeling loved and sending out love, asking permission before you touch, transmuting sexual urges into other energies, and healing past pains.

Fortunately, people now feel less stigmatized when seeking help when faced with problems such as abuse. Following a tantric lifestyle that fosters kindness toward oneself continues this healthy attitude that problems are not shameful defects or disasters, but opportunities for personal growth. Couples and even extended family groups can seek help together, consistent with the tantric spirit of empathy, caring, and extended community.

Dr. Judy's TantrAdvice

Encourage children to open their hearts more readily to others of different backgrounds. Do the same, and you might be surprised at the love that comes your way!

A Healthy Way to Get High

Now that you know about tantric practices, you might be willing to see how the type of exercises, including breathing and generating energy, can pale the pursuit of artificial highs through drugs and alcohol. Why take drugs and risk those dangers when you can get the same—and *better*—effects the natural, tantric way? Here are just a few examples:

➤ The Shakti shake, fire breath, Osho meditation, lama breaths, freestyle dancing, and sexercises can get your adrenaline going in the same way as the dangerous drug, speed.

➤ The meditative practices, such as chanting "om" and alternate nostril breathing, can make you as calm as taking a downer. Best of all, you get to control it all!

➤ Breathing and sending energy through your body can make your brain explode in the same way as mind-altering drugs. Try doing the bandhas (muscle holds described in Chapter 5, "Prep Your Body Temple of Love") and hold the breath before you shoot it through your chakras. You'll get a better, more natural blast than any drug can give you, with no complication, addiction, or side effects. Pleasure is at your fingertips. Take it in through the nose (your breath that is,) and blow your mind!

Tantra as a Healing Force in the Face of Illness

Tantric sex utilizes energy to heal pains stored in the body. These do not just apply to sexual hurts from past sexual experiences but to emotional wounds that are associated with hurts, rejections, and even to real physical illnesses. The techniques work because they give a person control over his or her energy, help them build powerful pools of energy through the sexual charge, and then direct their energy.

Directing energy through tantra practice is consistent with techniques used to heal serious illnesses, by helping patients use imagery to identify where bad cells are and direct their good cells to overcome the bad ones. This can be used in many disorders, even life-threatening illnesses such as cancer.

Ecstasy Essentials

Imagery techniques give patients control over their illnesses. Famed medical doctor and cancer specialist Bernie Siegel has been recommending these techniques and successfully using them with his patients for years.

California tantra teacher Diane Greenberg specializes in helping women with cancer by teaching them tantric sex techniques. "My major approach, and the belief that I teach women, is that being turned on is a major healing force," says Greenberg. She notes that this life-threatening disease insults a woman's sense of femininity, and that drugs often cause what she labels "a libido-ectomy" or an excising of sex drive.

Greenberg invites women to consider that even during a cancer crisis, a woman can still enjoy her sexuality and sense of womanhood. She encourages women to be present to their feelings, to give attention to their yoni and breast areas, and to use breathing and mudras to send love, energy, and "juice" to their own body and to their partners. Greenberg insists that women should not ignore their anatomy and genitalia, as many do when their libido is low and embarrassment about their body is high. Greenberg helps them reframe what is and is not lovely (such as mastectomy scars), and encourages them to let love heal. "Magic happens," says Greenberg, "when women with cancer practice tantra and suffer less."

How Tantra Promotes Tolerance and Diversity

We cannot avoid news stories about tragedies that evolve from racial, ethnic, and lifestyle diversity. Religious groups are still killing each other. Prejudice against people who choose different lifestyles—homosexuals, transgendered people—still runs rampant. History is full of wars that create an "us against them" mentality.

Yet we are becoming a global community, with all races, cultures, and creeds blending to create a new breed of human. Groups with alternative lifestyles have formed communities and action organizations. The tantric lifestyle fosters cooperation and trust rather than distrust and aggression. A generation of humans embracing tantra is capable of breaking the cycle of dysfunction and destruction by fostering a desire to support rather than destroy others.

How Tantric Sex Can Help Heal the World

Tantra communities often network to come together at times of *harmonic convergence* to anchor in peace and love for the planet. It happened after the World Trade attacks, when members of the tantra community sent out e-mail messages requesting people to all pray for peace at exactly the same time. Other tantra practitioners practiced sex magic, as described in Chapter 15, "Make It Juicy with Magic and Play." During the height of sexual energy arousal, they sent out healing love energy to the world.

A lofty goal, indeed—tantric sex saving the world! Yet, practicing tantric sex can actually help bring about more peace in the world. The fact is, the happier you are with yourself, the more tolerant you are of others. The more satisfied you are with your relationships, the more willing you are to treat others well and see to it that they are as happy as you are.

Tantric practices help you go beyond this patriarchal world of dominator consciousness in which one feels superior over the other, and enter a world of balance, harmony, and peace. Through tantra, you realize that nothing in the human condition is alien to yourself and begin to feel your sisters and brothers and other creatures that share this world with you. Once you feel others, you can no longer wish them ill or harm them. With this new

Ecstasy Essentials

Diversity expert and tantra teacher John Hill travels around the country teaching organizations how to become more tolerant of differences in race, age, and sex. He says, "When we realize that we are all the same, we can approach people with the respect they deserve, which will not only benefit the individual but the entire organization, with ripples felt in the larger community."

Tantra Tutorial

Increasingly, research is focusing on energy transmission for healing. Deepak Chopra's Center for Well Being is collaborating with the Institute of Noetic Sciences and Bastyr University, along with federal monies from the National Institutes of Health, on "The Neural-Energy Transfer Project" to scientifically explain the power of prayer.

paradigm, you change individually, and the planet as a whole changes, to create a true partnership society with equality for all.

> ### The Least You Need to Know
>
> ➤ Studying tantra connects you to a global tantric community that can provide you with a sense of belonging and mutual caring.
>
> ➤ The practices of tantra can heal the wounds of abuse and put an end to the victim/victimizer cycle of abuse.
>
> ➤ Tantric practices hold the power to help heal many physical and emotional illnesses, even those that are life threatening.
>
> ➤ The tolerance and understanding necessary to heal racial and international tensions is facilitated by tantric practices, that teach people to come from love.
>
> ➤ Love, honor, and respect for oneself and partners consistent with a tantric lifestyle can extend to the larger community and the world, creating the potential for peace.

More About Tantra

Glossary

amrita   Female ejaculate, also called the nectar of the goddess, and considered a blessing for the partner and the fountain of youth.

bandha   Muscular lock, used to direct and intensify sacred energy.

beloved   A person with whom you share loving energy at the most committed level, and with the highest of intentions toward your mutual good.

bindi   A decoration that tantric women place on the third eye; to dazzle, but also to aid the woman and her partner in focusing during meditation. The word formally means "seed" or "dot," which symbolizes the union of male and female. Red dots are received from the mother, and white dots from the father, at conception.

bliss   An extremely ecstatic and expansive feeling often characterized by clear light that fills the mind and body.

chakra   A center of energy, in the shape of a wheel, that emanates from certain body areas or centers, and is the focus of concentration in tantric sex practices. The seven centers are located at the base of spine, genitals, belly, heart, throat, forehead (third eye), and top of the head.

daka   The Sanskrit name for a highly trained male who helps arouse blissful sexual energy in another who wants to learn tantric practices. A male healer who embodies Shiva energy and serves Shakti unconditionally, considered a priest who could be versed in many disciplines including healing, yoga, sexuality, philosophy, psychology, and metaphysics.

dakini   The female equivalent of the daka. The Sanskrit name for a highly trained female who helps arouse blissful sexual energy in another person who is learning tantric practices. Also a goddess or priestess who is a healer and, like the daka, can have varied expertise in a number of disciplines.

deity-yoga   The practice of aligning oneself with a deity in meditation for the specific purpose of attaining the qualities embodied by that deity.

deva/devi   Another term to refer to gods and goddesses respectively, a deity, cosmic power, or holy creative force.

empowerment   An initiation into tantric practices, used in modern times to refer to personal strength to follow one's path with convictions and overcoming any fears.

energy   The life force from within that can be pooled internally and then channeled to create magnificent results in the inner and outer worlds.

goddess/god deities   Spiritually enlightened, powerful, erotic, sexual, or fertility related energies worshipped in ritualistic ways. Refers to ancient beings as well as every contemporary woman and man, each equally deserving of being treated with respect and honor.

grounding   Connecting solidly to the earth; feeling secure and centered within one's body, as through the energy of the first (base) chakra.

healer   A person who facilitates the growth of another while being clear of personal needs or demands.

holding the space   Contributing your positive energy to whatever is happening to make the environment or people safe.

initiation   A process by which an authorized teacher trains you in specific practices and deems that you are ready for these.

inner flute   A clear breathing pathway through the energy centers (chakras) of your body, so that you can almost hear the air in a flutelike sound, traveling through your body.

kundalini   Blissful energy dormant within the spine until activated by tantric practices. Often depicted as a coiled serpent that moves up the spine.

lingam   The phallus. A man's "wand of light" derived from the word "linga," meaning pillar of adoration and worship.

maithuna   Elaborate tantric ritual with many ceremonial steps, usually culminating in some form of sacred sexual union.

mandala   A diagram symbolic of a message about life and death and the nature of being, used as a tool for meditation. The design often depicts animal forms, nature scenes and particular deities and evokes their properties or aspects.

mantra   Recitations (of words, phrases or sacred Sanskrit syllables) used in practicing meditations, the repeating of which focuses attention and invokes spiritual powers.

meditation   Concentration that stills the mind to allow pure energy to exist without the interference of thoughts or emotions.

mudra   Sacred hand gestures to focus the body's energy with intention.

nadis   Subtle nerve channels related to physical body and energy healing.

nirvana   Reaching the highest state of bliss and enlightenment that is liberated from the attachment to worldly possessions. Also considered as the ultimate spiritual peace that transcends birth and death so that the soul no longer needs to incarnate on the earth plane.

prana   Energy, air, breath, life force that is generated in the body by nurturing, healing, physical, and mental practices, healthy eating and devotion to self-transformation and enlightenment.

puja   A specific ritual, or sacred circle of worship performed by a group of people.

rituals   Actions that are special or ceremonial in nature. Those done during tantric lovemaking include bathing, making dedications of love, and setting intentions.

safe space   The experience of being protected from danger, either referring to a physical location or to the ambiance created by the people present. This facilitates free expression.

Sanskrit   The ancient sacred Hindu language in which most religious texts are written, which expresses a total philosophical, scientific and religious body of knowledge about spiritual and sacred practices to reach higher states of consciousness. The word means "perfect" or "complete."

separation   The sensation of being apart from others, created by our thinking that we are different, or by withholding emotions or thoughts.

sexual healing   An experience in which a healer facilitates someone in a session where sexual energy is aroused and allowed to be expressed for the person's highest good.

Shakti   A name used to refer to the ultimate energy created by the force of the feminine, and any woman as a goddess. Also the name of a Hindu deity who represents the divine mother and lover who unites with Lord Shiva for blissful consciousness.

Shiva   A name used to refer to any man as the ultimate representation of male energy. Also, the cosmic masculine force capable of creation or destruction, the divine male, worshipped in tantric practices and manifested in many forms, who combines with Shakti for blissful union.

Shiva/Shakti mudra   An exercise of bringing the energy up from the earth (the source of feminine Shakti energy)into the heart area and bringing it down from the sky (the source of male Shiva energy) into the heart area.

shushumma   The central energy channel, visualized as a tube of light in front of the spine.

spooning position   A position where one partner lies against the other with his chest pressed against her back, meant to create connection or provide safety and protection.

329

tanghka Sacred paintings, usually of deities and other life forms, that represent universal themes and forces. Focusing on the images assist in the attainment of various states of consciousness and awareness of the nature of life and death.

tantra Sanskrit word for sacred teachings and practices that lead to high states of bliss and enlightenment. A mystical and spiritual system that combines philosophy, psychology and cosmology and transmutes energy in order to achieve a balance between opposites and the integration and evolution of mind, body and spirit. Characterized by an honoring of the goddess, uniting with god energy.

tantric sex Using the teachings of tantra in the sexual union to reach high states of bliss and enlightenment.

tantric sex master A person trained in tantric sex practices who can teach others on the path.

tantric temple Your body, in the sacred act of giving and receiving pleasure for yourself and your partner; also, any place in which you engage in tantric lovemaking rituals (bedroom, another room in the house, hotel room that you specify as a sacred place for lovemaking for even one night).

tantrika Any woman practiced in the art of moving sexual energy to reach higher states of consciousness and bliss for herself and a partner. In ancient times, a woman expert in the arts of lovemaking.

third eye The symbolic eye on the forehead between our two eyes that is a focal point for concentration toward higher states of consciousness.

transmuting energy Moving energy from one energy center to another, such as using the breath to pull energy up from the sexual center into the heart area.

vajra A Sanskrit term for the male genital organ, or lingam (also called a jewel, or dorje in Tibetan), symbolic of power, indestructibility and great worth. Considered a magical weapon or thunderbolt, it is depicted in an emblem or forged into a three-dimensional object with two crown-like shapes connected with a ball in the center. The male symbol is combined with a bell, symbolizing the female, to create a union of both energies.

visualization The use of creative imagination in meditation to conjure up states of being.

yab yum A pose used in many tantric sex practices in which woman sits astride her partner, facing him so that their chakras are aligned to facilitate their connection. Their feet can meet behind each other's backs, to further encircle them.

yang Energy that manifests as masculine energy, symbolic of qualities that are active, analytic and associated with the heaven and father. Meant to unite with yin (feminine) energy in order to achieve balance necessary for enlightenment.

yantra Mystic geometrical diagram used for healing meditation.

yin Energy that manifests as feminine, considered symbolic of receptivity, nurturance, earth and all that is opposite to yang energy. Meant to unite with yang in order to achieve balance and wholeness, necessary for enlightenment.

yoga A physical discipline that conditions the body as a vehicle through which the mind can attain higher states of consciousness.

yogi/yogini Sanskrit names to refer to gods and goddesses (devas and devis) or classes of spiritual beings, as well as those males and females who engage in yoga practices.

yoni Sanskrit word for the vagina, a woman's sacred temple, the symbol of Shakti or female power.

Appendix B

Workshops, Web Sites, Teachers, and Tantra Communities

Listed here are some helpful resources for you to start—and continue—your practice. I've listed whatever information the source provided. Once you get started, you'll inevitably link from one site to another and find what you need. Get in touch with me (see ad page) with any questions.

Teachers and Workshops

Here is information about various people and places you can explore for more information about tantric practices and training experiences. The list includes contact information for tantra teachers and resources referred to in this book to help guide your choice of what's best for you. These offer a variety of services, including events, workshops for individuals and couples, various levels of advanced work, private coaching, and teacher trainings. Their sites also offer books, videos, CDs, clothing, and other items for tantric practice.

Tantrika International
Executive Director: Antoinette Asimus
1-888-TANTRIKA (1-888-826-8745)
E-mail: tantrikaIn@aol.com
Web site: www.tantrikainternational.com

Weekend workshops and week-long trainings at introductory and more advanced levels given by trained teachers in the Tantrika International tradition founded by Bodhi Avinasha, author of *Jewel in the Lotus* and *Living in Bliss*. Comprehensive approach unifies mind, body, and spirit to harness sexual energy to higher states of consciousness and ecstasy. Also offers teacher certification, books, videos, and other items.

Charles and Caroline Muir
Source School of Tantra
P.O. Box 1451
Wailuku, HI 96793
808-572-8364
Fax: 808-572-8622
E-mail: tantra@mauigateway.com
Web site: www.sourcetantra.com

A yoga master and sexual healer for over 20 years, the Muirs are pioneers in the field of tantra in America and offer a wide variety of courses for beginning or advanced singles and couples, including certification for teachers. Thousands of men and women have taken their weekend workshops with special emphasis on freeing—and healing—sexual energy and honoring the goddess. Books and videos on "conscious loving" and secrets of female sexual ecstasy as well as other items are also available.

Butterfly Workshops
Founders: Laurie Handlers and Joshua Smith
3701 Reno Road, NW
Washington, DC 20008
202-686-7440
E-mail: info@butterflyworkshops.com
Web site: www.butterflyworkshops.com

Called "the place where people fly," this committed couple offers workshops on subjects like bliss, ecstasy, and personal empowerment; courses in creative techniques like Yogaboxing; and vacation retreats in the U.S. and abroad for individuals and couples at all levels. Also sells clothing, jewelry, videos, books, music, and artwork.

Carla Tarantola
718-899-2267
E-mail: carla@tantranewyork.com
Web site: www.TantraNewYork.com

Private tantric energy sessions for men, women, and couples; and tantra seminars and workshops for small and large groups in New York and around the country. Carla has 20 years as a yoga instructor and relationship counselor.

Celebrations of Love
Founder: Lori Star
c/o Sunrise Center
45 San Clemente Drive, Suite C-200
Corte Madera, CA 94925
415-924-LIVE (415-924-5483)
Web site: www.celebrationsoflove.com

Comprehensive programs of tantric study from a variety of teachers, and weekend and other vacation retreats as well as celebratory evening events. Popular courses in "Tantra, Healing, and Sacred Sexuality" and "Breath, Love, and Passion," also in communication and massage.

Robert Frey
P.O. Box 1006
Studio City, CA 91614
818-784-0110
E-mail: Robert@sacredtantra.com
Web site: www.SacredTantra.com

Leads or co-leads workshops and tantric events, especially with original music. Background in meditation and Sufism, Buddhis and counseling.

Sky Dancing Tantra
Founder: Margo Anand
P.O. Box 2967
San Rafael, CA 94912-2967
415-454-6030
E-mail: skyoffice@infoasis.com
Web site: www.margotanand.com

A pioneer of tantra and student of Osho, Anand's brand of tantra, Skydancing, is taught by her trainees in the U.S., while she does special weeklong workshops and trainings. Author of many books on tantric sex, including *The Art of Sexual Magic*, she is currently pursuing a life-long dream to set up a spiritual church.

Marci Javril
13428 Maxella Avenue #136
Marina del Rey, CA 90292
310-306-9838
Web site: http://vitalenergycenter.com/classes.html

Certified body worker, massage therapist, talented intuitive healer, and tantric sex teacher offers certification courses in bodywork, as well as tantra events, courses, and coaching for men and women.

Taoist Sex
Universal Tao Center Co. Ltd.
Founder: Mantak Chia
274/1 Moo 7, Luang Nua, Doi
Saket, Chiang Mai 50220, Thailand
1-66-53-495-596
Fax: 1-66-53-495-852
E-mail: universaltao@universal-tao.com or info@tao-garden.com
Web sites: www.universal-tao.com, www.multi-orgasmic.com

Expert in Eastern Taoist techniques in sexuality for men and women, Mantak Chia has been teaching for three decades. He has written many books on these techniques and offers trainings at his retreat center in Thailand.

335

Quodoushka
Deer Tribe Metis Medicine Society (DTMMS)
408-443-3851
Web sites: www.Spiritualsexuality.com, www.dtmms.org

Native American Indian tantric tradition that uses breathwork and other rituals of special sexual skill to achieve overall well-being.

The Art of Being, LLC
Founder: Alan Lowen
P.O. Box 790269
Paia, HI 96770
808-572-1435
E-mail: jan@theartofbeing.com
Web site: www.theartofbeing.com

Workshops include "Body, Heart & Soul" tantra trainings and "The Universal Experience."

Teachers in a Male/Female Team

Dick and Antoinette Asimus
Cincinnati, OH
1-877-931-3030 or 513-931-3030
E-mail: adasimus@fuse.net
Web site: www.tantraheart.com

Experienced tantric couple, married in loving union for 30 years, lead evening events and workshops in their local area and around the country, in the tradition of Tantrika International.

Steve and Lokita Carter
Institute for Ecstatic Living
1-877-982-6872 or 707-928-6964
Web site: www.ecstaticliving.com

Trained tantra teachers also expert in techniques of massage and watsu (healing in water). They also coordinate Skydancing tantra workshops.

William Florian and Christina Sophia
962 Dorthel Street
Sebastopol, CA 95472
707-524-7898
E-mail: williamflorian@aol.com or christinasophia@aol.com
Web site: www.TantraDance.com

Organizes parties and tantric gatherings for evenings or weekends in romantic and exotic environments, and workshops in tantra and sensual dance, with performances of tantric love rituals, god/goddess dance massage, and sensual feasts.

Mark (Umeshanand) Michaels and Patricia (Veenanand) Johnson
Kailash Center for Personal Development, Inc.
1992 Commerce Street, #301
Yorktown Heights, NY 10598
914-962-7328
E-mail info@tantrapm.com
Web site: www.tantrapm.com

Devoted married couple who combine contemporary Western tantra with a traditional, lineage-based approach. They also offer distance learning programs with Dr. John Mumford, a leading figure in contemporary tantra now living in Australia.

Francesca Gentille and Brian Bourke
The LifeDance Center
510-465-2320
E-mail: sacreddancer@mindspring.com
Web site: www.lifedancecenter.com

Co-directors of the LifeDance Center, they teach sacred sensual dance, and give workshops in conscious flirting and relationship skills. Developing tantra community at www.ishtartemple.org to raise awareness about positive sexuality.

Workshops for Special Populations

College Students

Meghan Lambert and Ryan Deluz
E-mail: dolphintantra@yahoo.com or ryanoflight@hotmail.com

College-age couple trained by Tantrika International hold events and workshops especially for college students.

Teen Tantra

Shavana Fineberg, Ph.D.
E-mail: shavana@indra.com
Web site: www.teentantra.com

Psychologist offers workshops for teens to develop self-esteem and relationship skills using tantric consciousness.

Gay Men

Bruce Anderson
E-mail: Bruce@gaytantra.com
Web site: www.gaytantra.com

Classes on tantra for gay men given by California-based tantra teacher, using Kriya Jyoti Cobra Breath, massage, and other tantra techniques.

Disability

Mitch Tepper, Ph.D.
Web site: www.sexualhealth.com
Extensive Web site about all aspects of sexuality, including disability.

Singles

Web site: www.talkinghearts.com
Ceremonies and workshops on "Conversations That Matter" especially for Singles.

Cancer

Diane Greenberg
415-898-7510
E-mail: keener58@hotmail.com

Tantra educator certified by the Muirs' Source School of Tantra. Greenberg is also a sexual healer and advocate for women who specializes in helping women with cancer heal.

Related Trainings

Tantra Sound Toning
Ohana of Joy
Founder: Karin Schelde
P.O. Box 1173
Haiku, HI 96708
1-800-841-7457 or 808-249-6434
E-mail: Karin@soundandvoice.com

Talented healer gives workshops and private coaching in using voice, sounds, chanting, and other breathwork exercises for transformation, expansion of ability to communicate, healing, and empowerment. Also offers videos, audiotapes, and CDs.

Spinal Alignment
Lexi Fisher D.C.
Abundant Health Associates
Palm Springs, CA
760-327-4041
Web site: www.abudndanthealth.org

Tantra teacher also trained in nutritional counseling and special techniques to keep the spine healthy.

New Relationship Choices
Deborah Anapol
415-507-1739
Web site: www.lovewithoutlimits.com

Runs events, workshops, and intensive trainings for individuals and couples interested in new lovestyle choices, based on her book, *Polymory, the New Love Without Limits*. Also offers video, *Erotic Spirituality*, based on the first Celebration of Sacred Sexuality Conference she organized.

Sasha and Janet Lessin
1371 Malaihi
Wailuku, HI 96793
1-877-244-4103 toll free or 808-244-4103
E-mail: planetsexy@aol.com
Web site: www.schooloftantra.com

Committed couple who runs evenings, parties, workshops in their home in Maui and in other parts of the country. Experienced in tantra, as well as yoga and breathing techniques, and specialize in creating tantric polyamorous communities.

Related Centers for Personal Growth

Osho International
210 East 68 Street
New York, NY 10021
212-585-3666
Fax: 212-879-8680
E-mail: osho-international@osho.com
Web site: www.osho.org
Also contact: Karuna Kress, Ed.D., Director, Center for Consciousness
P.O. Box 186
Easthampton, MA 01027
413-527-2697 or e-mail NEITC@earthlink for Osho-related workshops

Extensive organization dedicated to the teachings of the "spiritually incorrect mystic" Osho, which includes a meditation resort, books, tapes, a magazine, and teachers all over the world who offer classes.

Harbin Hot Springs
P.O. Box 782
Middletown, CA 95461
1-800-622-2477
E-mail: reception@harbin.org
Web sites: www.harbin.org or www.harbinhotsprings.com

Retreat center north of San Francisco known for its hot spring pools, that hosts conferences and workshops of various healing topics, led by noted experts in various healing arts fields. Clothing-optional vacation spot also offers evening events such as dances and prayer circles.

Omega Institute
150 Lake Drive
Rhinebeck, NY 12572
1-800-933-1001
E-mail: registration@eomega.org
Web site: www.eomega.org

A healing center headquartered in upstate New York that it also organizes journeys to other parts of the country and abroad. Holds over 250 workshops throughout the year related to health and wellness conducted by noted experts, and sponsors wellness vacations and a wide variety of healing services.

New Life Expo
218 West 72nd Street
New York, NY 10024
212-787-1600

Hosts occasional weekend-long health fairs where a wide variety of health providers exhibit their services and experts lead panels and classes.

The Prophets Conference
1-888-777-5981
E-mail: prophets@greatmystery.org

Travel programs and weekend conferences with renowned experts and avant thinkers in a wide spectrum of worldviews, from philosophy to spirituality.

Body Electric
6527A Telegraph Avenue
Oakland, CA 94609-1113
510-653-1594
E-mail: bodyelectricweb@aol.com
Web site: www.bodyelectric.org

Offers workshops and retreats in healing arts that celebrate the erotic body.

Retreats and Gatherings

Paradise at Harmony
Juliana Dahl (Shakti Joy), Ph.D., M.A., C.S.S.E,
7647 Lefthand Canyon Drive
Jamestown, CO 80455
1-888-416-3522 or 303-413-9073
Fax: 303-413-9072
E-mail: info@sacredsexyes.com
Web site: www.sacredsexyes.com

Colorado mountain retreat center with indoor pool/spa and river grounds for relaxation and vacation pleasure. Also offers healing work on sacred sexuality for individuals and couples.

Goddess Gatherings
Founder and Priestess: Marylyn Motherbear Scott
707-937-3629
E-mail: motherbearscott@mindspring.com

Annual weekend of workshops to empower women to develop self-awareness and self-esteem, and to connect with their feminine spirit and power. Held in a retreat camp in California.

Living Ecstasy Institute, American Tantra
Paul Ramana Das and Marilena Silbey
415-499-1769
Fax: 415-499-9163
E-mail: yaluie@pacbell.net
Web site: www.3mmagic.com

Offers playshops, monthly parties, and musical events. Also produced a video, *Intimate Secrets of Sex and Spirit,* on pleasuring techniques, specializing in using sound, consistent with Ramana Das' musical talent. Solo concert pianist has CDs for lovemaking.

Related Courses (Not Necessarily Tantra)

Human Awareness Institute (HAI)
1-800-800-4117
E-mail: office@hai.org
Web site: www.hai.org

Workshops on all aspects of sexuality and intimate relationships, including topics as "Love, Sex, and Intimacy."

Woman Within, Inc.
1-800-732-0890
E-mail: wwithin@aol.com
Web site: www.womanwithin.org

Offers many workshops and support groups for women's empowerment and healing.

Mankind Project
1-800-870-4611
Web site: www.mkp.org

Offers "The New Warrior" training for men, originally called "The Wildman Weekend," for initiation processes and empowerment for men.

Dennis Mead-Shikaly
541-488-7800
Fax: 541-488-2730
E-mail: info@sacredrelationships.com
Web site: www.sacredrelationships.com

Workshops by two male facilitators on "Healing Relationships with Father: Leaving My Father's House," to help women face and transform unresolved issues related to their father, which impede their relationships with men. Uses meditations, music, visualization, guided imagery, journaling, group discussion, and individual process work.

Web Sites

www.tantra.com
Founder: Suzie Heumann
707-823-3063

A pioneer Web site that extensively covers the products and services in the tantra community, including a wide range of videos, books, audiotapes, and CDs. Also produced a video, *The Ancient Secrets of Sexual Ecstasy*, featuring many tantra experts and techniques. A good source to get an idea of the breadth of products in the field of tantra.

www.sexuality.com
E-mail: contact@sexuality.com

A site that offers information about a wide range of sexuality issues from sexual harassment to bondage, as a clearinghouse for information on the field in general.

Tantric Tools

Books

Here are some books that I recommend on tantra and related topics.

Tantric Sex

Jewel in the Lotus and *Living in Bliss* by Bodhi Avinasha (Sunstar Publishing, 1994, and Tantrika International, 2002).

The Art of Conscious Loving by Charles and Caroline Muir (Mercury House, 1990).

The Encyclopedia of Sacred Sexuality: From Aphrodisiacs and Ecstasy to Yoni Worship and Zap-lam Yoga by Rufus Camphausen (Inner Traditions, 1999).

Spiritual Sex: Secrets of Tantra from the Ice Age to the New Millennium by Nik Douglas (Pocket Books, 1997).

Sexual Energy Ecstasy: A Practical Guide to Lovemaking by David and Ellen Ramsdale (Bantam Doubleday Dell Publications, 1993).

The Essential Tantra: A Modern Guide to Sacred Sexuality by Kenneth Ray Stubbs (JP Tarcher, 1989).

The Tao of Love and Sex: The Ancient Chinese Way to Ecstasy by Jolan Chang (Viking Press, 1993).

The Art of Sexual Magic: Cultivating Sexual Energy to Transform Your Life by Margot Anand (Putnam Publishing Group, 1996).

The Yin Yang Butterfly by Valentin Chu (Putnam, 1993).

Ecstasy Through Tantra by John Mumford (Llewellyn Publications, 1988).

Healing Love Through The Tao: Cultivating Female Sex Energy and Taoist Secrets of Love, and *Cultivating Male Sexual Energy* by Mantak Chia (Healing Tao Books, 1991 and 1984).

The Complete Idiot's Guide to the Kama Sutra by Johanina Wikoff and Deborah Romaine (Alpha Books, 2000).

Related Books on Tantra and Healing

Introduction to Tantra: A Vision of Totality by Lama Yeshe (Wisdom Publications,1987).

Tools for Tantra by Harish Johari (Density Books, 1986).

Secrets of Western Tantra: The Sexuality of the Middle Path by Christopher S. Hyatte, Ph.D. (New Falcon Publications, 1989).

The Tao and *The Tree of Life: Alchemical and Sexual Mysteries of the East and West* by Eric Steven Yudelov (Llewellyn Publications, 1996).

The Tantra Experience: Discourse on the Royal Song of Saraha and *Tantric Transformation: Further Discourses on the Royal Song of Saraha* by Osho (Rebel Publishing House Pvt. Ltd., 1978).

Tamang Shamans by Larry Peters (Nivala, 1998).

Sex

Generation Sex by Dr. Judy Kuriansky (Harper, 1996).

The Clitoral Truth: The Secret World at Your Fingertips by Rebecca Chalker (Seven Stories Press, 2000).

Sex for One by Betty Dodsen (Harmony Books, 1987).

Forbidden Art: The World of Erotica and *Visions of Erotica* by Miss Naomi (Schiffer Books, 1998, 2000).

The Art of Arousal by Dr. Ruth Westheimer (Artabras, 1997).

Relationships

The Complete Idiot's Guide to a Healthy Relationship by Dr. Judy Kuriansky (Alpha, 2001).

The Complete Idiot's Guide to Dating by Dr. Judy Kuriansky (Alpha, 1999).

The New Physics of Love: The Power of Mind and Spirit in Relationships (audiocassette program) by Henry Grayson (Sounds True Inc., 2000).

Getting Together and Staying Together: Solving the Mystery of Marriage by William Glasser, M.D. and Carleen Glasser (HarperCollins Inc., 2000).

The Unimaginable Life by Kenny and Julia Loggins (Morrow, William and Co., 1998).

Music

Here are some CDs that are excellent for meditation, massage, and lovemaking—personal favorites that are regularly in my CD changer.

Sex 'n' Violets and *Songs of the Earthschild*
Jaiia Earthschild
808-573-4284
E-mail: jaiia@Earthschild.com
Web site: www.Earthschild.com
Beautiful songs about learning how to love oneself, be honored by a beloved, and care for the planet.

Music to Disappear In II, The Tantric Wave, The Calling
Raphael and Kutira
Kahua Hawaiian Institute, LLC
1-877-524-8250 or 808-572-6006
E-mail: info@KahuaInstitute.com
Web site: www.KahuaInstitute.com
Ritualistic music and pulsating chants that puts you in spiritual love mood, or relaxed or undulatory oceanic trance states. Instrumental or voice tracks guide you to an ecstatic experience.

Trance, Bones, Endless Wave
Gabrielle Roth
The Moving Center and Raven Recording
1-800-76 RAVEN or 212-760-1381
E-mail: ravenrec@Panix.com
Web site: www.gabrielleroth.com
An extensive library of selections of trance dance and urban primitive music for dancing and inspiring the soul, moving spirit, and activating ecstasy. Universal rhythms free the body and the mind also used in Roth's popular workshops.

Journey into Love, Return, and *Hidden Waters/Sacred Ground*
Sophia
Ivory Moon Recordings
1-800-515-8515
Profound yet simple songs that lead to deep Tantric embrace.

Spirit of Love
Awakening Heart Productions
409-835-7327
Collection of inspiring songs that touch our heart.

Sounds True
Web site: www.soundstrue.com
Music to put you in the mood for love.

Opening to Love
Robert Frey
818-784-0110
E-mail: Robert@scaredtantra.com
Web site: www.sacredtantra.com
Chants that inspire loving feelings.

Ecstatica 1 A Sound Track for Lovers, Love's Healing Touch, River of Romance
Paul Ramana Das
U-Music, Inc.
415-499-1769
Primal, playful, passionate, or percussive sound track for love experience that goes through seven different sensual soundscapes to a blissful completion.

Bruch Violin Concert No. 1 and Brahms Violin Concerto Op. 77
By Hideko Udagawa
London Symphony Orchestra
CHANDORS Records Ltd.
Web site: www.amazon.com
Classical music facilitating romance.

The Essence
Deva Premal
White Swan Music
303-494-9060
E-mail: swan@netone.com
Web site: www.mitendevapremal.com
A definitive chant album.

A Gift of Love: Deepak and Friends with the Love Poems of Rumi
Rumi
raSa Music
E-mail: aum@rasamusic.com
Web site: www.rasamusic.com
Recitations set to music to create the spirit of ecstatic love.

Inner Journey
Metamusic
Interstate Industries, Inc.
804-263-8692
E-mail: Interstate@Hemi-Sync.com
Web site: www.Hemi-Sync.com
Ethereal sounds and a special method of synchronizing brain spheres to relax and give free reign to the imagination.

Spiritual Environment Tantra
Anugama
Meistersinger Music USA Inc. Nightingale Records
520-733-9382
Fax: 520-722-8293
E-mail: meistersinger-us@TheRiver.com
Web site: www.meistersinger.com
The first half is more energizing and sexually stimulating. The second half stimulates the feminine and meditative side of sexual energy.

Songs to Shiva
Vyaas Houston and Mark Kelso
The American Sanskrit Institute
845-986-8652
Collection of ancient Sanskrit songs to Shiva, the great god.

ORFF—Carmina Burana
Saint Louis Symphony Orchestra and Chorus
BMG Music
Web site: www.amazon.com
Classic operatic piece evoking dynamic moods.

Graceful Passages: A Companion for Living and Dying
Michael Stillwater
415-492-0123
E-mail: music@innerharmony.com
Web site: www.innerharmony.com
Healing music with contemporary chant and intuitive singing, to evoke the preciousness of life.

Enhancing Sensual Pleasure and many other selections
Steven Halpern
Sound Wave Rx/ESP Productions
1-800-909-0707
Web site: www.stevenhalpern.com
Stimulates passion with subliminal affirmations.

Chakra Chants
Jonathan Goldman Etherean Music
1-888-384-3732
Web site: www.Etherean.com
Resonates and aligns energy centers of the body with sounds designed to balance the physical, emotional, mental, and spiritual bodies.

Spirit in Sound Chant the Best of World Chant
Robert Gass
Spring Hill Music
303-938-1188
Traditional and contemporary chant from the world's greatest chant artists.
Companion to Gass's book, *Chanting: Discovering Spirit in Sound* (Broadway Books).

Tantric Sexuality
The Mind Body and Soul series
New World Music Inc.
1-800-771-0987
Facilitates and enhances tantric practice, especially ecstatic breathing.

Videos

Many of these videos are geared toward tantric sex; others are geared toward sexuality in general.

Kama Sutra, Tantra and Tao, Hot Sex in Erotic Art, The Ecstasy of Exotic Sex, The Amazing G Spot and Female Ejaculation, and many others
Access Instructional Media (AIM)
16161 Ventura Blvd., Suite PMB 328
Encino, CA 91436
1-800-772-0708
Web site: www.sexualintimacy.com
A wide variety of expertly produced videos, some specifically geared toward tantric sex practices, with detailed instructions and demonstrations that are excellent how-to guides. By sexologist Michael Perry.

Secrets of Female Sexual Ecstasy
Charles and Caroline Muir
Source School of Tantra
P.O. Box 69
Paia, HI 96779
808-572-8364
Fax: 808-572-8622
E-mail: tantra@mauigateway.com
Web site: www.sourcetantra.com
Depicts sexual loving with exquisite art and original music, showing secrets of erotic kissing and touch, facts about male ejaculatory control, female sacred spot (G spot) massage, and female ejaculation.

Intimate Secrets of Sex and Spirit
By Marilina and Paul Silbey
Sexually explicit and entertaining video shows a variety of ways to enhance experiencing your body as a vibrant temple of divine energy.

Kama Sutra, The Art of Making Love and *Kama Sutra II*
Penthouse
A Vision
75 Rockefeller Plaza
New York, NY 10019
Beautifully shot videos with explicit demonstrations of positions and ancient love arts by modern-day couples.

Sluts and Goddesses: Video Workshop: How to Be a Sex Goddess in 101 Easy Steps
By Annie Sprinkle
Beatty/Sprinkle, 1992
Gates of Heck
1-800-213-8170
Web site: www.gatesofheck.com
A workshop for women on tape, showing tantric and Taoist principles along with very advanced activities such as group masturbation, shaving, and gender play.

Video Portrait of a Woman's Sexuality Seminar and *Viva La Vulva*
Betty Dodson Productions
P.O. Box 1933
Murray Hill
New York, NY 10156
212-679-4240
Web site: www.bettydodson.com
Sexuality pioneer shows women how to reclaim their erotic bodies and eliminate body shame. Teaches self-loving in a group seminar, combined with breathwork and heightened awareness of body sensations to increase pleasure.

Better Sex video series
The Sinclair Institute
P.O. Box 8865
Chapel Hill, NC 27515
1-800-955-0888
Web site: www.intimacyinstitute.com or www.sexedvideo.com
An extensive library of videos on sexual topics, from fantasy and aids to advanced lovemaking techniques.

The Secrets of Sacred Sex
Healing Arts
1-800-2 LIVING
Video that shows tantric lovemaking with commentary by experts.

Sensual Escape, Urban Heat, and other titles
Femme Productions
302 Meadowland Drive
Hillsborough, NC 27278
1-800-456-LOVE (orders, catalogs); 1-888-416-6130 (wholesale orders)
Web site: www.royalle.com
A library of erotic videos from a woman's perspective that has erotic as well as romantic themes.

Caballero videos
Especially selections of Andrew Blake.

Catalogs and Gifts

Most tantra sites and teachers also offer various items for sale, so check Appendix B, "Workshops, Web Sites, Teachers, and Tantra Communities." Here are some examples of special sites for items related to tantra.

Eve's Garden
119 West 57th Street
New York, NY 10019
1-800-848-3837
E-mail: huntress@evesgarden.com
Web site: www.evesgarden.com
An extensive catalog of videos, books, oils, vibrators, clothing, and other aids, all meant to empower women and celebrate female sexuality; the boutique in New York offers a discreet place for men and women to shop.

Taylor Soma Lamborne
Nectar Products: Sensual Tools for Tantra
4950 Coronado Avenue, Suite I
San Diego, CA 92107
619-226-6969
E-mail: nectarprod@earthlink.com
Web site: www.LoveNectar.com
Boutique of tantric aids and gifts.

E-sensuals
1-800-9-TANTRA
E-mail: e-sensuals@tantra.com
Web site: www.tantra.com
Probably the most extensive clearinghouse and selection of all items relevant to tantra and tantric practice.

House O'Chicks
2215 R Market Street
San Francisco, CA 94144
415-861-9849
Fax: (415) 626-5049
E-mail: Dorrie@houseochicks.com
Web site: www.houseochicks.com
Vulva puppets of silk, velvet and gems, made to order ($200)

Tantra Goddess/God Wear

Silk Angel Productions
808-573-1124
Special-order handpainted silk sarongs ($90–$150) with designs featuring mermaids inside a unicorn, lavender hibiscus flowers, or ocean scene with dolphins; silk chiffon jackets; velvet dresses.

Sacred and Erotic Art

Hrana Janto
10 Waterside Lane
New Paltz, NY 12561
845-658-8319
E-mail: hj@hranajanto.com
Web site: www.hranajanto.com
Illustrations, graphics, paintings; posters of sacred art and myth; folk and fairy tales in historical, cultural, or fantasy style; goddesses; historical scenes; lovers. Also, goddess oracle card set.

Paul Heussenstamm
949-497-2708
E-mail: heartcenter@mandalas.com
Web site: www.mandalas.com
Custom paintings of mandalas, commissioned art of male and female unions surrounded by geometric figures and nature forms with ruby and crystal stones. Also runs workshops in California and around the world on "Discovering Your Soul Mandala" to connect with your "inner artist" and explore the soul.

Meadow
108 Sheldon Road
Pine Bush, NY 12566-5518
845-744-4847
Fax: 845-744-4852
Illustrations, paintings, sculptures on many subjects including eroticism. Developing "Woodrock Sanctuary" art park, a healing center and wildlife sanctuary.

Al Hughes
212-330-9070
New York-based illustrator specializing in fashion, children's books, and celebrity caricatures.

Index

A

Abuse, healing cycles, 322-323
activation, 27
adornments, 199
advanced aids, 212-213
advanced practice, 201-202
  advanced aids, 212-213
  advanced tuning in, 210
  advanced visualization, 209
  base chakra pleasuring, 211-212
  deity yoga, 210-211
  mudras, 209
  passion positions and acts, 206-209
  snake dance, 203-204
  white tantra twosomes, 204-206
aerobics, 68
AFE (anterior fornix eroge-nous) zone, 169
affairs
  handling, 276-279
  reasons for, 277
affirmations, 125
  sex, 188-189
afterplay, 104
age
  changes, facing, 285-286
  empty nest syndrome, dealing with, 288
  menopause, dealing with, 285-286
  mid-life crises, dealing with, 286-287
  youthfulness, maintain-ing, 283-292
Aghora, 51
agreements, honoring, 274
aids (sex), 212-213
air yoga, 74-75
Al'Lat, 50
alchemical marriages, 298
alcohol, avoiding, 323-324
alignment and aloinment, 269
allowing pleasure, 11
alphabet orgasms, 168-169
altars, building, 90
alternate nostril breathing, 114
Amazing G Spot and Female Ejaculation, The, 235
ambiance
  considerations, 87
  sex, preparing, 88-90
American Pie 2, 238
amrita flow, 284
amrita, 188
Anand, Margot, 236
Ancient Secrets of Sexual Ecstasy for Modern Lovers, 236
androgyny, 23
anger, diffusing, 110-111
animals, tantric, 300-301
anterior fornix erogenous (AFE) zone, 169
anywhere-in-your-body orgasms, 170
appearance, considerations, 82, 84
"Arm and Hammer First Impression Study," 84
aromatherapy, 101
aromatic room oils, 88
Art of Sexual Magic, The, 197
artificial highs, avoiding, 323-324
attachment, overcoming, 115-116
attire
  dressing up, 86-87
  gods and goddesses, 199
  tantric clothes, 86
Avinasha, Bodhi, 37, 203
Awakening Heart, *Spirit of Love*, 230

B

Bairab (Shiva), 46
balancing male/female ener-gies, 111-115
bandhas, 67
base chakra pleasuring, 211-212
bathrooms, lighting, soften-ing, 84
baths
  bathing him, 136
  music, 84
  rituals, 84-86
  sharing, 84
  taking, 84
  traditions, 85
  water jets, 86

battles, relationship controls, 115
beards, shaving your partner's, 84
bedroom bodybuilding, 179-180
beds
    mattresses, 89
    preparing, 89
    sexual associations, 89
    sheets, 89
belly dancing, 192
belly hold (bandhas), 67
beloved partners, 24
Benzai Tennyo, 49
Berkowitz, Bob, 239
bindis, 199
bliss, 95-96
Bliss, 6, 238
bliss breathing, 35
blocks (mind), clearing, 117
body
    abusing, 62
    advanced exploration, 103-104
    affirmations, 62
    appreciating yours, 295
    homeplay, 62-65
    left side, yin representation, 22
    loving, 62-65
    right side, yang representation, 22
    taking care of, 27
body dust (Kama Sutra), 200
books, resources, 199
Bourke, Brian, 246
Brahma (Hindu God), 46
breathing, 29
    bliss breathing, 35
    chakras, 33-37
    circulating breathing, 35
    clear channels, 37
    cobras, 36
    complete breathing, 34
    ecstatic breathing, 35

energy, synchronizing, 96
exercises, 34-36
fire breathing, 34
heart rate, increasing, 75
incorrectly, 30-31
lama breathing, 78-79
nostril breathing, 113
partner pelvic passion breathing, 36
practicing, 30
reciprocal breathing, 34
synchronizing, 34
transmutation breathing, 154-155
yawning, 30
Britton, Patti, 235
Buddhism, 308
building altars, 90
Buller, Carlton J., 221
Burning Man festival (Nevada), 56

C

Cadell, Ava, 164
calling on women, 123-124
calming energy, 74
cancer patients, tantra classes, 338
candles, using for ambiance, 88
Carter, Steve and Lokita, 104
cat pose, yoga, 66
ceremonies (tantric marriage)
    feasts, 259
    guest participation, 260
    marriage, 258-259
    music, 259
    special ceremonies, 260-269
chakras, 31-33
    base chakra pleasuring, 211-212

breathing, 33-37
chakra thumps, performing, 76
energy centers, 37
evaluation chart, 32
examining, 62
sounding, tantric music, 232-233
Chalker, Rebecca, 129
chants, 233
    male/female enegy balancing, 114
    Om Mane Padme Hum, 39
Chao Mae Tuptim, 50
cheating. *See* affairs, 277
chemicals
    endorphins, 6, 172
    oxytocin, 6, 172
    phenylethlyamanime, 7
Chia, Mantak, 8, 209
Chopra, Deepak, 325
circling couple celebration, 175
circulating breathing, 35
clear channels, breathing, 37
clearing orgasms, 162-163
Clitoral Truth, The, 129
clitorises (pearls), 26, 64
clothing
    dressing up, 86-87
    gods and goddesses, 199
    tantric clothes, 86
cobra poses
    breathing, 36
    yoga, 66
coccyx bone (chakra energy center), 37
Cocoon, 163
college students, tantra workshops, 288
colors
    male/female, 115
    tantra, 65-66

commitment, tantric sex, 16-17
communication, practicing, 202
complete breathing, 34
Complete Idiot's Guide to a Healthy Relationship, The, 112
Complete Idiot's Guide to Dating, The, 112
connecting, 245
conscious flirting, 245
Conscious Loving workshop, 125
control, relationships, battles over, 115
Conversations with the Goddess: Revealing the Divine Power Within You, 50
corkscrew technique (massage), 140
cosmorgasms, 162
costs, workshops, 315
counterparts, gods/goddesses, 53-54
couple cobras pose, 178
couple connect pose, 174
couple cuddle pose, 179
Cranes with Necks Intertwined, 23
criticisms, Western revitalization, 10
crystal onyx massage eggs (sex toy), 197
crystal wands (sex toy), 198
Cybele, 51
cybertantra, 293-295

D

Dahl, Juliana, 341
dances
    belly dancing, 192
    ecstatic dance, 192
    hand dance, 191
    performing, 76
    snake dancing, 203-204
    Sufish, 79
    temple dance, 193
dancing, 173
    importance of, 189-190
    mirrors, 190-191
dangling duos pose, 176-177
Das, Paul Ramana, 341
dates, tantra dates, going out on, 93
deaths, partners, dealing with, 288
dedications, tantric marriage ceremonies, 259
deities. *See* gods and goddesses
deity yoga, 210-211
delaying ejaculations, 146-147
    partner help, 155-156
    sexual kung fu, 152-153
    technique comparisons, 153-154
    techniques, 151-152
    transmutation breathing, 154-155
desire
    expressing, 26
    sex, increasing, 75
desperation, overcoming, 115-116
dimmers (lighting), 88
disabled people
    tantra realtionships, 299-300
    tantra Web site for, 338
diversity, promoting, 324-325
Double Love Blasts, 127
Douglas, Nik, 236
dragon goddess, enflaming, 207-208
dressing up, 86-87
drugs, avoiding, 323-324
Duphiney, Rundy, 179
Durga, 48
Dynamic Meditation, 37

E

ears, stimulating, 101
earth to sky salutes, 204
Earthschild, Jaiia, 236
    Sex 'n' Violets, 231
eating healthy, 70
Ecstasy of Exotic Sex: The Joys of Total Sexual Ecstasy, The, 235
ecstatic breathing, 35
ecstatic dance, 192
Egypt, gods, 53
Ehmka, Greg, 102
ejaculations
    delaying, 146-147
        expectations, 149-150
        partner help, 155-156
        sexual kung fu, 152-153
        techniques, 151-154
        transmutation breathing, 154-155
    fast, reasons for, 149-150
    injaculation, 152
    male sexual response cycles, 151
    mechanics of, 150
    orgasms, compared, 150
emotions
    See also specific emotions
    overcoming, 117
    releases, 108-109
empathy, 115
empty nest syndrome, dealing with, 288
Empusae, 50

endorphins, 6, 172
energetics, 31
energy
  chakras, 31-33
    energy centers, 37
  connecting, energy cen-
    ters, 166-167
  drawing, massage, 138
  energy booster checklist,
    279
  entrances, 24
  External Relationship
    Energy, 277
  Extra Relationship
    Energy, 277
  gods/goddesses, drawing
    from, 55
  increasing, 75
    chakra thumps, 76
    dancing, 76
    fantasizing, 78
    freeing your mind, 78
    lama breathing,
      78-79
    pelvic thrusts, 77
    sacrum taps, 75-76
    shakti shakes, 78
    streaming, 76
  levels, rating, 74
  love energy, sending, 322
  male/female, balancing,
    111-115
  NRE (New Relationship
    Energy), 277
  relaxing, 74
  sexual, 24
  synchronizing, 96-99
  tragedies, sending,
    320-321
energy booster checklist,
  279
energy pathways, 7
Epstein, Donald, 70
Erzuli, 50
excitement stage (male sexual response cycle), 151

exercises
  bedroom bodybuilding,
    179-180
  breathing, 34-36
  dancing, 173
    belly dancing, 192
    ecstatic dance, 192
    hand dance, 191
    snake dancing,
      203-204
    temple dance, 193
  love muscle exercises, 172
  partners, 179-181
  partner pelvic thrusts,
    172-173
  pass up the pass exercise,
    246
  pubococcygeal muscles,
    68
  steel ball exercise, 245
  workouts, 68
    videos, 237
  yogaboxing, 181-183
exploration, bodies,
  advanced exploration,
  103-104
External Relationship
  Energy, 277
Extra Relationship Energy,
  277
eye gazing, energy, synchronizing, 97-98
eyes, stimulating, 100

F

faces, stimulating, 100
fantasies
  channeling, 12
  performing, 78
fears, facing, 123
feasts, tantric marriage ceremonies, 259
female/male energies, balancing, 111-115

females
  calling on, 123-124
  homosexual relation-
    ships, 298
  juicyness, 188
  pleasing, 121-131
  sexual healing,
    217-219
  yin representation, 20-22
fertility festivals, Japan,
  55-56
festivals, gods/goddesses,
  55-57
figurines (gods and god-
  desses), 199
Fineberg, Steven, 289
fingernails, keeping clean,
  82
fire breathing, 34
Fisher, Lexi, 69
flirting, conscious flirting,
  245
Florian, William, 192
food
  healthy, 70
  tantric marriage cere-
    monies, 259
Forbidden Art, 199
Free Like a Dolphin, 289
freeing your mind, 78
Frey, Robert, 104, 109
  Opening to Love, 231
friend participation, tantric
  marriage ceremonies, 260
full stop technique, 208

G

G spots, 169
Gaia, 50
games (sex), 194-195
Gate feasts, 193
gatherings, 316
  gods/goddesses, 55-57
gays, tantra classes,
  297-298

genitals
  describing, 63-65
  examining, 62
  terminology, 25-26
geriatrics, tantric sex,
  284-285
gifts (sex), 199-200
  finding, 200
global community (tantra),
  320-321
god areas, pleasing, 141
goddess bags, preparing, 135
goddess space, pleasuring,
  130
goddesses, 46-53
  Al'Lat, 50
  attire, 199
  Benzai Tennyo, 49
  Cybele, 51
  dragon goddesses,
    enflaming, 207-208
  Durga, 48
  Empusae, 50
  Energy, drawing from, 55
  Erzuli, 50
  festivals and gatherings,
    55-57
  figurines and statues, 199
  Gaia, 50
  gods, counterparts, 53-54
  Greece, 50
  Hindu, 48
  Kali, 49
  Lakshmi, 48
  Maeve, 50
  Mboze, 50
  middle east, 50
  modern-day figures, 53
  Mother Maui, 50
  near east, 51
  Odude, 50
  Pele, 50
  Qadesh, 50
  Riannon, 50
  Ruth, 50
  Saraswati, 49

  Shekinah, 50
  Tap-tun, 50
  Tara, 48
  within, 54
gods, 46-53
  Aghora, 51
  attire, 199
  Egypt, 53
  energy, drawing from, 55
  festivals and gatherings,
    55-57
  figurines and statues, 199
  goddesses, counterparts,
    53-54
  Greece, 51
  Hindu, 51
  Japan, 53
  manifestations, 46
  modern-day figures, 53
  Musuri-Kami, 53
  Osiris, 53
  Ra, 53
  Shiva, 51
  within, 54
  Zeus, 52
gods/goddesses
  past life connections, 213
  roles, integrating,
    44-45
granting permission, sex, 26
grasping, pleasurable, 11
Greece gods/goddesses,
  50-51
Greenberg, Diane, 324
growth, sharing in, 275
guest participation, tantric
  marriage ceremonies, 260
guides
  finding, 305-309
  importance of,
    304-305
  Osha, 310
  trainings, 310-311
Gutenberg, Steve, 163

H

hair, washing, 84
hand dancing, 191
Handlers, Laurie, 193
hands, stimulating, 101
harmonic convergence, 325
head lifts, yoga, 66
heady trip technique (massage), 140
healers, 311-312
healing, 6
  abuse, 322-323
  illnesses, 324
  parents, 300
healing. *See* sexual healing
heart rate, increasing,
  breathing, 75
hearts, holding, 98-99
hermaphrodites, 23
Heussenstamm, Paul, 40
higher selves, 10
Hill, John, 325
Hindu gods/goddesses, 48,
  51, 308
Hindu fire ceremonies, 267
holding hearts, 98-99
homeplay, 62-65
homosexuals, tantra work-
  shops, 297-298
hooking up, 245
Hot Sex in Erotic Art, 199,
  235
How To Love A Nice Guy, 246
hygiene, considerations, 82

I

illnesses, healing, 324
in-between spots, 152
incense, 88
infidelity, fantasies, channeling, 12

inhibitions, relaxation of, 15
Initiate Secrets of Sex and Spirit: How to Worship Each Other in Bed, 236
injaculation, 152
inner flutes, 33
inner guidance, 102
inner smile, 38
intentions
    lovemaking, 92
    setting, 122
Internet
    cybertantra, 293-295
    global community, 320
    resources, 238-239
Ishtar, 47

J

Jacobson, Kirby, 203, 308
Jagger, Chris, 239
Japan
    fertility festivals, 55-56
    gods, 53
Javril, Tantrika, 190
Jewel in the Lotus, 37
jewelry, 199
Johnson, Patricia (Veenanand), 98
Journey Into Love, 230
Joys of Everyday Rituals, The, 286
juicyness, women, 188

K

Kabazzah, 208
Kali, 49
Kama Sutra, 25
Kama Sutra body dust, 200
Kama Sutra II: The Art of Making Love, 236
Kama Sutra series, videos, 235-236

kareeza, 154
Kivin method, 208
kunda gland (chakra energy center), 37
kundalini energy, 37
    snake dancing, 204
kundalini glands, 64

L

labels
    genitals, 25-26
    partners, 24
ladder technique (ejaculation control), 152
Lakshmi, 48
lama breathing, performing, 78-79
Lamborne, Taylor, 197
laughter, importance of, 189
left side (body), yin representation, 22
lesbians, tantra relationships, 298
levels
    energy, rating, 74
    sex drives, excelling, 165
lighting
    bathrooms, softer, 84
    candles, 88
    dimmers, 88
limbic system, 38
lingam (penis), 26
lingam love strokes, 138
lingam mudras technique (massage), 140
lion's play exercise, 110
Living in Bliss, 333
love, sex, importance of, 160
love arrow show exercise, 103
love muscle exercises, 63, 172
love rituals, honoring, 90-92

love toys, 89
lovers table pose, 178
Loving More magazine, 277
lubricants, 198

M

Maeve, 50
magic (sex), 196-197
maithuna love ritual, 203
male sexual response cycles, stages, 151
male/female energies, balancing, 111-115
males
    females, pleasing, 121-131
    gays, 297-298
    pleasing, nights of pleasure, 134-144
    sexual healing, 219
    yang representation, 20-22
mandalas, 40, 199
manifestations, gods, 46
mantra designs, 199
mantras, 39
marriage ceremonies (tantric), 258-259
    feasts, 259
    guest participation, 260
    music, 259
    special ceremonies, 260-269
massage, 140
    corkscrew technique, 140
    heady trip technique, 140
    lingam mudras technique, 140
    natural rabbit fur massage mitts, 198
    palming the crown technique, 140
    sexual energy, drawing, 138

massage mitts, 198
masturbation, 65
mattresses, beds, 89
Mboze, 50
meditation, research, benefits of, 7
medulla oblongata, 37
mega-orgasms, 162-163
menopause, dealing with, 285-286
Michaels, Mark (Umeshanand), 98
micro movements, 202
mid-life crises, dealing with, 286-287
mind
    blocks, clearing, 117
    freeing, 78
mindfulness, 5-6
mirrors, dancing, 190-191
misconceptions, tantra, 5, 11-12
modern-day gods/goddesses, 53
Money, Sex, Power and You: Transforming Your Ego, 102
morning blessings, 109
Mother Maui, 50
mouths, stimulating, 100
movies, 238-239
mudras, 209
Muir, Charles, 109
Muktananda, 8
multiple orgasms, 163
music
    baths, 84
    choosing, 230
    lovemaking, 89
    resources, 346-349
    tantric marriage ceremonies, 259
    tantric music
        appreciating, 232
        chakra evocation, 232-233

chants, 233
choosing, 229-231
recommendations, 230
themes, 231-232
Music to Disappear In, 231
Musuri-Kami, 53
myths, tantra, 11-12

N

names, women, changing, 49
natural rabbit fur massage mitts, 198
nesting, 161
network spinal analysis (NSA), 69
Nevada, Burning Man festival, 56
New Relationship Energy (NRE), 277
nights of pleasure
    night 1, 134-144
    night 2, 139-143
    night 3, 143-144
nine levels of orgasms, 163
noses, stimulating, 100
nostril breathing, male/female energies, balancing, 113
NRE (New Relationship Energy), 277
NSA (network spinal analysis), 69

O

obsessions, purging, 116
Odude, 50
Om Mane Padme Hum, 39
ooo-ahhh exercise, 167
ooo-ehhh exercise, 167
ooo-uhhh exercise, 168
Opening to Love, 231

opposites
    balancing, 22-23
    relationships, 295-296
orgasm stage (male sexual response cycle), 151
orgasms
    ejaculations, compared, 150
    nine levels of, 163
    types, 160-164
        alphabet orgasms, 168-169
        anywhere-in-your-body orgasms, 170
        clearing orgasms, 162-163
        cosmorgasms, 162
        mega-orgasms, 162-163
        multiple orgasms, 163
        simultaneous orgasms, 163
        stock market orgasms, 164
        tantric orgasms, 163-164
        TTOs, 164
        valley orgasms, 164
Osho, 9, 37, 78, 310
Osho International, 78
Osiris, 53
overdependence, overcoming, 115-116
oxytocin, 6, 172

P

pacing windows, 246
painting toenails, 84
paintings, 199
palming the crown technique (massage), 140
panic, purging, 116
parents, healing relationships, 300

pareos, 86
partner passion pods, 99
partner pelvic passion
  breathing, 36
partner pelvic thrusts,
  172-173
partner pelvic supports,
  176-177
Partner Sexual Review, 113
partners
    asking for help, 80
    attracting, 249-253
    beloved, 24
    breaking up with,
      275-276
    death of, dealing with,
      288
    exercising with,
      179-181
    making time for,
      109-110
    meeting, 245-253
    persuading, 272-274
    relaxing, 125-127
    worshipping, 46
pass up the pass exercise,
  246
passion pods, 99
pearls (clitoris), 26
Pearls of Delight, 212
Pele, 50
pelvic thrusts, 77,
  172-173
pelvis hold (bandhas), 67
penises, terms, 26
permission, sex, granting, 26
Perry, Michael, 235
pets, tantra for, 300-301
PFZ (posterior fornix zone),
  169
phenylethlyamanime, 7
pituitary glands, 37
plants, tantra, 301
plateau stage (male sexual
  response cycle), 151

playing, sex, 188
    dancing, 189-191
    games, 194-195
    importance of, 188
    laughter, 189
    sensuous eating,
      193-194
    sex gifts, 199-200
    sex magic, 196-197
    toys, 197-199
playshops, 316
pleasure, allowing, 11
pleasure promise coupons,
  200
pledges, tantric sex,
  16-17
positions
    advanced aids,
      212-213
    advanced passion posi-
      tions and acts, 206-209
    advanced tuning in, 210
    advanced visualization,
      209
    base chakra pleasuring,
      211-212
    deity yoga, 210-211
    mudras, 209
polarities, balancing,
  22-23
polymorous relationships,
  276
pompoir, 198
poses, yoga
    advanced aids,
      212-213
    advanced passion posi-
      tions and acts, 206-209
    advanced tuning in, 210
    advanced visualization,
      209
    advanced white tantra
      twosome, 204-206
    base chakra pleasuring,
      211-212

circling couple celebra-
  tions, 175
couple cobras, 178
couple connect, 174
couple cuddle, 179
dangling duos,
  176-177
deity yoga, 210-211
lovers table, 178
mudras, 209
partner pelvis supports,
  176-177
squat to stand support,
  175-176
positions
    partner passion pods, 99
    spoons position, 129
    yab yum, 23-24
    yoga, 66-67
posterior fornix zone (PFZ),
  169
practice
    advanced practice,
      201-202
        advanced aids,
          212-213
        advanced tuning in,
          210
        advanced visualization,
          209
        base chakra pleasuring,
          211-212
        deity yoga, 210-211
        mudras, 209
        passion positions and
          acts, 206-209
        snake dance,
          203-204
        white tantra twosomes,
          204-206
    maithuna love ritual, 203
    rituals, 202
    sharing, 203
    snake dancing,
      203-204

practices (teaching), starting your own, 312-315
practicing communication, 202
practitioners, 311-312
prana, 100
pubococcygeal muscles, strengthening, 68

Q

Qadesh, 50
Qigong, 68
quickies (sex), 146-149

R

Ra, 53
rabbit fur massage mitts, 198
radio shows, tantric related, 238-239
Raphael and Kutrina, *Music to Disappear In*, 231
rating energy levels, 74
readiness, tantric sex, 15-16
Real Sex, 238
relationships, energy booster checklist, 279
rebirthing, 116
reciprocal breathing, 34
red, 65
relationships
    affairs, handling, 276-279
    agreements, honoring, 274
    control, battles over, 115
    cybertantra, 293-295
    ending, 275-276
    homosexuals, 297-298
    maintaining, 274
    obstacles, overcoming, 275

opposites, 295-296
    parents, 300
    pets, 300-301
    plants, 301
    sexual relationships, 111-113
    tantric relationships, persuasion, 272-274
    tolerance, 276
relaxing energy, 74
relaxing into ecstasy, 202
relaxing partners, 125-127
religions, 308
research, meditation, benefits of, 7
resistance, dissuading, 273-274
resolution phase, 129
resolution stage (male sexual response cycle), 151
revitalization, tantric sex, 7-9
Riannon, 50
right side (body), yang representation, 22
rituals
    love rituals, honoring, 90-92
    maithuna love ritual, 203
    practicing, 202
    tantric marriage ceremonies, 258-267
River of Romance, 231
Roles, god/goddess, role integration, 44-45
romance, preparing for, 124
Roth, Gabrielle, 37
    Waves, 231
Ruth, 50
Ryan, Meg, 163

S

Sachidananda, 8
sacraments, 89

sacred sectors, 299
sacred sex, 10
sacred space (feminine divine energy), 26
sacred-erotic bellydances, 192
sacrum (chakra energy center), 37, 75-76
sacrums, 64
Sanskrit names, changing to, 49
Sanskrit: Tantra, 4
Saraswati, Sunyata, 37, 49
Schubach, Gary, 131
sealing the penis (ejaculation control), 152-153
Secrets of Female Sexual Ecstasy, The, 236
semen retention (Taoism), 146
sensate focus, 154
sensations
    sexual, awareness of, 102
    stimulating, 99-101
sensuous eating, 193-194
separation anxiety, overcoming, 111
settings
    changing, 89
    considerations, 87
    sex, preparing, 88-90
sex
    affirmations, 188-189
    afterplay, 104
    appearance, considerations, 82-84
    desire, increasing, 75
    energy, 24
    fears, facing, 123
    intentions, 92
    love, importance of, 160
    making time for, 82
    permission, granting, 26

playing, 188
    dancing, 189-191
    games, 194-195
    importance of, 188
    laughter, 189
    sensuous eating,
        193-194
    sex gifts, 199-200
    sex magic, 196-197
    toys, 197-199
preparing for, 124
quickies, 146-149
sensations, awareness of,
    102
settings, preparing, 88-90
taking turns, 122
youthfulness, maintain-
    ing, 283-292
Sex 'n' Violets, 231
sex drives
    levels, excelling, 165
    transmuting, 165
Sex in the City, 238
sex therapy, tantric sex,
    compared, 153-154
sex toys, 89
sexual energy, connecting,
    energy centers, 166-167
sexual healing, 216-222
    abuse healing,
        221-222
    conclusions, 224-225
    effectiveness, 226
    men, 219
    rules, 223-224
    women, 217-219
sexual kung fu (ejaculation
    control), 152-153
sexual relationships,
    111-113
    control, battle over, 115
    Partner Sexual Review,
        113
shakti shakes, performing,
    78
sharing, practicing, 203

shaving beards, 84
sheets, bedding, 89
Shekinah, 50
Shiva (Hindu God), 46, 51
Shiva Shakti mudra exercise,
    165-166
shower rituals, 84-86
Silbey, Paul Ramana Das
    Silbey, *River of Romance*,
    231
simultaneous orgasms, 163
singles
    attracting someone,
        249-253
    loving yourself,
        244-245
    meeting someone,
        245-253
sitiphilia, 194
Sluts and Goddesses, 236
snake dancing, 203-204
Sophia, *Journey Into Love*,
    230
soul mates, finding,
    249-250
special ceremonies, tantric
    marriage ceremonies,
    260-269
spines, examining, 69
Spirit of Love, Awakening
    Heart, 230
spiritual emergencies, 204
spontaneity, passionate
    embraces, 82
spoons position, 129
Sprinkle, Annie, 236
squat to stand support,
    175-176
squeeze technique (ejacula-
    tion control), 151
stages, male sexual response
    cycle, 151
Stamp, Terence, 238
Stassinopolous, Agapi, 50
state of bliss, 95-96

statues (gods and god-
    desses), 199
steel ball exercise, 245
Stillwater, Michael, 234
stimulating senses,
    99-101
stock market orgasms, 164
*Stolen Innocence: The
    Autobiography of a Lost Soul*,
    222
stop-start technique (ejacu-
    lation control), 151
streaming, performing, 76
stuffing, 154
Sufish, 79
superficiality, seeing
    beyond, 45
sweat ritual, 260
symbols, male/female, 114
synchronizing
    breathing, 34
    energy, 96-99

T

T'ai Chi, 68
tantra, 4
    colors, 65-66
    misconceptions of, 11-12
    myths, 11-12
    origins of, 4
    revitalization of, 7-9
*Tantra and Tao: The Ancient
    and Erotic Techniques for
    Incredible Sexual Pleasure*,
    235
tantra dates, going out on,
    93
tantra teachers, scams, 12
tantra true love quiz, 248
tantric clothes, 86
tantric getaways, 316
tantric marriage ceremonies
    feasts, 259
    music, 259-260

special ceremonies,
260-269
traditional marriage ceremonies, compared,
258-259
tantric music
appreciating, 232
chakras, evoking,
232-233
chants, 233
choosing, 229-231
recommendations, 230
tantric marriage cere-
monies, 259
themes, 231-232
tantric orgasms, 163-164
tantric sex, 3
benefits of, 13-15
misconceptions of, 5,
11-12
myths, 11-12
objectives of, 4-5
reasons for, 12-13
sex therapy, compared,
153-154
tantric sex communities,
316
Tantric Sexuality, 37
tantric transformation
orgasm (TTO). *See* TTO
(tantric transformation
orgasm)
tantric triggers, finding, 102
tantric twosome trestles,
205-206
tantrika, 192
Tantrika International, 75
tantrikas, 197
*Tao for Women, Cultivating
Female Sexual Energy,* 209
Taoism, 308
*Taoist Secrets of Love,
Cultivating Male Sexual
Energy,* 209
Tap-tun, 50
Tara, 48

Tarantola, Carla, 173, 204,
284
teachers
finding, 305-309
Osha, 310
trainings, 310-311
techniques, integrating, 317
teens, tantra workshops, 289
teeth, brushing regularly, 82
temple dance, 193
temples, tantric rituals, 57
ten-minute connections,
109
terminology
genitals, 25-26
partners, 24
terms of endearment, 125
testicle tug technique (ejaculation control), 151
thangkas, 199
themes, tantric music,
231-232
therapists, 311-312
third eye, opening, 37
throat hold (bandhas), 67
thunderbolts (penises), 26
time, making, 109-110
toenails, painting your partner's, 84
tolerance
promoting, 324-325
relationships, 276
touch, senses, stimulating,
101
toys (sex), 197-199
advanced aids,
212-213
finding, 200
traditional marriage ceremonies, tantric marriage
ceremonies, compared,
258-259
tragedies, energy, sending,
320-321
transitions, tantric love,
287-288

transmutation breathing,
154-155
transmuting sex drives, 165
Tratak (eye gazing practice),
98
triggers (tantric), finding,
102
true tantric sex partner quiz,
248
TTOs (tantric transforma-
tion orgasms), 159, 164
tubs (bath), water jets, 86
tuning in (advanced), 210
twin souls, 250
twosome trestles, 205

U

urethral openings, vaginas,
64
urethras, 64

V

vaginas (yoni), 25
clitorises, 64
examining, 63
urethral openings, 64
urethras, 64
vajra (penis), 26
valley orgasms, 164
VAT (Video Assisted
Therapy), 234
vibrators, 199
Video Assisted Therapy
(VAT), 234
videos, 199, 234-237
general sex, 237-238
goddesses, 236
Kama Sutra series,
235-236
tantric sex, 199
workouts, 237
Vishnu (Hindu God), 46

visualization (advanced), 209

vows, tantric marriage ceremonies, 258

W

water exercises, 104

Watsu Water Shiatsu, 104

Waves, 231

Web sites, resources, 238-239

weight lifting, 68

Welch, Tawhnee, 163

Western revitalization
    criticisms of, 10
    tantric sex, 7-9

When Harry Met Sally, 163

White (tantric color), 65

white tantra twosomes, 204-206

witnesses, 39

women
    calling on, 123-124
    homosexual relationships, 298
    juicyness, 188
    names, changing, 49
    pleasing, 121-131
    sexual healing, 217-219
    yin representation, 20-22

workouts, 68, 237

workshops
    costs, 315

worshipping partners, 46

X–Y–Z

X spots, 169

yab yum, 23-24

yantras, 39

yawning, 30

yin and yang (body representations), 20-22

yoga, 66
    air yoga, 74-75
    bandhas, 67
    cat pose, 66
    cobra pose, 66
    exercises, 179-181
    head lifts, 66
    resting pose, 66
    poses
        advanced aids, 212-213
        advanced positions and acts, 206-209
        advanced tuning in, 210
        advanced visualization, 209
        advanced white tantra twosome, 204-206
        base chakra pleasuring, 211-212
        circling couple celebration, 175
        couple cobras, 178
        couple connect, 174
        couple cuddle, 179
        dangling duos, 176-177
        deity yoga, 210-211
        lovers table, 178
        mudras, 209
        partner pelvis presses, 176-177
        squat to stand support, 175-176
    yogaboxing, 181-183

Yoga Nidra, 321

yogaboxing, 181-183

yoni (vagina), 25

yoni show exercise, 103

youthfulness, maintaining, 283-292

Zeus, 52

CONTACT DR. JUDY

Dr. Judy is an expert on relationships, sex, dating, and love, as well as other topics like creativity, brain styles, the psychology of current events, and trends. Get your copy of her books at your local bookstore or amazon.com (English and foreign language versions):

The Complete Idiot's Guide to Dating (Alpha, 1999). Everything you need to know about how to meet your mate.

The Idiot's Guide to a Healthy Relationship (Alpha, 2001). Everything you need to know about making a love relationship last.

Generation Sex (Harper, 1996). A collection of touching questions on a massive range of topics about sex—with advice you won't find anywhere else—and good humor! Culled from questions from the radio show *LovePhones*, including comments from rock stars.

How To Love A Nice Guy. A helpful and effective 10-step program to learn to be attracted to nice guys instead of bad boys. Also appropriate for guys who keep going for the "wrong" girls who don't return their interest. Log on to www.brides.com for Dr. Judy as advisory board member, or contact Dr. Judy at the following numbers.

Contact Dr. Judy at **apoll143@aol.com**, or call Alissa at 718-761-6910 or beep 917-354-3029, to inquire about the following:

___ Giving a lecture, seminar, workshop, keynote speech. Especially designed for your needs, on tantric sex, love, sex, and relationships.

___ Private counseling session in person or by phone. Individuals and couples, from a unique approach unifying mind, body, and spirit, combining a variety of techniques.

___ Hosting your event. ("The Dating Game" for *Details* magazine, Calvin Klein Menswear, Bloomingdales stores, Volunteer Recognition Programs for New York Cares, JC Penney's community drug awareness).

___ Consulting for your company (on trends, women, men, youth).

___ Judging your contest (Revlon's Most Unforgettable Woman, Lane Bryant's Real Woman, Close-Up Rap 'n Roll).

___ Being your spokesperson. (Universal Studios Florida "Theme Park Therapy," Durex World Survey, Virginia Slims Opinion Poll, Holiday Depression, Church & Dwight, "First Impressions" campaign, Organon's blues in the bedroom, and www.matureamerica.com).

___ Designing your campaign for public affairs or advertising (perfumes, soft drinks, Herpes Awareness).

___ Being on your advisory committee/board (*Brides* magazine, Environmental Visionary Efforts, Planned Parenthood the Vice Chair of the Foundation of American Women in Radio and TV, Board of TV Academy in New York).